# Introduction to Politics

Dedicated to our parents, Gladys and Ken Gill,
Ada Ponton and in memory of Jack Ponton

# Introduction to Politics

## Third Edition

Geoffrey Ponton and Peter Gill

BLACKWELL
Oxford UK & Cambridge USA

Copyright © Geoffrey Ponton and Peter Gill, 1982, 1988, 1993

First published in 1982 by Martin Robertson & Company Ltd
Reprinted 1983

First Blackwell Publishers Ltd edition published 1984
Reprinted 1986, 1987

Second edition published 1988
Reprinted 1989, 1992

Third edition published 1993
Reprinted 1993, 1995, 1996

Blackwell Publishers Ltd
108 Cowley Road
Oxford OX4 1JF, UK

Blackwell Publishers Inc.
238 Main Street
Cambridge, Massachusetts 02142, USA

*British Library Cataloguing in Publication Data*
A CIP catalogue record for this book is available from the British Library

*Library of Congress Cataloging in Publication Data*
Ponton, Geoffrey.
Introduction to Politics/Geoffrey Ponton and Peter Gill — 3rd edn
p.  cm.
Includes bibliographical references and index.
ISBN 0–631–18784–7 (pbk)
1. Political science. I. Gill, Peter, 1947–. II. Bretherton, Charlotte.
III. Title.
JA66.P66   1993                                    92–39485
320—dc20                                              CIP

Typeset in 11 on 12½ pt Sabon by Graphicraft Typesetters Ltd., Hong Kong
Printed in Great Britain by TJ Press, Padstow, Cornwall

This book is printed on acid-free paper

# Contents

# Tables and Figures

# Preface to the Third Edition

In the light of the many dramatic changes in the world of politics since the publication of the second edition, we have taken the opportunity to revise the text thoroughly. The collapse of the Soviet Union has left confusion and uncertainty in its wake. The legacy of Soviet politics, however, will remain an important feature of the new Europe for some time. In the circumstances, we have decided to continue to use the Soviet Union as a case-study, while we also consider the events that led to its breakup. Charlotte Bretherton has written two new chapters on global politics.

Geoffrey Ponton
Peter Gill
November 1992

## Preface to the Second Edition

In this second edition we have updated the text to take account of developments since 1982. New questions have been added at the end of chapters, and we have thoroughly revised the Further Reading references to include recently published material.

We have amended and updated our discussion of models in chapters 3 and 4, and have included a new chapter on state structures to provide a clearer link between the consideration of analytical models and ideologies in Part I and the later discussion of the country case-studies. We have added a chapter on local politics to improve the discussion of subnational politics. The main structural change that we have made is to bring forward the material on politics and government at the national, subnational and supranational levels before we deal with legitimacy, socialization and elections. We feel that this reflects the fact that the study of the state has been restored to relative pre-eminence in recent years compared with the 'inputs' of the political process.

Geoffrey Ponton
Peter Gill
February 1988

## Preface to the First Edition

This book developed from the authors' dissatisfaction not only with lectures as a mode of teaching politics, but also with existing introductory works on politics. Both, in their different ways, tend to assume the existence of a generally accepted body of knowledge or 'conventional wisdom' which requires to be passed on to students before they are in a condition to discuss the issues raised. We believe it is better that people to be involved actively in learning as soon as possible, especially in an area such as politics where the generally accepted body of knowledge is small compared with other disciplines. Therefore, we have tried to write a book which raises questions as much as, if not more than, it answers them. The study and practice of politics involves many pitfalls, and we hope to have provided an introduction to these problems. Because we do not believe that there is some objectively ascertainable view of 'real world' politics which simply waits to be revealed, we have dealt first with methodological problems so that by the time we deal with the more descriptive material on British, Soviet and American politics the reader should be well aware of the impact of his or her own background, values and attitudes on the perception of politics.

The book aims to provide a readable and useful introduction to politics for the general reader as well as the student. However, it is in the first place intended for use as an introduction for students. While it can be adapted for use in accordance with whatever arrangements the teacher deems suitable, it was primarily envisaged as the basis for a discussion-centred course in politics. The length of the chapters, with a couple of exceptions, is such that they are suitable for a week's reading and discussion.

The Questions for Discussion at the end of each chapter are not designed simply to test comprehension of the ideas discussed in the chapter, but are also aimed at getting people to think about the implications of those ideas beyond the confines of the chapter. The particular questions we raise are those which strike *us* as important; we hope many others will occur to the reader. Similarly, the Further Reading is suggestive rather than definitive. Both we and our students have found these references useful; clearly, lack of time and access to libraries may prevent the reader from following up many of them. Other readings may prove as good as or better than ours; it does not matter. What does matter is that readers gain as wide a variety of views and interpretations as they can.

Since we do not believe that there can be such a thing as a 'value-free' or 'neutral' approach to the study of politics, we should make our own values explicit rather than try to slip them past the reader's guard under the guise of 'academic objectivity'. While we have our differences, we might both be characterized as 'leftward-leaning sceptics'. Therefore, if what we write excites criticism and questioning then we shall consider that we have been successful.

We would like to thank Penny Gill and Tom Rowbottom for their assistance, the various typists who have helped produce the typescript, and colleagues and students for their comments and suggestions.

Geoffrey Ponton
Peter Gill
July 1981

# Part I

## The Study of Politics

# 1

# The Meaning and Scope of Politics

## The Approach

In approaching the study of a new subject we must first be clear in our minds as to the area of knowledge we intend to explore, and how we shall go about it. This involves making some basic assumptions. In some disciplines, such as the natural and biological sciences, there are widely agreed definitions as to the area of study covered by such terms as 'physics' or 'biology'. Within such disciplines there are also accepted standard definitions and assumptions. However, such definitions may undergo considerable changes over time. There is always some doubt as to the exact location of a subject's boundaries – what is to be included and what omitted. Other areas of study interrelate with and encroach on the chosen field, confusing the situation further. This raises the question of whether the boundary between one subject and another is too artificial, a hindrance rather than an aid to understanding. Should we therefore adopt new ideas to provide a more analytically useful definition of our subject? Should our chosen subject be seen as a separate discipline at all?

It is important to remember that areas of academic study are abstract creations of our minds. They are an attempt to identify a viable field for examination in a world that at first seems a confusion of unordered and unanalysed information. But these defined areas of study – politics, biology, sociology and the like – do not actually exist in this carefully delineated manner in the outside world as our senses perceive it. In that world thoughts and actions occur at various times and places in a continuous, overlapping, disordered flood.

The overall understanding of a subject depends on the set of interrelated concepts – the framework or model – that we use to interpret the world. These concepts and models are not objective realities but analytical tools. It is not surprising, therefore, that scholars give a great deal of attention to the assumptions and prejudices that underlie their approach to their subjects. Such assumptions and prejudices inevitably colour our understanding of everything. More important, sometimes such assumptions and prejudices are subconscious and therefore not easily recognized or comprehended by ourselves. Thus, for example, it is fundamental to our analysis whether we assume an essentially materialistic interpretation of the world, or that nothing can be understood apart from a metaphysical insight and knowledge. It also matters a great deal whether we see politics as mainly concerned with the activities of a few 'great' people, or as receiving its impetus from the needs and drives of groups or the masses. How we understand politics will often depend on what we emphasize. Is politics, for example, primarily concerned with the resolution or containment of differences? Is it necessarily a public activity or can it be defined to include private areas of human social life such as the family? Does politics necessarily involve an ethical dimension, that is does it involve the ought as well as the 'is'? What is the ultimate goal and purpose of political activity? Does it in fact have an ultimate goal? And so on. The way in which these questions are answered gives focus and direction to our whole understanding of politics.

## Concepts

A model (a mental or theoretical framework) is composed of a set of interrelated concepts. 'Politics' is itself a concept. A concept is simply an idea defined in the mind as an aid to understanding; it is not given – we do not search for some 'objective' meaning. Nor is there an authority that can tell us definitively what a concept like politics 'means'. What we have to do first is examine what the concept means to recognized authorities, and then attempt to discover a core of meaning common to all, or most, of these authorities. Our own use of the concept will depend on this more or less common core of meaning, together with the refinements that we ourselves introduce to adapt the concept to our immediate purposes. Thus it is best to regard a concept not as something given and objective; rather, it is a tool that, while it has a broad purpose, can be adapted and refined for particular and specialized needs. A great deal of our study will be concerned with defining concepts, without which real understanding of the subject is impossible. Some fundamental political concepts are discussed in chapters 3 and 4.

## Models

It is our minds that impose order, and therefore meaning, on our thoughts and actions. Our brains assemble the sense data and organize them into a comprehensible form. Some data are ignored or relegated to the subconscious. The rest are ordered by connecting and interrelating key concepts in frameworks which are called models. Through them we make sense of our relation with the world. The use of models and its implications is discussed more fully in chapter 5. It is through a model, or mental framework, that we understand the world. Without it we would not be able to comprehend or relate to the world. This mental framework is not simply contained within our brain, clear, complete and identical in each of us. It is to a large extent created and developed out of the sum of our social experiences. People in different cultures will analyse and understand the world in different ways according to their various life experiences. No two human beings comprehend things in exactly the same way, although there are significant areas of similarity, otherwise we would not understand each other at all.

Therefore, our only means of understanding the world is in our own minds and is only to a limited extent under our own control. However, any model must also contain analogical and rational relationships between its parts that make sense to others as well to us. If the logic behind our mental framework has meaning only for ourselves (for example because it is based on false premises, circular arguments or exclusive metaphysical beliefs), we will not be able to communicate meaningfully with our fellow human beings – we will appear to be insane.

## A Definition of Politics and Political Activity

The most basic concept in the study of politics is that of 'politics' itself. A working definition of politics is: the way in which we understand and order our social affairs. This applies especially to the allocation of scarce resources, and its underlying principles. It also involves the means by which some people or groups acquire and maintain a greater control over the situation than others. Thus politics is above all an activity – concerned with people's social and material relationships, expressed in various ways in different places and continually changing through time. Clearly, therefore, politics is closely related to many other fields of knowledge, for example economics (material relationships), sociology (social relationships), geography (the spatial dimension) and history (the temporal dimension).

What distinguishes 'political activity' from 'politics' is action towards others. While people may think about politics, it is of no significance to anyone else, including the analyst of political life, until they act on their thoughts, whether verbally or physically. Let us consider the way in which the concept of political activity is used in everyday life in Great Britain. For example, it is often said that in Northern Ireland 'terrorism' will never succeed and ultimately there must be a political solution. What is meant by a political solution in this context and why is 'terrorism' not considered to be a political activity by the proponents of the argument? It is argued that political activity takes place only between certain individuals and groups that are publicly recognized as having an accepted right to behave in a certain way, and according to certain common recognized and enforceable rules. Groups and individuals without this legitimacy, or which act outside the rules as defined by the same public authorities, are deemed to be acting outside the arena of politics.

It will be seen that, in these cases, the types of activities regarded as political are delimited by one set of interested parties. The governmental authorities and political parties define their relations and activities as political, while excluding from the definition the activities of the terrorists. The Provisional Irish Republican Army (IRA), on the other hand, consider that they are involved in activities whose aims are unequivocally political – a restructuring of the political arrangements in Ireland. When captured and convicted they assert a right to be treated not as common criminals or even as prisoners of war but as political prisoners. The British government briefly recognized this special status, then regretted it and now holds that no such category of prisoner is recognized in English or Scottish law. The protagonists in this dispute therefore each define the term 'political' to advance their particular cause, a fact that has profound practical implications.

Another example of the significance of defining activities as 'political' or 'non-political' is the question of whether sports players, actors or show-business personalities should compete or perform in regimes disapproved of by their own government or a strong body of opinion at home. Until recently, many people objected to sporting or cultural relations with South Africa. A capitalist regime may have disliked such links with a communist regime, and vice versa, while others protest about relations with regimes that are thought to abuse human rights. When such controversies arise, it is common to hear people deplore the intrusion of politics into the sphere of sport or the arts. What is meant by 'politics' in this context? Since it is hardly the case that in sport and the arts there are no disputes over the allocation of public resources (that is political questions), at one level the argument seems to be that the intrusion of politics on what are considered to be private, non-political, activities leads to the abandonment of rational procedures and criteria (equated with 'common sense' and 'reasonableness'). In fact, what it often means is that habitual behaviour or vested interests are being disturbed. No social activity can consider itself exempt from potential wider public concern when it impinges on matters of controversy and disagreement, such as discrimination against sections of the community. Political arguments are not necessarily any more unreasonable than any other sort of argument.

At another level, since governments and political parties are very obviously involved in making decisions about both sport and the arts, the argument for keeping out politics may be no more than an attempt to camouflage political goals in the hope of generating support for them. For example, the South African government used to employ the 'keep politics out of sport' argument while strenuously attempting to induce foreign sports players to break the international boycott of sporting links with the country and thus legitimate its policies on apartheid. Communist and liberal democratic governments have also promoted sport to raise the status and prestige of their regimes. More generally, nationalist, racial and other concerns will impart political overtones to sporting achievements, and performers and artists are also likely to express themselves in ways that have profound political implications. Therefore, whatever the views of others, from the point of view of the student of politics, sport and the arts are areas in which political activity can be expected and where it can often be seen taking place.

Indeed, while what is considered to be the proper sphere of political activity will vary from time to time and from place to place, the student of politics cannot in principle exclude the possibility of political activity in any sphere of human social life at any level, from the smallest of groups, such as the nuclear family, to the activities of international organizations.

The Soviet Union presented an especially interesting example of the concept of political activity. For some (for example Crick, 1982), politics implies a public arena in which the dialogue and contest essential to political activity takes place. It is argued that this is typical of liberal democracies such as Great Britain and the United States. Before the advent of Mikhail Gorbachev as general secretary of the Communist Party of the Soviet Union (CPSU) in 1985, such a public arena barely existed. What was termed 'public discussion' was, rather, explanation and elucidation. Contested argument occurred only in closed party and governmental commissions and committees, and in backstairs disputes (Hough and Fainsod, 1979, pp. 285–93). The use of public media to strengthen one's political position was rare and usually very discreet. Khrushchev was a notable example of a Soviet politician who used the media for this purpose, and conservationists sometimes 'went public' in an attempt to protect the environment. Under Gorbachev there was an explosive expansion of public discussion of a variety of political issues and social ills. But can we say that there was such a thing as political activity in the Soviet Union before 1985? We would argue that recognizable political activity was present. Argument and discussion did take place in the decision-making process. The activities indulged in by party and government officials, however restricted, were similar to those engaged in by people we call politicians in Western liberal democracies. It would be extremely misleading to imply that there was a fundamental absence of discussion in deciding questions concerning the social order.

The restricted nature of the public arena in that regime does not affect the conclusion. To require a very open public arena for discussion seems to narrow the definition unduly and to restrict political activity to a particular set of economic and social arrangements, that is liberal democratic ones. Political activity may be far more restricted in some regimes than in others, but it is difficult to envisage a regime, however authoritarian or autocratic, where some degree of political activity does not take place at various levels within itself and between it and other regimes.

Such a definition leads to further questions. What are people doing when they engage in political activity? How do we recognize political behaviour or a political idea? We defined politics as being concerned with the arrangements for ordering our social affairs and the degree of control that individuals and groups have over it. It is essential that all participants should have some potential influence and that the relationships between individuals and groups should to some degree be flexible and susceptible to change. People who can do absolutely nothing to influence their situation cannot act politically. Social relationships that are rigidly governed and controlled by custom, law or technical rules also have a low political potential. In most societies there is some restriction on the types of public political activity as we have defined them, but the degree of restriction varies considerably. Some societies are, or claim to be, comparatively open, that is the opportunity to participate in the process by which society orders the allocation of resources is widely distributed throughout the population. In other societies this opportunity is restricted to comparatively few elite groups or even to a few individuals. These are frequently referred to as 'closed' societies. Whether and to what extent the ability to participate can be translated into power to affect decisions remains to be discussed.

## Conclusion

Politics is a concept that we employ as part of the models, or mental frameworks, through which we interpret and try to understand the world around us. Our understanding therefore depends at least partly on how we define politics and political activity. There is no 'correct' definition of politics or its related concepts, and the term is variously defined according to the different uses to which it is put. These include attempts by revolutionaries to win support or by politicians in or seeking power, or as the basis for generalizations about political life made by political analysts. In each case we should ask why politics is defined in a particular way. At this point it seems best to retain a broad approach and to accept the possibility of labelling as political a wide range of activities, institutional arrangements and ideas.

## Questions for Discussion

1   What do you consider to be the essential core meaning of the concept of 'politics'?
2   What are the advantages and disadvantages of studying politics separately from the other social sciences, such as economics and sociology?
3   Does political activity require an open society with firmly established civil liberties? (What is an open society?)

## Further Reading

Laver, M. (1983), *Invitation to Politics*. Oxford, Blackwell, ch. 1.
Leftwich, A. (ed.) (1984), *What is Politics?*. Oxford, Blackwell, esp. chs 1, 4 and 8.
Machiavelli, N. (1961 edn), *The Prince*. Harmondsworth, Penguin.
Marx, K. (1967 edn), *The Communist Manifesto*. Harmondsworth, Penguin.
Meehan, E. (1986), Women's studies and political studies. In J. Evans et al., *Feminism and Political Theory*. London, Sage, pp. 120–38.
Zuckerman, A.S. (1991), *Doing Political Science*. Oxford, Westview, ch. 1.

# 2

# Approaches and Levels

## Introduction

We have defined politics as being concerned with the arrangements for ordering social affairs and with the degree of control individuals and groups have over this ordering. In this chapter we consider some analytical approaches to the study of politics, then go on to discuss the different levels of society at which political activity occurs.

## Approaches to the Study of Politics

Approaches to the study of politics and, consequently, definitions of politics have varied considerably in the past. For Plato the meaning of politics, as of everything else, was related to the search for the ideal society which alone gave meaning to the imperfect world of the senses. For many centuries after Plato, and throughout the medieval period, the preoccupation of students of politics (both Christian and Islamic) was essentially ethical – they were concerned with how human society ought to be ordered and governed within a religious context. After the Reformation in Europe such approaches were matched and modified by secular concerns – the primary need for the best secular order rather than a continual striving for perfect social harmony at one with the mind of God. Eventually, this led to the development of sociological, psychological and legal analysis. However, such thought was still dominated by the concepts of progress and the perfection of both the human individual and society. At first, these were seen as a real possibility attainable by human means, in contrast to the medieval Christian view of the inevitable inadequacy of purely human achievements. In the West such ideas seem less important today, in the face of disillusionment and cynicism bred by the apparently intractable problems of war and poverty. But while politicians in many states attempt simply to cope with crises pragmatically, idealistic notions of society still provide the impetus for much political action which may, as in Iran in 1979, culminate in revolution.

For the past century, in Western capitalist democracies politics has often been seen as an aspect of law, of the working and interrelationship of formal institutions like, in Great Britain, Crown, Parliament, Cabinet, Civil Service and the legal system. This preoccupation with legal and political institutions can be seen even earlier in the work of political philosophers from Aristotle to Locke who were concerned with how their preferred ends could be achieved in practice. But a variety of approaches have also developed, all centred around the concept of politics as part of social and psychological activity. The emphasis is on underlying motivations of political activity which are said to be material needs and psychological beliefs (the two motivations are not unrelated). There is a wide diversity of theories to assist the study of the political relevance of such needs and ideas. These range from theories of individualism to those of group politics and the class-conflict theories of Marxists. There is also a wide range of methods by which politics is studied, from a variety of descriptive or speculative approaches in history and philosophy, to the quantitative methods of the natural sciences, applied by the behaviouralists who believed them capable of producing precise and verifiable knowledge.

The two dominant approaches to politics are usually referred to as 'political philosophy' and 'political science'. The first is more speculative and normative and discusses how, for example, concepts of justice, liberty and democracy may be clarified and realized in practice. The second has developed in the nineteenth and twentieth centuries. After the Second World War there was an attempt to understand the analysis of politics as quantitative and inductive, akin to the supposed objectivity of the natural sciences rather than in an institutional-legal manner. More recently, there has been a return to an acceptance of the inevitability of a more contingent, subjective but also normative analysis of political activity. The approaches of political philosophy and political science to the understanding of politics are, in different ways, integrated with political activity. Political philosophy considers the significance of the rationalizations and explanations that justify and make sense of politics for those who are actively involved in the political process, and how societies may more often live up to their own frequently exaggerated claims. The political-science approach, with its various methods, was developed in the twentieth century as a reaction against both speculative political philosophy and the study of formal institutions. It was once argued against political philosophy that political analysis should be detached and value-free, using the quantitative tools and methods of the natural sciences increasingly facilitated by the rapid development of data-processing technology. It was argued against the institutional-legal approach that how people behave politically (and predicting how they will behave in the future) was more important than the purported workings of political institutions, but it is now realized that formal political and legal institutions and processes can and do affect behaviour and therefore cannot be ignored. Thus military, bureaucratic, police, legislative, executive and judicial institutions clearly have an independent impact on the behaviour both of those who are members of the institutions and of outsiders. There is also now a more realistic appreciation of the inevitable subjective element in political analysis and of the difficulty of subjecting fluctuating social behaviour to scientific analysis.

The major approaches to the study of politics today are, characteristically, the study of norms, institutions, structures and behaviour. As we have seen, the first of these is mainly concerned with the purpose and ends of politics and the last with the actual behaviour of individuals. Clearly, although they provide distinctive approaches to the subject, they are closely connected. For example, much, if not all, political behaviour is related to the desire to attain certain ideals. They in turn are also closely related to the other approaches – the study of decision-making in the context of laws, institutions and structures. As we shall see, the debate as to the relative importance in the political life of a people of, say, institutions, structures, behaviour and norms continues between the proponents of one and another approach. However, there are important interactions between all four main approaches to the study of politics, even if much research concentrates on just one or two of them, or to the relationships between them. We must also consider the structures that are more deeply rooted in society than these institutions, that is the division of social life into various routinized networks of relationships, such as those based on caste, religion, ethnicity, gender and class.

One other dimension of the debate between proponents of the various approaches has been the place of values. Political philosophy deals in a self-conscious way with values, while early behaviouralists claimed that their methods were value-free and eschewed any involvement in politics on the grounds that it compromised their objectivity. But, as was soon pointed out by critics, their meticulous study of data as found, with its implicit support of the status quo, was not necessarily any more value-free than speculations on what could or should be by a committed radical reformer. A growing realization of this (for example Easton, 1969) led increasing numbers of the profession to abandon their stance of pseudo-objectivity and to acknowledge the inevitable role of values in the study of politics. This has been effectively expressed by the remark that truth is 'not the ever-receding horizon but the ground beneath our feet' (Kaplan, 1964, p. 321). The actual manifestation of this varies widely, usually according to the values of the researcher, from the analysis of how governments could more successfully implement their chosen policies to radical proposals for change.

Thus the study of society cannot be completely objective: the values and interests of the observer will always intrude from the start, at the stage of choosing what and what not to study. Since complete objectivity is unattainable, it is important that students of politics make their own values clear so that others can judge their work in that light. Furthermore, it is important that statements are not made without supporting evidence, that an open mind is maintained towards evidence contrary to what is expected, and that findings are made available to others so that there is a possibility of genuine debate and discussion.

## Levels of Political Activity

### The Size of Political Groups

There are several approaches to the consideration of levels of political activity. It could be argued that as soon as two, or perhaps three, people come together there is the potential for political activity to occur. Such a group may co-operate or come into conflict over some choice to be made, but relationships of control and subordination, bargaining and compromise, may all be present as they set about ordering their affairs. The most common manifestation of politics at this level is the family group. But, while the significance of the political dimensions of the family should not be underestimated, they must be placed primarily within the private, rather than the public, domain of life, and we shall deal with them only in so far as the family is a key socializing influence on children.

More generally, small face-to-face groups are found everywhere in political life. From the committee of a tenants' association to the Security Council of the United Nations, the decisive political arena is frequently that of the small group. Beyond a certain size, usually a few dozen, it is impossible, in practice, for everyone in the group to participate in detailed decision-making. Groups of several hundred people – like a parliamentary assembly – can usually take broad, more generalized, decisions. Once the size of decision-making groups reaches thousands, order and coherence are difficult to maintain, and demagoguery can easily dominate proceedings.

## The Neighbourhood

An alternative, and perhaps more useful, way to distinguish more clearly between levels of politics is to use the geographical or spatial dimension. The 'lowest' level or, in spatial terms, the smallest arena of political activity in the public domain is the neighbourhood. Here the contest over the allocation of resources is likely to be concerned with housing, schools, roads, rubbish collection, public transport and so on. Because the size of the arena is small, the main actors may well be individuals. But, frequently, tenants' and residents' associations develop to provide both a forum for political debate within the neighbourhood and a means of using greater leverage against higher levels of the political process.

Organizations for monitoring and dealing with neighbourhood affairs exist in the United States and the former Soviet republics. In Britain the traditional officially recognized groups at this level have been the parish councils which still operate in rural areas and, more recently, neighbourhood councils (part of the central government response to the problems of the inner city), preservation societies, watch schemes and so on have been set up in many areas. Their role is defined as representative rather than executive.

## Local Politics

The next level is that usually referred to as 'local politics', although the population of the localities thus indicated ranges widely from a few thousand to a few million. What distinguishes this from the neighbourhood level is that it is the lowest level at which the 'who gets what, when and how' of politics is decided, usually with varying degrees of central government interference (see chapter 23). The actors in local politics vary, depending partly on the size of the local group. Groups and associations of those with an interest in the course of the local economy and the level of local services will be most active. In the United States and Britain, the larger the area concerned the more important the organized political parties tend to be. In the Soviet Union local cells and districts provided the lowest levels of party and state organization respectively.

## Regional Politics

In the three countries that we have chosen as case-studies, it is useful to distinguish another level of politics between the local and the national levels. It is difficult to make generalizations about regional politics because it manifests itself in different ways depending on the size, demography and governmental structure of the country. The fifty states that make up the United States of America are based partly on the early settled communities and partly on land acquired subsequently. They have provided a crucial arena and focus of identity for political activity in that country.

In the Soviet Union there were fifteen union republics (plus other autonomous republics and regions), of which by far the largest was the Russian Soviet Federative Socialist Republic with over 50 per cent of the population and 75 per cent of the land area of the Soviet Union as a whole. These political and administrative divisions were based on nationality. The cultural and economic differences such as those between the states of the United States were in the Soviet Union compounded by the even greater physical size of the country, and the language and nationality differences that existed, not only between the republics, but also within them. The now independent republics continue to have regional administrative arrangements, particularly to cater for the ethnic minorities within their borders.

The relatively small United Kingdom (geographically not demographically), with its unitary structure of government, makes use of the intermediate – regional level – primarily for the administration of various services (some privately run, some public) such as transport, gas, water, electricity and health. In England they do not provide a politically important focus of identity. It is different, of course, where the regions contain distinct nationalities other than the English. Irish, Scottish and Welsh nationalism have at various times had a considerable political impact in Britain (see chapter 22).

Currently, most of the discussion on this issue takes place within the context of a 'Europe of the regions'. The Assembly of European Regions, established in 1985, has 171 members drawn from both Eastern and Western Europe. Although it is defined as lying between central and local government, the concept of the 'region' covers a multitude of situations, for example Wales is a member although it is a nation, and so are most of the Scottish regional governments although they are, strictly speaking, local authorities. On the other hand, Belgium, Italy, Spain and France have all introduced less ambiguous structures of regional representation in the last twenty years (*New Statesman and Society*, 19 June 1992, p. 17).

## The National Level

The major focus of the study of politics in modern times has been the national level. This is largely because the nation-state has increasingly provided the major institutional setting for the allocation of resources and the main focus of people's identity for 300 years in Europe (less elsewhere). The collapse of the Soviet Union means that the last of the great empires has finally gone, leaving the nation-state as the main focus of political identity. There is frequently a poor fit between feelings of national identity and the formal boundaries of nation-states. The Soviet Union faced this problem (as do its successor republics) and so, perhaps, does Great Britain, to a lesser extent. Such national minorities join the many complex forces operating politically at the national level – the national organizations of groups, associations, parties, trade unions and representatives of lower levels of government in the case of the United States and Great Britain. In the Soviet Union the hierarchy of the CPSU used to provide almost the only official channel of influence. Many of the successor states, however, are developing a range of political institutions and activities similar to those in liberal democracies. They, too, have to contend with language and cultural differences.

Today the proliferation of nation-states, each with a seat at the United Nations, can obscure the fact that, apart from a recognition of their independence in international law, they are a very disparate collection of political entities. Some are very small, either in geographical area or with populations numbering a few hundred thousand, or both. Others cover vast areas with populations of hundreds of millions. Their origins may be located far back in history or be very recent. Some have 'natural' geographical and demographic boundaries. Others are the artificial creations of historical circumstances which may no longer be relevant to contemporary political realities. Their power and influence in the world, by virtue of their economic strength or military might, varies enormously. Similarly, power and prestige can, for a variety of reasons, wax or wane. The Soviet Union rose in power and prestige before its rapid decline. Great Britain has experienced a slow decline throughout the twentieth century. The United States finds itself in decline as an economic power in relation to the rise of such nation-states as Germany and Japan.

## The International Level

Finally, there is the international level. Conflict and co-operation between nation-states have always ensured an international dimension to politics. In this century international politics has acquired new importance with the occurrence of two world wars, the development of nuclear weapons capable of hitherto unprecedented destruction, and the development of complex economic interdependence. Again, there are various institutional manifestations of this, in military alliances such as the North Atlantic Treaty Organization (NATO) and the former Warsaw Pact, and in politico-economic alliances such as the European Community and the communist organization Comecon (the latter now dissolved in its old form). There are many forums for the discussion of international disputes, such as the United Nations and the Conference on Security and Co-operation in Europe, as well as the great variety of transnational organizations, both public and private, which are discussed further in chapters 20 and 21.

### Which is the Most Significant Level of Political Activity?

In this book we have chosen to follow the tradition of taking the nation-state as the primary focus of our discussion of political activity, but it is important to bear in mind that there are strong movements towards both more international political decision-making and, at the same time, a devolution or even dispersal of power from large nation-states to smaller political units – often states based on exclusively nationalistic criteria. The nation-state has certainly evolved and, in many ways, diminished in importance in the latter half of the twentieth century, in spite of the great increase in their number.

The European Community has adopted the principle of 'subsidiarity', which holds that political decisions should be taken at the lowest practical and effective level. At all levels there are similarities and differences in the way political activity is conducted. Politics, at whatever level, is concerned with the ordering of social affairs for the allocation of scarce resources, and with the means by which some people acquire greater control than others. As we have seen, what is likely to differ is the identity of the actors: the individual is the basic actor at all levels, of course, but while a few individuals may dominate neighbourhood politics, as we move up the levels, groups and organizations become increasingly important. Finally, at the international level, individuals, groups and organizations are joined by nation-states, as well as international and transnational organizations. The relations of actors and institutions to the various levels of politics are summarized in Table 2.1.

## Conclusion

We need to be aware, when studying politics, of the different emphases of philosophical, sociological and psychological analyses. Any approach we employ inevitably has value implications for our study. We should ask ourselves why it seems appropriate, at a particular time, to study politics from one perspective rather than another. On a deeper level, we should ask ourselves what is the kind of truth we are seeking to discover.

**Table 2.1** Levels of political activity

| Levels | Institutional manifestation (if any) | | | Actors |
|---|---|---|---|---|
| | *United Kingdom* | *United States* | *Soviet Union* | |
| International | United Nations (UN) European Community (EC) North Atlantic Treaty Organization (NATO) | | | Mainly national and international organizations and nation-states |
| National | Central government | Federal government | Federal government | Local and state bureaucracy, parties and groups |
| State | Not applicable | State governments | Autonomous republics and regions | Local and state bureaucracy, parties and groups |
| Regional | Scottish and Welsh authorities etc. | Not applicable | Not applicable | Local and state bureaucracy parties and groups |
| Local | District and county councils | Town and county councils, special districts | Local soviets | Neighbourhood councils, parties and groups |
| Neighbourhood | Community and neighbourhood councils | Community and neighbourhood councils | Neighbourhood meetings | Individuals and tenants' associations |

It is impossible within the space of a brief work to deal adequately with the manifestations of political activity at all the levels of society at which it occurs. While we shall focus predominantly on the national level, it is important to consider whether the models and concepts that we discuss are applicable at all levels, or at some levels rather than others. We must also ask: why do traditional studies of politics concentrate on the national level? And, even if this has in the past seemed to be the most fruitful arena of politics for study, is it necessarily so today and what may happen in the future? For example, what of arguments that the nation-state has outlived its usefulness and that government would be better split between subnational units (to increase the possibilities of participation) and international units (to make international political action *vis-à-vis* increasingly international economic problems more feasible)? At whatever level we study politics we must always consider which of the various approaches or combination of approaches is likely to be most fruitful for our understanding.

## Questions for Discussion

1  To what extent are different approaches to the study of politics mutually exclusive or, on the other hand, complementary?
2  Are political analysis and political action mutually incompatible?
3  Is there an ideal level at which most important political activity should take place?

## Further Reading

Blondel, J. (1978), *Thinking Politically*. Harmondsworth, Penguin, chs 2 and 3.
Leftwich, A. (ed.) (1984), *What is Politics?* Oxford, Blackwell, chs 5 and 6.
Leys, C. (1983), *Politics in Britain*. London, Heinemann, ch. 1.
Miliband, R. (1977), *Marxism and Politics*. Oxford, Oxford University Press, pp. 17–22.
Randall, V. (1991), Feminism and political analysis. *Political Studies*, 34 (3), pp. 513–32.
Zuckerman, A.S. (1991), *Doing Political Science*. Oxford, Westview, chs 3 and 6.

# 3

# Key Concepts (1): Power, Authority and Legitimacy

## Introduction

As we saw in chapter 1, political concepts are ideas that we use as aids to understanding. They are crucial elements in the analytical models discussed in chapters 6 and 7. In this chapter we examine some concepts which are central to the study of politics, in the belief that words such as 'power' and 'influence' must be carefully defined so that analysis can go beyond the often superficial nature of 'common-sense thinking' and analysts can communicate with each other with a minimum of misunderstanding. Throughout, the criterion employed in evaluating the definition of concepts is not whether it is 'right' or 'wrong' but whether it is analytically useful – whether it helps our understanding.

## Power

For many analysts of politics, power is not just one important concept among many, but it is the central concept of the discipline. Shortly, we shall compare power with some of its related concepts, influence, legitimacy and authority, but for now let us define power as 'the ability to get others to do what you wish, assuming this is different from what they would otherwise have done, with the use or threat of sanctions if necessary'. The notion of sanctions or coercion is what distinguishes between power and influence, influence being power without sanctions. Sanctions may be either positive (for example rewards of money or position) or negative (punishment or exclusion from participation). The centrality of power to the study of politics may now appear clearer. It exists in all political processes, however democratic they may be. In all known political processes there comes a point when someone, or a group of people, will be obliged to do something they would otherwise not do: power is being exercised over them. This is never a simple one-way relationship between governor and governed. The most autocratic of rulers necessarily has his or her power circumscribed in various ways. There are limits to what even the most subservient subjects will tolerate without at the very least becoming demoralized and developing passive resistance. No ruler can survive without significant support from some groups, whose interests will always have to be considered. Even rulers who claim divine sanction, or divinity, have not been immune from overthrow, as the pharaohs in Egypt and the dalai lamas in Tibet have discovered. As Nicholas II, the last Tsar of All the Russias, is said to have remarked, he could issue orders, but the difficulty was getting them carried out.

In the complex industrial societies of the world today the situation is even more confusing. For such societies to operate effectively they must have the general support and co-operation not only of special groups such as the army, but of the masses as a whole. Not that there are no particularly influential groups whose support is essential, but in modern society there are many of these. Hence the exercise of power is the result of a good deal of manoeuvring for position and of placating of interests. It involves the use of persuasion rather than the issuing of orders. If we take the British Prime Minister and the President of the United States, both of whom have frequently been described as very powerful, we shall find that, while their consent and support are necessary for major projects to be accepted, they are seriously constrained in the decisions that they make by pressures from influential individuals and groups, by the need for party support and by the desire to be re-elected within a relatively short time. In addition, there are often strong external pressures from international commitments. These may arise from, for example, a weak economic position making the wishes of the International Monetary Fund extremely significant, or from the harsh realities of military defeat, as the United States discovered in Vietnam.

In the Soviet Union the General Secretary of the CPSU was the most powerful person in the state, yet Stalin had to struggle to consolidate his position over rivals throughout the 1920s.

Khrushchev was overthrown when he upset and alienated the major interests of Soviet society. Brezhnev's hold on power visibly weakened as he contended with ill health and increasingly intractable economic and social problems. Gorbachev achieved great things by the exercise of his power as general secretary, but he released forces that he could not control and, in the end, his decrees were ignored. He could not prevent the breakup of the Soviet Union. His successors, the presidents of the post-Soviet republics, are also trying to establish themselves, and Boris Yeltsin, the President of Russia, has more than once been checked by the Russian parliament.

The most obvious question in any country's politics appears to be: where does power lie? It is an important question, but that any answer can, in fact, be only partial or possibly even misleading. The assumption that the source of power can be located may be erroneous. Power may be fleetingly exercised and its location ever changing. The question of where power resides, and how it should be studied, is bound up with the debates over whether we should study institutions or structures (discussed in chapter 2). It is also at the very heart of the dispute between proponents of the pluralist, elitist and Marxist models which we shall examine in chapters 6 and 7.

Pluralists are interested in the exercise of power where it can be observed. This means that they concentrate on the making of decisions in the policy-making process. Even if this cannot be observed directly, it can be reconstructed from participants' accounts, with a view to reaching conclusions as to who was more powerful than whom and so on. The advantage of this method is that, given sufficiently accurate information, it may be possible to identify clearly who wields influence or power and with respect to what areas of policy. On the other hand, it has the drawback of assuming that the decisions made in this relatively open forum are indeed the most important ones. Critics of pluralism sometimes argue that difficult or more far-reaching issues never reaching this stage of decision-making, being instead repressed by techniques such as manipulation of the media or simply turning a deaf ear, for example race relations or housing in Britain. In public, politicians refer to race relations as a problem of community relations, which is a politically manageable way of dealing with racial problems. They are reluctant to accept that racism may be endemic in many government, private and police organizations, and to discuss its eradication. Similarly, at a time of scarce resources, the housing issues concentrate on whether the country can afford to continue to subsidize public housing far more than on whether it can afford to continue to subsidize owner-occupation through tax relief on mortgages.

In the Soviet Union most decisions were taken in private, there being no real public arena for political discussion and debate. Decisions were then presented to the country for 'discussion' (that is elucidation), wrapped in the ideological rationalizations of Marxism-Leninism. An idealized picture was presented which ignored unwelcome realities. Sometimes these much more subtle exercises of power may be 'observable' in the sense that a 'decision not to decide' may be made by a group. Frequently, such exercises of power are not ascertainable, simply because the group concerned does not have to take a decision; its shared belief that such a matter is not a 'political' issue is enough to ensure that it never arises. If we accept the possibility that this could happen, then we are faced with the tremendous methodological problem of demonstrating that it actually does happen. How can we demonstrate the exercise of power where it occurs solely in the minds of some participants? This has led some analysts, particularly those of the elitist school (see chapter 6) to study the social backgrounds of top decision-makers. Their likely attitudes and behaviours over a range of issues, including those where apparently little overt debate takes place, are inferred from their backgrounds. While it is difficult to see how else to investigate this area, it is, clearly, fraught with dangers.

The discussion about power has been taken a stage further by Marxist and neo-Marxist analysts, who argue that concentration on the making of either positive or negative decisions is essentially misleading. They see the very structure of social and economic life as organized so that it operates inevitably in the interests of the ruling class, who do not have to reinforce explicitly their dominance in every action they take. Socialization through the family, education and the media ensure that acceptance of the basic structures of capitalism is so widespread that anyone contesting them is immediately classified as an extremist or a utopian dreamer. Similarly, in authoritarian communist states the norms of official Marxism-Leninism were taken for granted which bolstered the power of ruling elites. Many writers view this as just another aspect of power. For example, Lukes (1974) speaks of it as the 'third dimension' of power, but for the sake of clarity we consider it useful to view this as 'control'. In terms of the existence of sanctions and of people's behaviour being changed from what it would have been, control is the same as power. Where it differs is that even the power-wielders may not be consciously aware of why they are acting as they are; in an important sense, they are as much victims of the structural constraints as those over whom power is wielded. For example, an employer issuing redundancy notices to some of his or her work-force is not necessarily aware of exercising power over the work-force. He or she may, indeed, be genuinely upset in sacking them, but the need to make profit in a capitalist system may mean that such action cannot be avoided if the firm is to avert bankruptcy. It is the employer's decisions that control the situation, subject to any resistance that the work-force can mount. Again, this causes acute methodological problems. How can we ascertain the exercise of control in situations where none of the participants is consciously aware that it is happening? In some respects, it may be possible; for example, the content of education and the media can be examined for indications of the basic assumptions, attitudes and beliefs that are being transmitted to the population, but then we come up against the problem of interest – in whose interest is it that certain attitudes are transmitted and certain social and economic structures preserved? We shall consider this in the next chapter, but before that there are two other concepts closely related to power that should be mentioned.

## Authority and Legitimacy

Authority is closely connected with power, but again it is useful to distinguish the concepts. We can define authority in the same way as we have defined power, with an additional factor, that those over whom power is exercised must believe that the power-wielder has the moral right to exercise power and to employ sanctions if necessary. For example, I may be able to persuade you, by some combination of threats, to give me a proportion of your income, but it is extremely unlikely that you would acknowledge my moral right to do so. In other words, I may be able to exercise power over you, but it cannot be called authority. On the other hand, you may grumble at paying a proportion of your income to the state in the form of tax but you probably acknowledge the state's authority to demand it. To be able to replace power with authority is thus the aim of all governments, if only because it makes the task of governing much easier than having to rely entirely on rewards and punishments.

This recognition of the right of an individual or group to rule is also referred to as 'legitimacy'. This may originate in various ways, for example, as first suggested by the German sociologist Max Weber, by way of a social tradition such as tribal chiefs or by reason of a person's charisma. Most commonly today, at least among nation-states, legitimacy is conferred by the observance of accepted legal or constitutional procedures, and the occupation and control of the requisite offices or institutions by those involved. The most common legitimating procedure in the world today is free election. President Gorbachev found his power and authority seriously undermined by the fact that he had never submitted himself to popular election. His main rival, Boris Yeltsin, took full advantage of this and made sure that he did get such popular electoral support.

Ideally, political decision-makers wish to maximize their authority or to legitimate power. As we have seen, it is possible to exercise power without authority for a time but it is a rather unstable situation, for rulers without legitimacy are obliged to rely more on coercion. But is it possible to possess authority without power? In some cases rulers overthrown by a *coup d'-état* but who escape into exile may continue to be seen by a greater or lesser proportion of the people as the legitimate rulers of the state, but they may retain little power to give effect to their wishes. On the other hand, those seizing power hasten to acquire legitimacy so that their exercise of power and authority will not have to rely excessively on coercion. They will often go through the legal and constitutional forms and procedures in order to claim legitimacy. Others, like the Bolsheviks after the 1917 revolution, will seek to persuade people to accept a new form of legitimacy. In the case of the Bolsheviks, it was the assumption of power by the industrial masses following the inexorable logic of history. But recognized, accepted legitimacy takes time to establish and consolidate – as the Bolshevik revolutionaries discovered. There is also room for much debate over the extent to which legitimacy represents the genuine rather than the manipulated feelings of the people. This is discussed in more detail in chapter 24.

## Conclusion

Concepts are the significant components of models. We have suggested that the phenomenon of power, and its related concepts of influence, authority and legitimacy, are central to the study and understanding of politics. The crucial outstanding questions remain, however, of where power resides in societies, how it is exercised and the best means of studying it. These questions are closely related and an answer to one more or less determines the answer to the others. The models of democratic politics, which are discussed in chapters 6 and 7, give different answers to these questions.

## Questions for Discussion

1  Is there one acceptable definition of power?
2  Devise an outline for a study of where power resides in an institution or community with which you are familiar.
3  Between 1990 and 1993 the British government levied a local poll tax (the community charge). What do the circumstances surrounding the initiation and repeal of this tax tell us about the legitimacy of the government's actions?

## Further Reading

Ham, C. and M. Hill (1984), *The Policy Process in the Modern Capitalist State*. Brighton, Wheatsheaf, ch. 4.
Lukes, S. (1974), *Power: A Radical View*. London, Macmillan.
Miller, D. (ed.) (1991 edn), *The Blackwell Encyclopaedia of Political Thought*. Oxford, Blackwell, pp. 28–31, 397–400.
Schwarzmantel, J. (1987), *Structures of Power*. Brighton, Wheatsheaf, introduction.
Tinder, G. (1986), *Political Thinking: The Perennial Questions*, 4th edn. Boston, Little, Brown, ch. 4.

# 4

# Key Concepts (2): Ideology, Interest and Choice

## Ideology

'Ideology' is a concept that is widely used but its meaning is not always precisely defined, or if it is the meaning applied to it may vary from user to user. Broadly speaking, ideology refers to a more or less coherent set of ideas that provides a guide to action. Many people have tried to distinguish the more 'official' or codified collections of principles or ideas found, for example, in communist systems from the ideas found in liberal democracies, which have no official authorization and which are not necessarily set out in definitive texts. This distinction is unhelpful, however. It is easy to point to the contrast between the authoritative citing of Marxist-Leninist principles in the Soviet Union and the 'unofficial' expressions of opinion in liberal democracies, but there is a wide consensus, both among ruling groups and further afield, concerning the generally accepted ideas of liberalism and democracy. Pressures to conform can be brought to bear on those who dissent from these views too openly. A clear example in liberal democracies is the concept of individualism – the central value to society of the individual human being whatever his or her station in life. From this principle many applications and practices are derived: equality before the law, the rights of private property, universal suffrage, the equal value of each vote, and other characteristics of liberal democracies.

The assumed, orthodox political philosophy underlying the thinking and rationalizations of the political process is of the greatest importance in giving a sense of common purpose and understanding to the great majority of the population. It creates a sense of identity between citizen and citizen, and between controlling groups and the great mass of the people. It is intended to create and sustain a sense of unity within what may be a great diversity of subcultures. Social and political pressures, or even coercion, may be used to preserve this outward sense of unity. Thus the many nationalities of the Soviet Union, the various ethnic groups that emigrated to the United States and the four nationalities plus ethnic minorities in Great Britain can, in principle, identify with each other as believers in communism or liberal democracy as appropriate.

The United States provides us with a very good example of this. The massive immigration into the country in the late nineteenth and early twentieth centuries brought millions of people from religious and cultural backgrounds quite different from those of the earlier North European immigrants. The process of Americanization undergone by these people in schools and the workplace presupposed an ideology of 'Americanism' which could be passed on. This resulted in some practices that may appear rather crass to Britons (for example the saluting of the flag), but it should be remembered that similar processes go on in all systems. They were less subtle in the United States because of the need for the rapid inculcation of national loyalty into new citizens. There were strong pressures to conform.

In the Soviet Union there was an ideological belief that the people were building a new, ideal form of society – communism – which would produce a better type of human being – 'new Soviet man' (*sic*). While different cultural traditions would remain, society would be united in a common purpose at the political and social levels. Once again, an intense political socialization programme was introduced in education, the workplace and elsewhere. Ceremonies and symbols (for example the 'Lenin corner' in schools) abounded to reinforce the point. Alternative ideologies were condemned and forbidden, or strictly circumscribed.

An essential characteristic of ideology is that its basic ideas are capable, on a day-to-day basis, of being stated as self-evident, not needing rational, systematic justification and explanation. Phrases such as 'in accordance with the revolutionary principles of Marxism-Leninism', 'this is a free country', 'equality under the law' evoke a response in the audience of emotional identity with the utterer of the sentiments. To question such statements is considered ridiculous or even disgraceful. Discussion of the pros and cons becomes at best an academic exercise, at worst incomprehensible or threatening to the audience. Such an ideology is considered to be a vital cementing force by controlling groups, who will seek to define and preserve it. It will be closely integrated with their understanding of history, myth and tradition (which are discussed in chapter 10). Interpretation of these sets of ideas, interlinked and integrated as they are, is intended to be a vital element in binding the citizens together in common understanding and common loyalty.

In the past Marxist analysts have suggested that it is the successful imposition of this 'dominant ideology', or 'hegemony' (as the Italian Marxist Gramsci would have it) by the ruling class, through their control of socialization and the intellectual life of capitalist societies, that enables them to appear so tolerant of opposition. In other words, when the mass of the citizenry accepts as self-evident the superiority of capitalism, it is much easier to govern than if physical repression has to be used. A limited amount of 'opposition' is then permissible. Recently, however, other analysts have suggested that it is not particularly clear that the working class does accept the tenets of ruling-class ideology. Studies of working-class attitudes and behaviour have indicated, rather, its frequent – if passive – rejection, and the maintenance instead of subcultural ideas, including a more realistic picture of the political strengths and weaknesses of the working class. It may be argued that this phenomenon is also found among religious and ethnic groups who play subordinate roles within the political process. Their normal quiescence is explained less, therefore, by ideological domination than by a realistic appreciation of, or 'pragmatic acquiescence' in, their position.

The collapse of the Soviet Union revealed that more than seventy years of intensive teaching of Marxist-Leninist ideology and the lack of opportunity for publicly expressing dissent failed to eradicate the influence of alternative sets of ideas, such as liberal democracy, nationalism and religion. Indeed, nationalism appears to have been strengthened in many areas because the administrative division of the country into units based on ethnic identity had given people a focus for national loyalty.

But whether or not the preferred ideology of the ruling group dominates society, ideology still provides, on the one hand, an important rationalization of the political process for its sympathizers and, on the other, a very important rallying-point and vehicle of opposition for groups critical of the process. Historically, the same ideology may be at one time a guidebook for revolutionaries, and at another an orthodoxy to be imposed by a ruling group. Thus liberalism was a revolutionary doctrine in the late-eighteenth-century war between the American colonies and Britain and, after the success of the Americans, it became established as the new orthodoxy. In late-nineteenth- and early-twentieth-century Russia Marxism was one among a number of competing revolutionary doctrines. From 1917 to the 1980s it became the orthodoxy to be pursued to the exclusion of all other doctrines. Meanwhile, alternative versions of Marxism continued to provide inspiration for revolutionaries elsewhere. It is important to remember that ideas often have a deep ethical and moral content which can galvanize people into taking drastic action. Ideas have potentially dynamic force and it is not enough to interpret politics simply as a cynical manipulation of the many by the few for the sake of power.

## Interest

The definition of 'interest' is, as we have seen, closely connected with that of power and subject to similar methodological difficulties. Interests are not the same as 'wants'. Someone may want a cigarette, but would probably also acknowledge that it would not be in their interest to smoke it because it would endanger their health. Pluralists, just as they concentrate on the most obvious and observable exercises of power, tend to take the most accessible definition of interest – people's interests are what they say they are. The problem with this definition in its simplest form is that it rules out any possibility that people's perceptions of their interests may be distorted by manipulations of the content of, say, education and the mass media. Given that people are presented with only a relatively restricted view of the possibilities open to them, this narrow definition of interests seems to be unduly inhibiting for the researcher. Many would agree that, ultimately, we do have to rely on people's own definition of their interests; to do otherwise is to substitute our definition of what people need for their own, and history is strewn with the corpses of those whose rulers knew best what was 'in their interest'. But people must be able to state their interest in conditions that are as free as possible from the distortions and manipulations provided by vested interests. Not only is this freedom extremely difficult to achieve, but it is not at all certain how we would know if we had achieved it! Therefore, this condition remains hypothetical.

One way of resolving the problem, suggested by authoritarian conservatives, is to give the state the right and responsibility to decide and enforce society's interests and priorities. Another possibility is provided by the structuralist school of contemporary Marxists. They reject any subjective view of interests and argue that true interests can be ascertained objectively within the context of capitalism only by reference to the existence of two opposing classes – the bourgeoisie and the proletariat – whose interests are entirely irreconcilable by definition. This is not open to validation or refutation – one either accepts or rejects the definitions. Others have suggested, however, that there is a way out of this apparent impasse. Saunders (1980, pp. 43–8) argues that it is possible to assess objectively whether interests have been met once the relationship between interest and the benefit from policies has been defined. For example, it would be possible to determine whether particular policies regarding housing or health care benefited some groups or classes more than others, and thus we could determine in whose interests the policies were administered, given that we could satisfactorily assume that better housing and health care are desired by (that is in the interests of) all, whether or not everyone recognizes the fact.

The pluralist response to this would be that it is still possible for groups to benefit *accidentally* from the policy process and that answering the question 'who benefits?' does not therefore enable us to conclude that we have also identified 'who rules'. We need to examine power and interest together: we are closer to identifying the ruling groups or classes when we find those whose preferences are most often translated into policies which in turn serve their interests.

## Choice

'Choice' is the last key concept to be considered here. We might have used the concept 'decision', but that would have given rise to a whole range of models dealing specifically with the process of decision-making by individuals, small face-to-face groups, firms, government departments and whole governments. These are clearly relevant to our purpose, but 'choice' is more useful, at this stage

simply as a slightly more general concept. The relationship between choice and power is close, as the following quotation from
the American political scientist Harold Lasswell makes clear:
'When we speak of the science of politics, we mean the science
of power. Power is decision-making. A decision is sanctioned
choice, a choice which brings severe deprivations to bear on anyone who flouts it' (quoted in Mackenzie, 1975, p. 173).

We suggested in chapter 2 that politics could be viewed as
operating at various levels, and so it is with choice and decision-
making, except that here we can start with the individual. For
example, how does the individual voter decide whether or not to
vote and how to vote, and why does an individual civil servant
or police officer choose to exercise discretionary power in one
way rather than another? Second, there is choice exercised by the
small group: what are the factors accounting for the decisions of
the numerous committees that permeate the political system? The
committee is ubiquitous in politics, ranging from the relatively
minor (such as the party committee in a ward) to the major (the
Russian Security Council, congressional committees in the United
States and the British Cabinet). Third, there is choice exercised by
the bureaucratic organization: how are decisions made by government departments and, indeed, the large number of private
and semi-public bureaucracies that increasingly dominate industrialized societies? The fourth level is that of whole governments.
This is probably the highest level at which it is possible to say
'so-and-so *decided* something'. Here one person or group of people
probably do endorse what then becomes a 'government decision'.
This cannot be said so easily of the final level, that is the choices
made by the entire political process or the country. Here any
choices or decisions made, as summed up in such headlines as
'America Moves Right', clearly do not derive from a decision in
the sense that an individual or a committee may make a decision.
They reflect instead a simple adding up of a large number of
individual preferences, through an opinion survey or election,
and the conclusion that they constitute some collective majority
choice or decision.

Each of these levels is, of course, larger and more complex and,
in fact, contains several examples of the previous level. Therefore, it may be argued, we cannot obtain a complete picture of
the choice-making process without examining the different levels
and the interaction between them. But it would be extremely
difficult to do this, and therefore when one level is being studied

various assumptions have to be made about the impact of other levels. This is yet another example of the abstraction and simplification processes that necessarily go on in the study of such complex realities. For example, in studying a large bureaucracy one is interested primarily in the interaction between the small groups (consultative committees and informal groups of work colleagues) that make up the department. Certain assumptions have to be made about the interaction within those groups and the psychologies of the individuals who compose them. However, we must always be alert to the fact that choices and decisions are frequently not actually made at the level that formally ratifies and announces that choice, for example a decision of 'Her Majesty's Government' in Britain will almost certainly have been taken within one section of one department and ratified by a higher authority.

Finally, let us consider how choices are finalized in any group, however large or small. There are basically three ways in which this can be done: in the words of a well-known book *Fights, Games and Debates* (Rapoport, 1960), or violence, numbers and words. The first of these is possibly the oldest method employed in any situation where unanimity on some course of action does not naturally prevail. It is not uncommon for force to be used or threatened, either to speed up the choice-making process or as a negative sanction against anyone breaking ranks later.

We would probably all agree that 'words' are a rather more civilized, if at times very frustrating, way of making choices. What could happen here is that a group faced with a choice agrees in advance that no decision will be finalized until there is unanimity or until everybody at least feel able to tolerate the decision. The smaller the group, and therefore the narrower the range of original preferences may have been, the more this is workable, of course. But the principle is enshrined in the European Community, where many decisions have to be agreed unanimously by the member countries. The end result is usually a compromise that all the member states can live with.

The third method of making choices – 'number', or voting – is the one with which we are probably most familiar in any group other than very small ones. The second method – waiting until everyone finds a choice at least tolerable – is possibly the fairest method, but it has the big disadvantage of being extremely time-consuming, if it does not result simply in deadlock. The idea of voting is in effect a pragmatic solution to the problem. Even if a group chooses to decide on the basis of votes, it remains to be ascertained just what size of majority is acceptable. Frequently, decisions are made on the principle of a simple majority, that is more voting *for* than *against*, regardless of how many abstain; but sometimes special majorities are required if the group's own constitution or rules are to be changed, for example in the United States constitutional amendments require two-thirds majorities in each house of Congress and then ratification by at least three-quarters of the fifty states.

The problem with voting (as with many other solutions adopted for pragmatic reasons) is that it cannot always be guaranteed to produce an accurate reflection of the preferences of the group. This is because the process of simply aggregating any number of individual preferences does not by any means produce a genuine collective preference. It is, for example, well known that the final decisions of any committee can depend as much on the order in which the votes are taken as on the actual first preferences of the members. But more often than not it works. In other words, people generally accept the result of a vote even though it reflects poorly the genuine collective preference. This brings us full circle back to power and legitimacy. Why and under what conditions do people accept the result of such votes? Do people really believe them to be the best available option? How are people convinced that it is in their best interest to accept the result? Why and under what conditions do people decide not to accept the verdict of voting procedures? These are all questions to be pondered.

## Conclusion

Ideology has been defined as a more or less coherent set of ideas that provides a guide for action. An ideology enables people to understand events and to decide their reaction by referring back to its major principles. Sometimes an ideology is adopted consciously; more frequently, it is taken as self-evidently true. To the extent that an ideology is shared among a people, it can provide a sense of identity and unity. Some would argue that this is manufactured to such an extent that the resulting ideology is a major tool by which the ruling class maintains its dominance in capitalist societies, adjusting its interpretation of the ideology in the process. However, the extent to which people can be dominated in this way is questionable. It seems that ruling ideologies may be more or less dominant depending on a wide variety of conditions. Ideology is important in the study of politics not only because it provides rationalizations for the dominance of some groups by others, but also because it frequently provides the rationalization and inspiration for revolts against dominant groups and classes.

The problem with the study of interest is whether we accept people's own definitions of their own best interests and deny the possibility of their being distorted, or we substitute our own view of their interests based on our supposedly superior insight. To decide between them we shall have to make some assumptions regarding at least short-term interests. How can this be done, avoiding the two pitfalls identified above? How are the incredible number and variety of politically relevant choices and decisions made within the political process to be studied? We need to avoid, on the one hand, drowning in detail and, on the other, over-simplification, particularly in relation to the complex inter-action between the various levels at which choices are made. Again, the answer is likely to lie in the use of models while main-taining a keen awareness of their shortcomings (see chapters 5, 6 and 7).

There will never be agreement on the ideal method of finaliz-ing choices. All existing methods have drawbacks. Violence may be most effective in the short run, but it is the most unfair and probably the least stable in the long run. Unconstrained debate is possibly the fairest but can be very frustrating, not to say exhausting. The use of numbers, that is a voting procedure, is the most frequently used method which manages to avoid the ex-treme unfairness of force and the time-consuming nature of endless debate. But it is only a pragmatic solution which can produce some strange results and which is itself subject to manipulation by some to the detriment of others.

## Questions for Discussion

1  Are ideas the central dynamic of a political system or merely one influence among many?
2  How can we relate the impact of government policies to the notion of the people's interests?
3  What is the fairest method for any group to adopt as a way of reaching decisions? (What are your criteria of fairness?)

# Further Reading

Barry, N. (1990), Ideology. In P. Dunleavy, A. Gamble and G. Peele
(eds), *Developments in British Politics* 3. Basingstoke, Macmillan,
ch. 2, pp. 17–41.

Evans, A.B. Jr (1992), The crisis of Marxism-Leninism. In S. White, A.
Pravda and Z. Gitelman (eds), *Developments in Soviet and Post-
Soviet Politics*, 2nd edn. Basingstoke, Macmillan, pp. 22–42.

Foley, M. (1991), *American Political Ideas*. Manchester, Manchester
University Press, introduction and conclusion.

Held, D. (1987), *Models of Democracy*. Cambridge, Polity, chs 5–8.

Jones, B. (1991), Political ideologies. In B. Jones (ed.), *Politics UK*. Hemel
Hempstead, Philip Allan, chs 7–10.

King, R. (1986), *The State in Modern Society*. London, Macmillan, chs
2, 3 and 6.

Lukes, S. (1974), *Power: A Radical View*. London, Macmillan.

Smith, G.B. (1992), *Soviet Politics: Struggling with Change*, 2nd edn.
Basingstoke, Macmillan, ch. 4.

# 5

# Models in the Study of Politics

## Introduction

As we noted in chapter 1, all of us construct models in our minds of the way in which the world works. In this chapter we shall look at some of them in more detail. Models act as frames of reference and enable us in our everyday lives to give meaning to isolated events by placing them a broader context. Then we can say, for example, that we understand why someone acted in a particular way, or why the government has, or has not, taken some particular action. Most of the time these models remain implicit; rarely do we think about them consciously, let alone subject them to critical examination. The academic study of any subject, including politics, is characterized, however, by much more explicit, self-conscious processes of model-building.

Definitions of a model are numerous in political literature but the basic concept is that of 'isomorphism'. Put simply, this means that there must be correspondence between the model and the thing it is modelling. This can be seen most clearly in the scale models of cars and ships which for some are toys but for engineers and navigators are working patterns. In the social sciences models assume the form of abstracted intellectual constructs, for example 'economic man', or 'ideal types' such as the model of bureaucracy advanced by Max Weber. In these cases the isomorphism between the model and the outside world is not as close as that in the scale model, but the model must contain the main features of the thing modelled. The extent of isomorphism varies between models: the 'ideal type' may be most useful as a yardstick against which to measure the deviations that occur in the world; other models attempt a closer approximation to that world.

## The Paradigm

Underlying these processes is the paradigm. The term has been defined in many different ways since its detailed elaboration by T.S. Kuhn (1962). The sense in which it is most often used by social scientists, which is different from Kuhn's original intention, is that of the methodological commitments shared by a particular scientific community. At its most general, we may refer to the paradigm dominant in contemporary Western society – in which knowledge derives not from metaphysical beliefs but from hypotheses submitted to critical and empirical evaluation. Alternatively, 'paradigm' can refer to the common traditions, assumptions and techniques of particular scientific disciplines as different as physics and politics. Without entering the debate as to whether the study of politics can ever be really scientific (whatever that means) in the same way as physics is, it is possible to identify certain paradigmatic procedures that must be followed if communication, debate and the evaluation of research are to be possible in the analysis of politics or any other social phenomenon.

For example, our explanations of phenomena must be logical. Let us say that our problem, or the thing to be explained, is: why does Mr Bloggs vote Conservative? Our answer to the problem or explanation is likely to derive from two sets of statements: the first a generalization such as 'all business people vote Conservative', and the other a statement of a particular fact such as 'Mr Bloggs is a businessman'. From these two statements it is reasonable to conclude that we have at least partly explained Mr Bloggs' voting habits. However, people being what they are, it is extremely unlikely that all business people vote Conservative; therefore in the social sciences we tend to employ 'probabilistic' generalizations such as '90 per cent of business people vote Conservative'. This inability to make universal generalizations is one important sense in which the analysis of politics differs in practice from that of physics.

More specifically, in figure 5.1 we identify three main paradigms which provide the basis upon which the study of the relationship of individuals and society has been constructed in the West in modern times. Within these paradigms, model-building

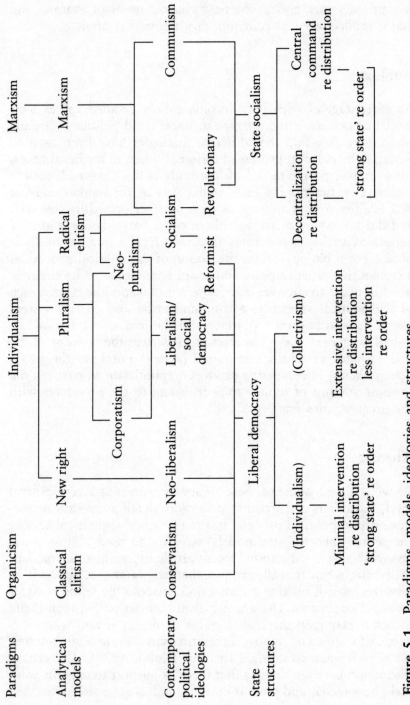

**Figure 5.1** Paradigms, models, ideologies and structures

is a primary task and in the next chapter we shall examine the major models used in contemporary political analysis.

## Analogy

An early stage of what may become a more detailed and explicit model of politics is the attempt to understand politics by means of analogy. We find that different analogies have been used to describe the political process at different times. In medieval times, for example, people talked of 'the body politic' in which society was seen as functioning in a similar way as the human body; it was healthy overall so long as each part performed its role well and did not try to usurp the role of other parts. Today a greater variety of analogies is employed, drawn from a number of disciplines. From biology comes the notion of the political process as a system that must respond and adapt to forces from its environment in order to survive; from cybernetics comes the related idea of the political system as a communication and control system steering towards certain objectives in the manner of a whale or a guided missile; and from economics derives the concept of the market-place in which consumers (voters) purchase the products (policies) of competing producers (politicians in parties), the greatest amount of money (power) going to the producers with the greatest sales (support).

## Theories

As we shall see, some of these analogies remain at a very general level, but others are articulated in more detail as models or theories of the political process. In the literature of political science the terms 'theories' or 'models' tend to be used almost interchangeably. It is not unusual for an article to use the term 'models' in its title when it really means 'theories', and vice versa. It is, however, worth making a distinction between the terms in order to avoid confusion. There is a logical connection between them: a model may gain the higher status of theory if and when it is subject to sufficient empirical confirmation – or, in Kuhn's terms, replaces former established theories (Kuhn, 1977). The crucial distinction between them is that theories purport to explain political phenomena, and models do not; models are used to discover and/or to suggest political relationships and potentially fruitful avenues of research. The discussion in this chapter is concerned with models; few would argue that there are any theories of politics in the sense that we have defined them.

## Why Use Models?

The greater use of models (and attempts at the construction of explanatory theories) in political studies in the modern era is in large part a reaction against what was termed 'hyperfactualism'. This consisted of the amassing of large amounts of information on the working of political institutions and then the exhaustive description of those institutions with little attempt to analyse their development over time or to compare them with equivalent institutions elsewhere.

With the post-war explosion in the means of processing, storing and retrieving information, the need to be selective became ever more clear. If one is to select some pieces from a massive reservoir of information about political systems, one must have some criteria for that selection. The model constitutes the analyst's criteria for selection and enables him or her to avoid drowning in a sea of information. We shall return below to some of the problems inherent in this matter of choice; indeed, since different models rarely agree entirely on what are the important features of political systems, it is necessary to consider the problems associated with the choice between models. Before that, however, let us consider just what it is that models do.

## What do Models Do?

It is possible to construct a lengthy list of what models are said to do for the analyst, but there are three basic functions. First, models help to *organize* the material. The amount of information available to political analysts is, in most cases, vast. As suggested above, what is needed is some criteria by which the information can be weeded for its relevance to the analyst's problem, organized in a coherent pattern and by which otherwise disjointed data can be related to demonstrate significant relationships.

Second, models perform a *heuristic* function – this is defined in Chambers Dictionary (1988) as 'serving or leading to find out'.

Once the relevant information has been selected and organized, the model may suggest other significant relationships that are worth researching further or, more generally, suggest other avenues for research that had not occurred to the analyst before the application of the model to the data.

Third, models may perform a *predictive* function. The application of the model to information concerning what happened, and its identification of important relationships and occurrences, may enable the analyst, by extrapolation, to predict future occurrences. The model's capacity for this varies from the highly specific to the fairly general. The former will tend to be quantitative, and is much used in economics, but is of less relevance to politics. The latter sort of prediction is made in politics and tends to be along the lines of 'if events *a*, *b* and *c* coincide, then *d* is likely to follow'.

## Choice of Models

The choice of a model will in the first place depend on its ability to do the job in hand. Therefore, the following questions should be asked. First, is the model relevant, is there sufficient correspondence between it and the phenomena in which we are interested? Second, is it economical, is it simpler than the situation to be modelled? If not, there is no point in employing the model. Then, does it organize, suggest and predict? (Deutsch, 1966, pp. 16–18). Given the practical problem of prediction in politics, a model should not be discarded because it cannot produce specific predictions of future events. It is enough if it can predict the possibility of future events and the relationships to be should be looked for.

In practice, however, the analyst is likely to find that several models meet this criteria. If so, how is a choice to be made? Ultimately, the analyst will choose the model that appears to be most suitable for use in the chosen area of research. Since there are no objective criteria for the choice of an area of research, the choice will depend on the subjective interests of the analyst or the pressures being brought to bear on him or her. In this sense analysts are like fishers: 'Conceptual models not only fix the mesh of the nets that the analyst drags through the material in order to explain a particular action; they also direct him to cast his nets in select ponds, at certain depths, in order to catch the fish he is after' (Allison, 1971, p. 4).

Therefore, it could be argued, using different models for the analysis of different parts of the political process will give a fuller picture of the whole. For example, if one is interested in decision-making, different models would seem to be particularly appropriate to the various levels at which decisions are made. A model derived from psychology about the way in which individuals make up their minds would be complemented by a model drawn from social psychology on the making of decisions by small face-to-face groups (such as the ubiquitous committee). In turn, these models would be complemented by one dealing with the behaviour of bureaucratic organizations. The most comprehensive picture of decision-making may thus be gained by the use of all these models. On the other hand, if one considers such models more deeply, it becomes clear that the factors and relationships identified as crucial by one model will be quite different from those identified as crucial by another. For example, if a bureaucracy takes a particular decision, is it best understood by reference to the psychological processes of one or two key individuals, by the pressures brought to bear upon them by their closest colleagues and advisers, by those brought to bear on them by other parts of the government machine (note the analogy) or, indeed, by none of these so much as by pressures generated elsewhere in the economy and society?

It could be argued that in the course of time academics will be able, after enough research, to ascertain the correct model or combination of models to be used by all analysts. However, this is highly unlikely, owing to the inevitably subjective component of knowledge. Both the selection of an area for research and, to a great extent, the selection of a model with which to abstract, organize, suggest and, possibly, predict in that area depend on the subjective interests of the analyst. These subjective interests, in turn, will not have been framed in a vacuum and are likely to reflect his or her attitudes as much towards different forms of political action as towards political analysis. In addition, it must always be remembered that political systems are dynamic – they are constantly changing, adjusting, and reforming themselves over time. Thus a particular model may become outdated and need to be modified or replaced. A change of place may also introduce new variables. This further strengthens the case for using more than one model for an in-depth understanding of political processes and for constantly testing models to ascertain their continuing relevance and validity.

### Paradigms, Models and Ideologies

The most fundamental differences between analytical models, their related political ideologies and consequent state structures derive from the different paradigms which, in turn, prescribe different research methodologies. We can identify four main paradigms with respect to the core relationships of individuals and society with which social and political analysis is concerned: liberalism, conservatism, collectivism and Marxism. The first, liberalism, which has constituted the mainstream of Western political theorizing since the eighteenth century, sees the individual as existing, both historically and logically, before society. Consequently, it is argued, the beliefs and behaviour of individuals, rather than society as a whole, must be the central object of analysis. Ideologically, the core of individualism relates to what are seen as individual rights, which should take priority over the collective needs of society. Government intervention in social and economic affairs is, in principle, to be minimized.

Conservatives reverse this relationship and emphasize the 'social whole' over and above the role of individuals. In terms of analysis, conservatives see the 'social organism' (the whole) as the key to understanding, since it is that which defines the position of individuals (the parts). In terms of ideology, this explains the conservative opposition to liberalism: individual rights, according to conservatives, may have to be subordinated to the good of the whole social organism (Schwarzmantel, 1987, pp. 216–21). What is good for the social organism is decided by those empowered to rule, which in practice means social, economic or military elites. Rights and duties are defined and enforced by these elites, who are sometimes legitimized by election. The government is seen as entitled to intervene to maintain an ordered and peaceful society.

Collectivism, which is essentially a modification of liberalism, is the belief that state intervention is necessary in order that the potential of individuals can be realized. Thus the state should promote social welfare to maintain a certain standard of living, and intervene to stimulate the economy and to minimize unemployment. Where liberalism and conservatism are essentially inegalitarian, collectivism is firmly rooted in the conviction that equality of treatment and opportunity should be promoted as a social good.

The labels 'liberal' and 'conservative' may give rise to some confusion. Political parties often call themselves by titles that do not accurately reflect their ideological leanings. So, in Great Britain the Conservative Party contains strong elements of liberalism in its beliefs, while the Liberal Democratic Party is influenced by collectivism. The Labour Party also embraces elements of both liberalism and collectivism. In the United States neither of the main parties – Democrat or Republican – rigidly adheres to an ideological position but the term 'liberal' in that country describes a position in support of collective welfare provision by the state.

Varieties of the Marxist paradigm have been dominant in many countries during the twentieth century, not least in the Soviet Union from 1917 to the 1980s. Marxism is distinctive for its rejection of the dichotomy between individual and society. At first sight, the Marxist view of 'totality' seems similar to conservatism in so far as it sees the significance of the individual (part) only in terms of his or her relations with other parts and with the whole society. However, what distinguished Marx from other theorists, conservative and otherwise, who had a view of the 'social whole', is the role of praxis, that is the interaction between people's consciousness of the world and their actions in transforming it. In terms of analysis, Marx's dialectical methodology involves constant shifting back and forth between the analysis of individuals, groups, classes and society as a whole. Politically, the implication of this is that only a total social transformation is capable of bringing about real change (Swingewood, 1975, pp. 34–9). Thus the Marxist criticizes liberalism for its concentration on the individual (a part) as separate from society (the whole); in particular, the liberal carrying out research treats the beliefs and actions of individuals as 'objective facts', whereas for Marxists 'Facts are not immediately given, concrete things, but exist within the specific totality of human, social relationships and institutions and are mediated by human consciousness and *praxis*' (Swingewood, 1975, p. 43).

## Conclusion

Figure 5.1 shows the basic paradigm within which the main analytical models used by contemporary political analysts have been derived. (In the next chapter, we shall concentrate on these models.) It also shows the political ideologies that relate to (and sometimes seem to merge with) these analytical models – and that provide the link between models and state structures. It is not possible to discuss the ideologies in any detail within the confines of this book but they are included in the figure in the interests of completeness.

Ideologies feature throughout the discussion of politics (see chapter 4). For now, we note that conservatism validates itself by claiming to be the expression of the natural, organic development of society, while Marxism claims an explicit unity between analysis and action in the notion of praxis. Models that derive from liberalism or collectivism have more frequently been promoted as 'objective', that is in some way free from contamination by values. As figure 5.1 shows, all analytical models have their ideological counterparts, and all analysis implies some form of political action or inaction even if it does not make it explicit. In turn, particular ideological views of politics have parallels in specific kinds of state policies (these are examined in chapter 11).

Since the ultimate choice of model rests with the subjective interests and values of the analysts, one criterion of that final choice is likely to be the analyst's own desires in favour of the status quo, reform, radical change or revolution. This means that students must develop a sceptical attitude towards everything that they read and hear about politics (including this present work). They should look carefully for the underlying assumptions and motivations of the commentators and be careful to acquire verifiable and concrete evidence for the conclusions they draw. It is necessary, in other words, to understand and place in context what is being said, why it is being said, the evidence that is being adduced to back it up, and the likely outcome of analysis of such evidence. Only then is it possible to understand, to analyse and to evaluate the problem in order to arrive at a thorough, reasoned conclusion.

## Questions for Discussion

1   How would you describe the model or analogy of the political process that you use (implicitly or explicitly) when you talk about politics?
2   If no models are value-free, what is their usefulness for analysis?
3   Is it practicable to use multi-model analysis?

# Further Reading

Deutsch, K. (1966), *Nerves of Government*. London, Free Press, ch. 1.

Ford, J. (1975), *Paradigms and Fairy Tales*, vol. 1. London, Routledge, chs 1 and 2.

Gamble, A. (1981), *An Introduction to Modern Social and Political Thought*. London, Macmillan, ch. 1.

Held, D. (1987), *Models of Democracy*. Cambridge, Polity, introduction.

McGrew, A.G. and M.J. Wilson (eds) (1982), *Decision Making: Approaches and Analysis*. Manchester, Manchester University Press, pp. 1–11.

Mayer, L.C. (1972), *Comparative Political Inquiry*. Homewood, Ill., Dorsey, ch. 7.

Reshetar, J.S. Jr (1989), *The Soviet Polity: Government and Politics in the USSR*, 3rd edn. 12. New York, Harper & Row, ch. 12.

Swingewood, A. (1975), *Marx and Modern Social Theory*. London, Macmillan, ch. 2.

# 6

# Models of Democracy (1): Alternatives

## Introduction

We suggested in chapter 5 that many models are likely to be a combination of the descriptive and the normative – the 'is' and the 'ought' – because of the subtle and essential part played by ideological paradigms and personal value judgements in the analysis of politics. Nowhere is this more evident than in models centred around the concept of 'democracy' (literally, 'government by the people'). That the concept nowadays has entirely positive connotations can be clearly seen in the keenness of most contemporary regimes to claim that they are 'democratic', while labelling their enemies as 'undemocratic'. This suggests that the concept may well be of little use in analysis, but it is important to consider the various meanings attached to it and to try to disentangle them.

First, democracy has not always had these positive connotations. Indeed, for most thinking people, up to about 100 years ago, democracy was to be avoided if at all possible, because rule by the people meant rule by the uneducated common masses – 'for the benefit of men without means', as Aristotle put it, writing in the fourth century BC (Aristotle, 1962 edn, p. 116). Similar fears were felt by the drafters of the American Constitution in Philadelphia in 1787. The elaborate checks and balances written into the Constitution were designed to prevent not only the resurgence of the sort of tyranny manifested by British rule which had been removed by the War of Independence, but also the potential tyranny of the masses, should the majority of propertyless people unite sufficiently to take political control of the country. In this chapter we shall consider the most common models of democracy and in the following chapter we shall examine some of the main debates between them.

## Pluralism

Pluralism is a model of democratic politics based on group activity. People have organized themselves into groups for political purposes since earliest times. Group activity, centred around Parliament in Britain, has been increasingly evident since the seventeenth century. The practice was, at first, severely frowned upon in principle even as it was widely indulged in. The official view was that a 'faction', as it was called, was tantamount to a conspiracy against the Crown. However, the King's ministers also found it necessary to organize their sympathizers to ensure a regular and reliable body of support. Many of these groupings were loose and temporary, but they illustrate a fundamental point: that organized combinations of people of more or less like mind can considerably increase the political impact of the individuals concerned. The tendency over the years has been for such groups to become more open and organized and for their behaviour to conform to understood rules. Other groups and organizations, representing various interests, were eventually formed late in the eighteenth century to reflect the growing political consciousness and activity away from Westminster. Ultimately, such groupings were to develop into modern political parties and pressure groups.

Liberal democratic ideology emphasized both the desirability and the possibility of maximum participation in the political process by individuals. With the growth of mass political movements in the nineteenth century, some people came to doubt the desirability of this, and argued that elite groups should rule. With the growing complexity of industrialized societies, others questioned the possibility of individuals having much impact. Early surveys of voting behaviour in the United States in the twentieth century showed that, regardless of the desirability or possibility of mass participation, it was simply not happening. Beyond exercising a periodic right to vote, most citizens did not participate at all in the political process.

Thus early versions of pluralism were developed to explain the workings of liberal democracies in terms of the activities of organized representative groups rather than individuals (for example Truman, 1951). With time, the model has been modified, but it is possible to identify the following key notions of the early model: all segments of society are capable of influencing government policy and with greater effect if they are formally organized; government policy is the result of bargaining and compromise between these groups; the role of the government is to set the parameters within which groups can operate, to act as umpire and to see that the participants observe the rules of the game. A stable and democratic policy-making process tends to result from this contest, for a variety of reasons: the groups accept the need for, and ultimate fairness of, the rules; membership of groups tends to be overlapping rather than exclusive, and for every group proposing a course of policy there will arise a countervailing group proposing the opposite. Therefore, in the long run, no one interest will dominate the process. All this takes place in an open society, characterized by civil liberties (especially freedom of speech and assembly) and free elections.

Nevertheless, the question arose of just how such a system could be reconciled with the notion of democracy as government by the people, which implies the maximum participation of the masses. The response to this was to look at practicalities. The direct political involvement of the entire people of a modern nation-state is considered to be impossible when very large numbers are involved. In any case, where such exercises in direct democracy have been tried, as in ancient Athens (although this would have involved no more than a few thousand people at most), further practical difficulties have been encountered. It is difficult to get a large assembly to act in a coherent and consistent manner, for example it can easily be swayed by demagogues or by other means of influencing it emotionally. Thus democracy had to be practised at one remove, by means of representative group leadership.

At an ideological level, liberals and social democrats in particular (see figure 5.1) argue that representative pluralism is the only practical form of democracy in the modern world of highly populated nation-states with complex, industrialized social structures. In an open society, where freedom of speech and of assembly are assured, grievances can be aired and anyone is free to attempt to form a group in order to bring pressure to bear on the government to adopt and implement policies favourable to the group concerned. Of course, not all groups can have everything their way and so there must be a spirit of compromise and understanding and a willingness to work towards an acceptable consensus. Thus the system is one that aims to create equilibrium and stability. Politics becomes a matter of marginal, incremental adjustment to maintain a more or less stable equilibrium between groups.

Many criticisms of the pluralist model have been expressed since it became the orthodox model of the political system in Great Britain and the United States from the 1950s. It was pointed out that the opportunity to form groups to pursue political interests may be inhibited by practical difficulties, like lack of finance or the problems of effective organization of widely dispersed individuals. Groups that do exist do not have equal access to decision-makers. Countervailing groups may not appear, or may be of quite different political strength to their rivals. Established groups can become quasi-official parts of the governmental system, making it very difficult for groups with alternative aims to get a hearing. It was also pointed out that it is unrealistic to think of government as merely an umpire between competing groups. The government itself is a collection of powerful interests with access to considerable resources and the ability to ensure that policy decisions are skewed towards what the government wants. A number of writers argued that the political system itself operated in a way that was biased in favour of certain interests (business, financial, military) over others. Finally, the model, ostensibly value-free, was accused of being implicitly supportive of the status quo, because it became a rationalization of the merits of incremental, rather than radical, change.

## Corporatism

Before leaving our consideration of models based on the relations between groups and government, we should take note of another possibility: corporatism. Historically, to describe a political and economic system as 'corporatist' was to equate it with the system that prevailed in Italy during its period of Fascist rule. At its simplest, this described a system in which industry remained in private ownership but was controlled by the state and used in the pursuance of an overriding 'national interest'. There was growing discussion of the applicability of the corporatist model to contemporary developments in Britain and elsewhere from the 1960s onwards. Cawson defines the concept as follows: 'Corporatism is a politico-economic system in which the state directs the activities of predominantly privately-owned industry in partnership with the representatives of a limited number of singular, compulsory, non-competitive, hierarchically ordered and functionally differentiated interest groups'. As he goes on to say, this definition 'focuses attention on the reciprocal relationship between the state and organized interests in society in respect of the formation and execution of public policy' (1978, p. 197).

From 1979 the British Conservative government, especially under Margaret Thatcher, pursued an unambiguously non-corporatist policy towards both unions and business corporations, telling them they must sort out their interests as best they could within the overall framework of the government's monetary and taxation policies. The disquiet that accumulated in the early 1980s in both union and business communities, however, over rising unemployment, the declining infrastructure and the collapse of manufacturing industry, produced a wide band of opinion across the ideological spectrum, stretching from the centre of the Labour Party through the Alliance (now the Liberal Democrats) to the centre of the Conservative Party (see figure 5.1) which would have welcomed some return to the corporatist trends of the mid-1970s. By the late 1980s, however, any remaining corporatist views had virtually disappeared.

## Neo-Liberalism or the New Right

In the 1970s growing dissatisfaction and disillusionment with collectivist and quasi-corporatist policies involving government intervention led many on the left and right of politics, both in Great Britain and the United States, to propose other options. The 'New Right', or neo-liberalism, was the most successful of these in attracting sufficient electoral support for an attempt at the implementation of neo-liberal policies. In the nineteenth century liberalism was a political creed identified with the concepts of individualism, free markets, civil liberties and limited government. Critics saw gross social inequalities at home and Britain's exposed economic position abroad as sufficient reason for developing collectivist policies in the twentieth century. The 1970s and 1980s saw a variant of nineteenth-century liberalism revived on the political right. As well as the belief in limiting the powers, intervention and expenditure of governments, there is hostility to the welfare state, which is seen as oppressive, unpopular and expensive; it is thought to be essentially coercive, towards both recipients and taxpayers. Neo-liberals advocate instead services based on market principles and private provision, with the government limited to providing a basic minimum of social welfare only.

A free market is regarded as essential to both economic and political freedom. Against 'state socialism', Hayek (1944) argues that central planning cannot accumulate sufficient information to reproduce the dispersed, multifarious and subtle knowledge of the market. Critics of the market theory argue that they fail to take into account changing conditions in the unregulated market, for example the growth of large monopolistic corporations in many areas of the market. Others question how the market can be seen as non-coercive in the light of large-scale unemployment. For Hayek, coercion is defined as the imposition of the arbitrary will of others; under this definition, unemployment is a misfortune but it is not coercive. On the other hand, it could be argued that impersonal economic and social circumstances can be just as coercive as the actions of individuals (Hindess, 1987, p. 129).

Analysis emphasizing the centrality of the market clearly derives from classical liberalism, but there is also an important strand of conservatism here. Hayek emphasizes the importance of the traditions and moral behaviour of the society in which the market operates. He sees a society evolving 'naturally' from the experience of successive generations; no body of theory or ideology could ever reflect the subtle complexities of real social and political relations. This argument is a substantial modification to the market theory, since it now appears that market mechanisms will work only in the right social and moral context. But, in general, for neo-liberals government interference on any but the most basic level is likely to be harmful. The condition of the poor is no better and may be worse with government intervention. Government is relatively insensitive to people's needs. Few actually advocate the abdication of the state from all responsibilities, but its role is ideally limited to certain areas: defence, law and order, and the provision of the most basic social welfare. In addition, governments may have to undertake minimal regulation in order to maintain conditions for the effective operation of the market.

Neo-liberals also emphasize the positive virtues of inequality rather than the welfare principles of collectivism which had been very influential (even in the United States) since the Second World War. Welfare policies are seen as essentially undermining initiative and self-reliance. Inequality encourages those with potential to succeed in mustering sufficient drive and ambition. Although social inequalities will increase, the beneficial effects of the extra economic dynamism will cause the material circumstances of everyone to improve. The standard of living will rise for all, although the gap between the most and the least affluent will increase. Neo-liberals criticize collectivists for defining poverty in relative terms – the poor understood as the least affluent section of society. Defined in this way, the poor are always with us, however much their relative standard of living improves. Neo-liberals would define poverty in absolute terms, as those without the basic necessities to sustain life. It is this level of basic provision that the state should provide – it should not seek to sustain comprehensive welfare programmes.

Neo-liberalism challenges not just corporatist analyses of politics, but also more commonly held pluralist ones. While organized interests provide the central feature of pluralist analysis and, ideologically, are seen as 'a good thing', neo-liberals argue that such interests distort the working of the political and economic market-place. For the new right, trade unions are the most notable and harmful example of this. Organized groups may thwart the most 'efficient' use of resources, especially when they form alliances with government bureaucrats who, for their own purposes, will encourage the spending of ever greater sums of money by the state. Elected politicians contribute to this 'pathology' by trying to outbid each other in the search for votes needed to win elections, and the result is an ever-growing public sector at the expense of the private sector (Barry, 1990, pp. 17–41).

## Marxism

In the nineteenth century there developed a group of models which took economic class as the most significant concept by which politics was to be understood. By far the most notable protagonist of class theory was Karl Marx and, largely as a result of his efforts, a great deal of thought and a huge literature has developed around this concept. For Marx, the true understanding of capitalist society could be achieved only by analysis based on its division into two fundamental classes: the bourgeoisie, who own the means of production, distribution and exchange and who thereby have power and control; and the proletariat, who, owning no property, can survive only by selling their labour, and who are therefore powerless and controlled. Capitalist societies are organized in the interests of the bourgeoisie – a small minority of the population – while the majority are obliged to sell their labour, without having any real control over their lives. Thus the majority contributes to the advancement of the interests of the minority. In fact, of course, there are significant social groups in addition to these two classes – for example small farmers, students, officials, managers and intellectuals – but, for Marx, the key to understanding the political process in capitalist societies is the extent to which these groups form alliances with one or other of the two main classes.

Since there are several different Marxist analytical models of politics, it is not surprising that there are different ideological positions accompanying them (see figure 5.1). The major distinctions lie between anarchism, socialism and communism, although it is often very difficult in practice to distinguish among them. Anarchists are characterized by their rejection of the possibility that the state, even when in the hands of the proletariat, is capable of being used as a temporary tool for furthering the revolution, while communists are prepared to accept the 'dictatorship of the proletariat' until the society is sufficiently revolutionized for it to be allowed to 'wither away'. Socialists, on the other hand, tend to be distinguished from communists and anarchists by their suspicion of the likelihood and possible consequences of the revolutionary overthrow of capitalism, and therefore tend to be committed to the gradual transformation of capitalism by means of liberal democracy. However, that there are also groups of 'revolutionary socialists' who challenge the symmetry of this simplified classification.

## Elitism

Elite models suggest that the important decisions in liberal democracies are taken by a single group – a ruling elite – rather than being the outcome of the pluralist competition between groups. The two main strains in elitist thought derive from different circumstances. The first, sometimes referred to as the classical school, was a conservative reaction to Marxist predictions of the inevitable fate awaiting liberal democracy. It is associated with the names of Mosca and Pareto. For Mosca, the political or ruling elite was composed of those whose natural aptitudes fitted them for this particular task, fortified by education and other social training. Pareto, however, saw elites as not so much based on the natural attributes of individuals in society but as an essential characteristic of all organizations beyond a certain size. Thus, decision-making in any large organization cannot, for sheer practical reasons, involve all personnel to any significant degree or at all. The decision-making power, he argued, inevitably falls into the hands of a small group, which is usually self-perpetuating, and acquires interests of its own, often at variance with the interests of the larger body. Such an elite usually becomes very firmly entrenched and virtually impossible to oust.

The second train of elitist thought was developed as a radical but non-Marxist critique of liberal democracy in America in the 1950s by the political sociologist C. Wright Mills. Mills argued that the critical decisions in the United States were being made at that time by a 'power elite' consisting of three sets of leaders – corporate, military and political. He was prepared to accept that, at what he called the 'middle levels of power', there could appear a pluralist interplay of competing interests, but this competition took place within the context of the decisions made by the power elite (Mills, 1956, pp. 242–97).

This elitist position was contested, notably by R.A. Dahl in his 'Critique of the ruling elite model', in which he defined a ruling elite as a 'minority of individuals whose preferences regularly prevail in cases of differences in preferences on key political issues' (reprinted in Castles et al., 1976, pp. 370–9). Dahl argued that it was meaningless to debate the relative power of politicians without specifying the scope of their power, that is those issues over which power could be exercised. Furthermore, elitist notions of generalized power over all major areas of decision were inadequate. Certainly, given the scale and scope of the activities of the modern state, it is difficult to imagine any one group effectively controlling events across the board. Dahl also argued that elitists tended to confuse actual control by elites with potential control. Often elitists would base their conclusions on studies of the backgrounds of those recruited to elites, which demonstrated that they tended to come from relatively narrow social backgrounds. Attitudes on policy issues would be inferred from these backgrounds and their ability to implement these preferences was assumed. In common with other pluralists, Dahl argued that only the study of actual decision-making could reveal whether their potential for control was realized.

## Conclusion

In this chapter we have discussed the major models used in the attempt to analyse politics less normatively and more empirically, to discover how liberal democracies and Marxist states actually operate. Marxism provides an explicit ideological link between analysis and action, but all the other models have their ideological counterparts, and the student of politics has to take care to distinguish the use of concepts and models as analysis from their use as ideology.

A central feature of these models is their use of different concepts of analysis – individual, group or class. This means that they will each tend to emphasize some characteristics of the political process rather than others. On the one hand, it could be argued that we shall obtain a more complete view of the political process by using aspects of each model (a multi-model approach), but on the other hand, this raises the danger of trying to take so much into account that we drown in detail. We must not forget that models must simplify if they are to be of use.

## Questions for Discussion

1 Is there a 'core meaning' of democracy that is applicable to all models that claim to be democratic?
2 Discuss the arguments for and against the proposition that groups are the most important units for explaining politics.
3 What would be the most significant aspects of the political process for (a) the neo-liberal; (b) the elitist; and (c) the Marxist?

## Further Reading

Cooper, J. (1991), Construction . . . reconstruction . . . deconstruction. In C. Merridale and C. Ward (eds), *Perestroika: The Historical Perspective*. London, Edward Arnold, pp. 161–7.
Held, D. (1987), *Models of Democracy*. Cambridge, Polity, chs 5 and 6.

Macpherson, C.B. (1977), *The Life and Times of Liberal Democracy*. Oxford, Oxford University Press, pp. 161–7.
Miliband, R. (1977), *Marxism and Politics*. Oxford, Oxford University Press, ch. 1.

# 7

# Models of Democracy (2): The Debate

## The Debate between Pluralists and Elitists

The essence of the debate between the pluralist and elitist models is the extent and significance of the conflicts observed in the policy-making process. For the pluralist, the conflicts between the leaders of various groups and government are the very stuff of politics; they represent far-reaching conflicts, and that nobody wins or loses outright demonstrates the fragmentation of power which they claim exists. For the elitist, the existence of these conflicts is less significant than that they take place within a more basic agreement as to the nature of society's political and economic institutions; here the key to understanding the political process is the maintenance by elites of their domination, and their belief that their continuance in power is in the best interests of all, transcending any specific disagreement over substantial policy questions.

Another aspect of the debate between pluralists and elitists is their disagreement over the methods to be employed in investigating power. This question was discussed in chapter 3 and illustrates the general point made in chapter 5, that the model chosen for analysis is likely to depend, ultimately, on the values of the analyst. For some, the elite, however numerous they are, do essentially form a privileged collection of people able to manipulate affairs in their own interests. It matters little that such elite groups in Great Britain and the United States are open, that is willing to admit new members. No one is admitted unless he or she has undergone a socialization process that has formed his or her attitude in line with those prevailing in the elite. Others believe that the democratic elements in the system – processes of election, supervision, control and accountability – make such a system quite compatible with the tenets of liberal democracy. To counter this view, it is said that, while elite members may argue among themselves, they will always unite to defend their common interest whenever it is seriously threatened.

Over the years, research evidence has raised serious doubts about pluralist arguments. For example, business and financial interests are often found to dominate, compared to other groups, such as consumers and employees. Others note the low level of active participation by group members (that is the domination of groups by a small leadership group). This has led a number of pluralists to shift their position to one sometimes characterized as 'neo-pluralist' (for example Dunleavy and O'Leary, 1987, ch. 6), which represents a partial synthesis with ideas derived from elite models. At the ideological level, however, neo-pluralists are still distinguishable by their commitment to liberal democracy. The mass of the people and the majority of the members of groups do not play a very active role except in sometimes insisting on a measure of accountability and control. But where individuals on their own are in a weak position *vis-à-vis* the state, with a group representing them, pluralists argue, they are considerably strengthened politically and the power of the state to ride rough-shod over their wishes is thereby weakened.

## Pluralism and Elitism in the Soviet Union and the Successors Republics

In the main, models of pluralism, elitism, plural elitism and neo-pluralism have been developed in the context of the study of liberal democracies. It is worth considering whether and to what extent they can be of use in the analysis of the politics of the Sovier Union and the successor republics. We cannot, of course, simply assume that models developed by Western analysts with respect to Western politics can be applied to the politics of states with completely different histories and traditions. Even more important, we should not make the mistake of thinking that, given time, politics in the former Soviet republics will inevitably develop along Anglo-American liberal democratic lines. Never-theless, it is important to ask what similarities, if any, can be detected between the processes of, say, the United States and the Soviet Union. It seems reasonable to propose that some idea of plural elites may be more productive than most. Ross noted:

> The natural conclusion is that the Soviet Union has evolved over time from a system where one interest (namely, Stalin's) governed its collective behaviour, to a system where the country's major interests (as embodied in the country's major institutional actors) meet at the apex of the regime, to be mediated and minimally satisfied. In sum, a kind of pluralism of elites and a related oligarchical rule has evolved from the totalitarian dictatorship as terror has been abandoned and revolutionary changes engineered from above have been forsaken. (Ross, 1980, pp. 267–8)

The events of the 1980s and 1990s have illustrated that, in fact, no effective 'pluralism of elites' was developing in the Soviet Union. *Glasnost* and *perestroika* released a great amount of pent-up frustration among a large number of interests – nationalist, economic, environmental, cultural, religious – which had found no way of expressing themselves with political efficacy under the old regime. In the early stages of independence no stable multi-party system developed in any republic, and pressure groups, too, are still feeling their way and trying to achieve a stability on which effective political impact can be based. It is clear that if recognizable, firmly established democratic institutions do develop, they will have their own characteristics and will not be mere copies of Anglo-American pluralism or other forms of Western democracy (Merridale, 1991, pp. 14–33).

## The Debate between Marxists and Elitists

The value of the Marxist concept of class as an analytical tool has been much debated, both among Marxists and between them and non-Marxists. For example, it is not only in capitalist societies that considerable power is exercised by those who do not actually own the means of production, distribution and exchange, in particular managers and bureaucrats, while intellectuals (in some cases employed by the state) may also have some influence; in communist societies, too, bureaucrats, technologists and managers came to exert enormous political power in the context of state, rather than private, ownership of the means of production. Thus the Marxist notion of the 'ruling class' may appear virtually indistinguishable from C. Wright Mills's idea of the 'power elite' (Mills, 1956) and, indeed, in their manifestation in day-to-day politics they are very similar.

There remain, however, important differences between the concepts. Let us examine two briefly. First, there is the question of the source of the ruler's power. For Marxists, the power of the ruling class derives directly from its ownership of the means of production, but elitists have argued that political power can derive from a variety of sources: status, education, wealth or the occupation of some key position. Western sociologists have used these criteria to distinguish between social groups in mapping the power relationships in contemporary capitalist societies, for example to show that elite educational background has a strong correlation with senior positions in the state bureaucratic structure. But the analysis often fails to relate this information to the location of the actual exercise of power or control in society. That a very high proportion of positions categorized as politically important in Britain are occupied by people educated at one of a handful of public schools and at either Oxford or Cambridge University, or that some sort of familial relationship can be traced among people in different but influential fields of activity, in itself, tells us nothing about the exercise of power.

Second, there is the question of in whose interest the few rulers rule. Elitists have tended not to dwell on this, suggesting that it is possible for an elite to rule in its own interest or in the interest of some other group or of the whole people. Marxists would deny the last two possibilities: for them, the ruling class rules in its own interest, that is to maintain and reproduce the conditions in which capitalism can survive and flourish. If any of their measures benefit other classes, they do so only accidentally or in order to legitimate the dominance of the ruling class in the eyes of the people.

But whose interests are served by the groups we have already identified as being neither in the bourgeoisie nor in the proletariat? We could assume that managers in large companies will serve the interests of the owners since that is what they are employed to do, but it still begs the question of whether the managers may not develop interests of their own, for example job security, which are opposed to the owners' interest in profit-maximization. With respect to bureaucrats employed by the state, we need to ask whether they may not develop interests and autonomous spheres of political action that could lead them to enact policies in opposition to ruling-class interests. Aspects of analysing power and interests have been examined in chapters 3 and 4.

## The Decline of Marxism

Alongside these theoretical questions, the bourgeois capitalist system, has, contrary to the expectations of early Marxist revolutionaries, shown a strong propensity to survive. Marxists expected it to collapse under the weight of its own internal contradictions as the conflicts engendered by irreconcilable class interests undermined the foundations of capitalism. But capitalism is an international system with such extensive ramifications that troubles in one part of the system can be borne by drawing on reserve resources elsewhere. In spite of the gross economic inequalities between classes and between states, the system has proved itself capable of significantly improving the material standard of living in the industrialized countries and the working class have made some positive political gains, such as the achievement of universal suffrage, the recognition of civil liberties and the establishment of strong trade unions and socialist and communist political parties.

This would have been enough to place contemporary Marxists in a rather different political and social context from their early forebears, but in the years following the Russian Revolution of 1917, the ostensibly Marxist-Leninist state of the Soviet Union developed along repressive, autocratic lines under Joseph Stalin. In spite of attempts to rationalize it by pointing to the enormous material difficulties suffered by the new state, this could not be seen as the dawning of a new liberated society. Marxist theory itself became stale and ossified, a rigid set of formulas instead of a living, developing tradition. After the death of Stalin in 1953, communists in the capitalist world attempted to rethink their position and to reformulate Marxism in terms that appeared realistic in, and relevant to, the prevailing conditions. The result was the burgeoning of several schools of Marxist thought and not a little controversy at both theoretical and practical levels. A more complicated and sophisticated analysis of the concept of class became acceptable, and the necessity of a social and political revolution was not inevitably interpreted as a dramatic and cataclysmic event (Smith, 1992, pp. 79–81). Such significant departures from traditional Marxist analysis caused strong dissent. Led by the Italian and Spanish Communist Parties in particular, the emphasis in what came to be known as Eurocommunism was on the real democratic gains that had been made in many capitalist countries after a hard fight and which could not be regarded simply as a sham. Moreover, the idea of a peaceful and orderly progression to the communist classless society by liberal democratic methods instead of violent revolution was assiduously promoted by some Western European communist leaders like Berlinguer of Italy and Carillo of Spain. The prospect of winning a share of power via the ballot box and of entering into coalition with capitalist political parties was now seriously contemplated.

Eurocommunists viewed the Soviet Union as a model of communism that had gone wrong, and argued that Western Europe required a different model, which built on national political traditions rather than on one that attempted to destroy them. This raised major questions for the communist movement: how would future communist societies differ from the Soviet Union? How could communism be achieved by compromising with the capitalist interests that dominated Western Europe? Was any transition to communism possible without a dramatic, probably violent, break with the past? Eurocommunism turned out to be the precursor of the collapse of neo-Stalinist communism. The Soviet Union and the communist states of Eastern Europe were increasingly unable to manage their economies efficiently and to keep up with the major technological (computer) revolution of the 1970s, which seriously undermined their political legitimacy. In addition, the arms race with the United States was a burden that the Soviet Union could not sustain. Eastern European states were more and more alarmed by the likelihood that a nuclear war between the superpowers would be fought in Western and Eastern Europe. There was growing evidence that the ideology of Marxism-Leninism had no real hold on the minds of the people of these countries. When the Soviet Union decided that it was no longer in its interest to sustain these regimes by force, they soon collapsed. The Soviet Union itself, undermined by economic crisis and nationalist demands, followed shortly after, breaking up into fifteen independent republics.

The future of Marxism as an ideology with practical political influence is problematic. It has been thoroughly discredited in all but a few countries, like China and Cuba, although it continues to provide inspiration to resistance movements in countries like El Salvador and South Africa. There is a possibility it could be revived, shorn of its Stalinist totalitarianism, as an alternative to capitalism and liberal democracy and in a form that will appeal to future generations.

## Democracy in Practice

The varieties of democracy observed around the world cannot be discussed independently of the social and economic circumstances within which they operate. The three main types that can be identified (there being numerous variations within each type) correspond to the first, second and third worlds in which the countries of the world are often divided in discussion of international affairs (see chapter 21).

The first world is characterized by industrialized economies run on capitalist principles and within liberal political frameworks. The economies of the second world are also industrialized, although usually less advanced than those in the first. Until the late 1980s, they were run on socialist principles of public rather than private ownership. Their political frameworks could have been described as non-liberal. The economies of the third world vary enormously but tend to be characterized by being predominantly agricultural. Some of these economies operate primarily on capitalist principles, some on socialist and some on neither, being basic subsistence economies run mainly on communal lines. The political frameworks also vary tremendously, but again tend to be non-liberal.

### The First World

In the liberal democracies of North America and Western Europe, Japan and Australasia, liberalism – in the sense of the freedom of individual choice within a market economy, which replaced the highly restricted social and economic relationships of feudalism – frequently predated democracy. This means that such rights were, in practice, at first restricted to property-owning elites. For many people, particularly women and ethnic-minority groups such as African-Americans, the right to vote came only after long and bitter struggles.

In the past hundred years or so the role of the state in liberal democracies has changed considerably. At one time it aimed to maintain the conditions within which the free market could develop and operate most efficiently. Later, it evolved into a more collectivist institution for performing a variety of welfare and regulatory functions aimed at compensating for some of the more drastic consequences of the free-market mechanism. The question is whether this change came about as the legitimate demands of the people were met by an essentially reasonable and responsible state, or because those in power came to appreciate the need to placate those getting least from the free market, lest they over-throw the entire political and economic system. In the 1980s there was a reaction (possibly temporary) against these collectivist policies (see chapter 8).

## The Second World

It may seem strange to discuss the discredited formerly socialist regimes of Eastern Europe in a consideration of democracy, but these regimes claimed not simply that they were democratic, but that their democracy was superior to that in the West, and their arguments must be considered. We in the West cannot claim that our form of democracy – liberal democracy – is the only true form, if only because the idea of democracy has been around for much longer than this particular variant. Liberal democracy has been made possible by certain social and economic features of society in Western Europe and North America. Even so, how can the notion of the 'dictatorship of the proletariat', even in theory, be compatible with the notion of democracy? Because, it would have been argued, the dictatorship is a necessary temporary period following the revolution that overthrows the capitalist/liberal democratic state. Once the capitalist order is abolished, classes, and therefore the need for the state, disappear and the higher form of communism is achieved. Even this temporary period of dictatorship is more democratic than liberal democracy, however, for where liberal democracy conceals the real rule of the minority (the capitalists) the proletariat's dictatorship establishes the rule of the majority (the workers).

How democratic was this system in fact? For example, were the workers in the Soviet Union able to make their views known to their political leaders and were those leaders responsible for their actions in the sense that they could be removed if their performance did not meet with approval? Of course, in the sense that we understand these processes, as they operate in the liberal democracies – freedom to dissent, competing political parties and regular competitive elections – the answer must be that the Soviet

Union was not democratic, if only because of the existence of just one party (the CPSU) and the relative lack of tolerance of dissent.

Thus, if our criteria for the existence of democracy are procedural – competitive elections, respect for minority rights and so on – the liberal democracies may well appear to be superior. But if we are more concerned with substantive rights such as the right to a job, decent housing and proper health care regardless of private wealth, we shall have to reconsider our views. The socialist countries claimed that they provided superior and more equal substantive rights than the capitalist liberal democracies. This gave them both their major justification for referring to themselves as democracies and their appeal as model societies to many third-world countries. However, many people both in and outside the second world would argue that their record in providing substantive rights was poor in practice (Sakwa, 1989, pp. 204–25).

## The Third World

Unfortunately, space does not permit an examination of third-world politics in any detail. On the face of it, many of these countries seem to have escaped the colonial domination of European liberal democracies only to come under the quasi-imperialist designs of the Soviet Union or the United States. However, while the developed capitalist and socialist states have had their client states in the third world, the emerging political processes in many of these countries are distinct from both liberal democracy and the Soviet model. There are both economic and political reasons for the rejection of liberal democracy, for example frequent chronic shortages of capital, and a belief that the traditional values of community are of greater importance than the individualism of the West.

While in the past there was a strong tendency towards one-party systems in many new nations such as Tanzania, Angola and Libya, this cannot be seen simply as an imitation of the CPSU model. First, single-party systems were the natural outgrowth of mass independence movements; and second, they were seen as more effective mobilizers of the population for the attempted solution of post-independence economic difficulties. They differed crucially from the single parties of the second world in that they represented a nationalist or racial revolution against imperialism and capitalism, rather than the class revolution of which European communist parties claimed to be the leaders.

The third-world countries are frequently closer to the second in their greater concern with ends – greater equality, prosperity and health – than with the niceties of the liberal democratic process. But many also see the desirability of remaining independent, both of the Soviet Union and the United States, whose motives in lending assistance to struggling new nations are rarely entirely philanthropic. With respect to procedural democracy, mass-based single parties sometimes enshrine a high degree of democracy within the party. Towards the end of the 1980s there was a growing movement for greater liberal democracy and electorally competitive party systems in many African countries, and in some countries it has been successful. But it must be remembered that the extent of democratic practice cannot be measured simply by the number of competing parties.

## Conclusion

Bearing in mind that it is a necessary simplification of an extremely complex political world, we suggested that there are three major varieties of the democracy system, each of which is critically related to particular social and economic factors. The different systems that claim to be democratic have different emphases, for example different weights are attached to procedural as opposed to substantial rights. It may be asked under what circumstances both of these could be maximized or whether, as some maintain, there must be an inevitable trade-off between freedom and equality.

Although all models are likely to include a normative element, the three models of democracy discussed in the chapter can be seen as primarily normative. Therefore, at some point we must grasp the nettle and decide which aspects and relationships are the most significant within the political process, which is an evaluative exercise in the last resort and likely to depend on the particular objectives of our study. There remains the question of whether pluralist, elitist and Marxist models are entirely incompatible. Would their selective use for the study of different types of power give us a more complete picture? For example, would not the pluralist model be more appropriate for the study of decision-making in governmental institutions, which takes place within the context of certain structural constraints that are better analysed using Marxist models?

In chapter 8 we shall examine in more detail how ideas of individualism, collectivism and state socialism have shaped the actual organization and practice of contemporary politics in the states on which we are concentrating our study.

## Questions for Discussion

1 Why do capitalism and liberal democracy seem to occur together?
2 What lasting influence, if any, has Marxism had on our understanding of democracy in the twentieth century?
3 Is it possible to devise one acceptable model of liberal democracy?

## Further Reading

Cox, A., P. Furlong and E. Page (1985), *Power in Capitalist Societies.* Brighton, Wheatsheaf, chs 3–5.

Crouch, M. (1989), *Revolution and Evolution: Gorbachev and Soviet Politics.* Hemel Hempstead, Philip Allan, ch. 3.

Dunleavy, P. (1986), Theories of the state in British politics. In H. Drucker, P. Dunleavy, A. Gamble and G. Peele (eds), *Developments in British Politics* 2, rev. edn. Basingstoke, Macmillan, pp. 373–90.

Ham, C. and M. Hill (1984), *The Policy Process in the Modern Capitalist State*, Brighton, Wheatsheaf, ch. 2.

Macpherson, C.B. (1966), *The Real World of Democracy*. Oxford, Oxford University Press, pp. 1–45.

Plamenatz, J. (1973), *Democracy and Illusion*. London, Longman, ch. 7.

Westergaard, J. and H. Resler (1976), *Class in a Capitalist Society.* Harmondsworth, Penguin, pp. 343–421.

# 8

# The Scope and Responsibilities of the State

## Introduction

Perhaps the most vigorous debate concerning the purpose and activity of the state in the twentieth century has centred on the extent of state intervention and control in the economy and society, together with the state's relationship with individuals, organized interests and classes. In liberal democracies there has been a tension between the tradition of individualism of the nineteenth century and the collectivism more characteristic of the twentieth. Recently, individualistic ideas, in the form of neo-liberalism, have reasserted themselves (see chapter 6). In socialist states there has developed a wide recognition that the attempt to achieve a close identity between state and society gave rise to rigid, authoritarian political structures that had long been in need of opening up (see figure 5.1).

## Liberal Democracy: Individualism

As we saw in chapter 6, the concept of the individual and of individualism has dominated the thought of Western Europe for several centuries. While its roots may lie in some elements of Christian philosophy and theology, it came into its own with the new flowering of knowledge in the Renaissance and the development of the liberal tradition (events that largely passed Russia by). The basic assumption of this school of thought is the supreme value and worth of the individual. Achievement is measured by its value to the individual human being; the social good is the sum of the individual human good; and human freedom is achieved by releasing the individual human being from as many restraints and restrictions (physical and psychological) as possible. On this basis a whole economic philosophy and practice (*laissez-faire*) was constructed, an interpretation of history developed, a science of psychology developed and, most importantly for our purpose, political attitudes and behaviour established. The epitome of political individualism in Britain was reached in the nineteenth century, when belief in the concept led politicians and others to proclaim the virtues of the absolute minimum of government interference in private and social affairs and of individual enterprise and responsibility. Perhaps the most prominent feature of the political philosophy of individualism was its heavy emphasis on the rights of private property, which has attracted the strongest criticism from Marxists and others. Ownership provides a means of control and hence of freedom – freedom from the need to work at the behest of others' needs and priorities, and therefore the opportunity for liberty and fulfilment as an individual and social human being.

John Locke, a prominent philosopher of political liberalism, wrote:

> Men therefore in society having property, they have such a right to the goods, which by the law of the community are theirs, that nobody hath a right to their substance, or any part of it, from them without their own consent; without this they have no property at all. For I have truly no property in that which another can by right take from me when he pleases against my consent. Hence it is a mistake to think that the supreme or legislative power of any commonwealth can do what it will, and dispose of the estates of the subject arbitrarily, or take any part of them at pleasure. (Locke, 1929 edn, p. 118)

Locke was one of the political philosophers most admired by the American founding fathers, and his thoughts on the importance of private property were reflected in the drafting and historical development of the American Constitution. In the political bargaining that led up to the ratification by the individual states of the new constitution drafted in 1787, it was agreed that Congress, when it first met, would immediately add a Bill of Rights to the document. This was achieved by the passage of what became the first ten amendments to the Constitution. The fifth of these reads in part: 'no person shall be . . . deprived of life liberty or property, without due process of law.' This protection was extended, on paper, by the Fourteenth Amendment of 1868, and the courts have used these clauses to uphold the right to keep slaves, declare unconstitutional minimum-wage and child-labour laws, and invalidate the rights of trade unions, among other things. Since 1937, however, the clause has been less important in this respect.

But the belief in the importance of the individual is still highly salient today. A comment on American politics is worth quoting: 'The focal point of political thought in the United States is the individual. From this base, all other relationships and values follow. The individual is the basic unit of politics, and the political system is erected for the individual's benefit' (Dolbeare and Edelman, 1977, pp. 154–5). From this come the two dominant realities of the American political economy – a capitalist economic system relying on individualistic materialism and a limited government which impinges on individual rights as little as possible.

While the notion of individualism represented a revolutionary break with the feudal past, the emphasis on private property as the basis for political rights was in effect highly elitist because a minority of men, and no women, had any property. Indeed, a prime object of the fifty-five men who wrote the American Constitution was to preserve their property. The massive inequalities in property holdings that characterized the eighteenth and nineteenth centuries were reflected directly in inequalities of political power, and much ingenuity was devoted to justifying this inequality on the grounds of breeding, education and race. As it became clearer, however, to those without power that formal legal equality, 'natural' economic forces and moral goodness could not secure them social justice, collective action grew in significance. Nevertheless, criticisms of individualism did not deter the advocates of a return to liberal principles when collectivist policies were running into trouble during the late 1960s and into the 1970s. Hence there developed neo-liberalism or the New Right – known in Great Britain as 'Thatcherism' after the prime minister who did most to reassert liberal, individualist principles in her government's policies (see chapter 6).

## Liberal Democracy: Collectivism

During the twentieth century many political systems with developed economies have undergone a considerable readjustment of philosophy, policy and structure, largely to take into account the increased political awareness and influence of the organized mass of the people. These changes centred around an enhanced role for the state in economic and social affairs, a departure from the dominant *laissez-faire* views of the nineteenth century. Broadly speaking, these changes, much less in extent than full socialism, have led to policies that are called 'collectivist', within a political structure called 'liberal democracy'. In Great Britain, for example (although collectivism is a widespread phenomenon), the decline of the Liberal Party and the rise of the Labour Party as an integral part of the political system, the mixed (part public and part private) economy and the development of the welfare state are the primary manifestations of collectivism.

Collectivism is characterized by the state developing many policies in (and assuming responsibility for) important aspects of the economy as well as social welfare. The influence of Keynesian economic theory during and after the Second World War led governments to believe that they had the means effectively to control and direct the economy in ways that would produce the resources to sustain an elaborate welfare state and the social rights that go with it.

The beginnings of twentieth-century collectivism can be traced to the growing realization of the extent of poverty in nineteenth-century Britain and the injustices (for example to the elderly) that it entailed. In addition, the low standards of education and health of the population became increasingly obvious. The 1870 Education Act was intended to do something about the former, while the poor quality of health among army recruits for the Boer War helped to give rise to the amorphous 'national efficiency' movement at the beginning of the twentieth century. This implied that there was a necessity for the state to take the initiative in reforms. A wide body of thought on the 'respectable' left (like Beatrice and Sidney Webb) advocated plans for bureaucracy-led reforms.

Politically, several writers have identified the main theme of politics after the First World War as an intention to incorporate the Labour Party and the trade union movement fully into the political system. This was intended to create a new basis for stability and legitimacy in a situation where the mass of the people were more politically active and whose co-operation was needed more than ever before. These state-led collectivist (interventionist) policies seemed desirable both to the Labour movement as a way to achieve the political goals and social reforms they desired, and to the ruling elites as a means of avoiding a serious undermining of the stability and power structure of the political system. The result can be considered a success from the point of view that a new consensus was established which flourished most obviously from the Second World War to the end of the 1960s. In the context of economic growth and full employment the future was viewed optimistically. Democratic practices were incorporated into the system but in a limited manner, while the role of the state was steadily extended. An all-party consensus had emerged by the late 1940s which accepted the nationalization of major industries and public utilities, together with a comprehensive system of social welfare. But this post-war collectivism was in some senses a retreat from levels reached in the Second World War. Many controls were abolished, and although the concept of national planning had been acknowledged (from the Barlow Report of 1939) it was not seriously attempted. More indirect intervention was adopted and financial interests regained their influence within a Keynesian context.

The collectivist policies and political society that emerged in the period after the Second World War saw attempts at a managed (mixed capitalist and state-controlled) economy on Keynesian lines and the increasing provision of social welfare. Until the 1970s, there was a broad consensus on this, and it gave rise to political behaviour in which elections became a time for promising further developments and improvements in social welfare, and in which numerous interest groups emerged in both the public and private spheres to negotiate the relationship of their interest to the state, and to campaign and create pressure for as generous a share of state-distributed resources as possible. One of the most notable advocates of post-war collectivism in Britain was Antony Crosland in his book *The Future of Socialism* (1956). He had a confident belief in the ability of governments to control the economy and to promote growth into the far future which would provide the resources for an ever-growing welfare state.

Even at the height of belief in this consensus in the 1950s the signs of misunderstanding and stress were evident. There was the idea, for example, that governments could ultimately 'control' private industry in the context of capitalism whereas, of course, private firms cannot be made to invest in ways in which a government may wish. There was never wide agreement that government could manage the economy better than the private sector, particularly after the repeated attempts to introduce an incomes policy. The political difficulties of imposing controls over trade unions meant that, in return for voluntary co-operation over incomes, the unions were able to gain some control over government policy. Another major interest group whose co-operation was required was the Civil Service, and some Labour ministers, in particular, were not satisfied that this had been achieved.

In the light of the relative decline of the British economy and the difficulties of financing social welfare and other policies, criticisms increasingly emerged. It was perceived that the demands made by particularly powerful interest groups on government resources meant that others lost out, whatever the merits of their case. Many people felt that the size and complexity of government administration led to inefficiency and contradictions, which were compounded by government intervention in areas like poverty or crime where, it was suggested, they had no effective means of action or of evaluating policies. Not everyone considers these criticisms to be valid although there is more general agreement that there has been a problem of rising costs. Some right-wing critics assume that goods and services not produced as commodities (like education) make no positive (measurable) contribution to social wealth. This is contentious, as is their view of the harmful effects of the cost of government policies growing faster than the economy as a whole, while the level of disposable personal income has grown more slowly. They also argue that the rewards of collectivist policies are often distributed not to those who are most in need, but to the relatively affluent (for example the middle class makes proportionately more use of the National Health Service than the working class) or to those who are effectively organized for industrial or administrative disruption.

A long-standing critic of collectivism was Frederick von Hayek (1944), who emphasized what he saw as the morally pernicious consequences of the welfare state. For him, welfare encourages dependence instead of personal responsibility and initiative, and also gives rise to coercion of both the beneficiaries of the system and the taxpayer. Above all, socially redistributive policies and the state's attempts to relieve poverty and maintain full employment threaten freedom, ultimately undermining social and political stability by inflation. Samuel Beer (1982) has argued that collectivism leads to 'pluralistic stagnation', the power of a number of interest groups to prevent government action. He suggests that parties make promises to win votes and then cannot implement them without increasing costs, taxation and, consequently, inflation.

A number of critics on both the right and the left saw 'demand overload' or 'crisis management' as the major problem of post-war collectivism. Various remedies were put forward, such as constitutional limitations on government power, or a reduction in the 'excessively' democratic character of liberal democracies. These were overtaken by events in the 1970s, when parties at last turned away from the collectivist orthodoxies of the previous decades and looked for radical left- or right-wing alternatives. Right-wing governments in Great Britain, the United States and elsewhere have attempted to implement more market-orientated economic policies and a reining back of government intervention and control. In many ways, they have turned to modified versions of classical individualism as a remedy for collectivist problems. This was the basis of neo-liberal, New Right policies in Great Britain and the United States during the 1980s. Nevertheless, the collectivist policies of the political and administrative structure created to sustain them remain largely intact at their core, even if expansion has ended and reduction and reorganization are now government priorities. Moreover, in Britain, collectivist policies have remained popular with the public.

## State Socialism

State socialism is one of the terms applied to the government and policies prevailing in the Soviet Union until the collapse of the system under Mikhail Gorbachev. Other terms, often explicitly hostile, were sometimes used in the West, like 'totalitarianism' or 'state capitalism'. In the Soviet Union itself the system was described (in the Soviet constitution of 1977) as 'a state of the whole people', while Brezhnev coined the phrase 'a developed socialist society'. Certainly, the Soviet state officially saw itself as socialist and moving steadily and inexorably towards full communism. (This should not be confused with any movement towards collectivism in liberal democracies which are based on the private rather than social ownership of property.) Marx had indicated the need for a strong state with unrestricted authority, particularly in the period following the revolution (the 'dictatorship of the proletariat') when the last vestiges of capitalism are removed and the system of socialism established – the transforming of property relations and the social and economic structures. It was also needed for defence from external enemies. But at the same time Marx insisted that the state should be absolutely accountable to the people. The state's aim is to limit its role to the co-ordination and direction of social life without coercion (Held, 1987, p. 125). In the longer term, Marx appears to have envisaged a state organized somewhat along the lines on which he understood the Paris Commune of 1871 to have been: participatory and self-governing, with much local control, unlike (as he saw it) the remote, elitist parliaments of liberal democracies. Faced with the crisis following the Russian Revolution, Lenin at first seemed to favour a participatory role for the people based on soviets and factory councils, but under the leading role of the Communist Party. The growing crisis of the times forced him towards a strong state and authoritarian measures. Debate continues today as to whether Lenin regarded it as a temporary measure or as an inevitable development of his principles and in line with his own real inclinations.

In fact, the failure of the revolution elsewhere, with the pressing need to feed the population and the urgency of massive industrialization, did push organization in an authoritarian direction. Lenin's early death in 1924 gave Stalin the opportunity to consolidate his power as party secretary throughout the 1920s. In many ways, it is the Soviet Union of Stalin's creation that has provided us with the main characteristics of Soviet socialism. The influence of his personality and policies could be seen until the late 1980s in the strong, authoritarian, bureaucratic society, the major role of the secret police (KGB), the façade of unity and a selective, one-sided interpretation of history. One of the main results of Gorbachev's policy of *glasnost* was the demand for the exorcizing of Stalinist influence over government and the interpretation of history. Thus, until the death of Stalin in 1953, an apparently monolithic and repressive society existed, with terrible crimes committed in its name. These included the elimination of the *kulaks* (wealthy peasants) during the collectivization of agriculture, and the purges and show trials of prominent Bolsheviks in the 1930s. But it could also boast of great achievements, for example near-universal literacy, massive industrialization and the successful but costly defence of the country from German invasion in the Second World War.

From the death of Stalin in 1953 up to the mid-1980s the Soviet Union was run on modified Stalinist lines. Khrushchev attempted to restore legality and the leading role of the Communist Party, together with a more relaxed attitude to the arts. From 1964 to 1982 Brezhnev initiated a period of consolidation and stability after the rather hectic Khrushchev years, but it degenerated into stagnation and corruption. The desire for reform was widespread, and the appointment of Mikhail Gorbachev to the party secretaryship (after the very short periods in office of the ageing and sick Andropov and Chernenko) was seen as heralding a new era of reform. Gorbachev was a party man, however, and it was probably thought that he would initiate reform strictly within the existing party-dominated structure.

The official political myth in the Soviet Union was that the Communist Party enshrined the essential democracy of the regime by effectively representing the interests of the people. There was no class conflict or vested interest outside the overriding values, policies and organization of the party. Through the party, Marxism-Leninism was interpreted to the people, and practical policies for its implementation were devised. Critics in the West saw the Soviet Union not as democratic but as an elitist and privileged party and government bureaucracy, which by controlling the means of production was fulfilling a capitalist role. Trotsky argued that the Soviet Union was a true proletarian state which had been perverted by the privileged bureaucracy. Variations on these models emphasize either the repressive (totalitarian) characteristics of the regime, especially in the Stalinist period, or the elitist, bureaucratic characteristics which were seen to be evident in the post-Stalinist period. Alternatively, 'convergence' models suggested that the similar economic and technological characteristics of all industrialized societies meant that political and social developments would also be similar, especially in the interdependence of the ruling organs (such as the CPSU) and other organized interests. But this was a sweeping assumption; even among liberal democratic states there are wide variations (Crouch, 1989, pp. 204–13; Reshetar, 1989, pp. 338–73).

The Soviet system was characterized by public ownership of virtually all business organizations and, even in the very limited private sphere, the absence of employer–employee relationships. There were elaborate formal institutions of social control (like the *nomenklatura*, the CPSU's means of controlling important appointments) and no checks and balances or effective means of accountability among political institutions. The open articulation of interests was difficult or risky. The party acted as the organ through which the benefits of co-operation were mediated. Its coercive and normative roles, prominent in the past, had been much reduced. The Soviet Union was no longer a society in the throes of revolutionary fervour. By the end of the Second World War it had become a legitimate system apparently based on legal, coherent and consistent authority with its own traditional values. Nevertheless, the system was having to face up to significant and growing social and economic problems. The economy was increasingly inefficient, the system of planning could not effectively supply the needs of industry or consumers. It was weakened by the unsuccessful attempt to keep up with Western defence expenditure and a failure to embrace the technological (computer) revolution of the 1970s. There was over-bureaucratization and corruption, a lack of participation except at mundane levels, and an inadequate system of accountability.

In calling for thoroughgoing reform, Gorbachev used the concepts of *glasnost* (openness) and *perestroika* (restructuring). He also said that he was aiming for a 'revolution without shots' ('revolution' is a very emotive word in the Soviet context). But, perhaps most significantly, he called for more democracy in Soviet life. This did not mean an adoption of liberal democratic values and institutions as understood in the West. The primacy and unchallenged role of the CPSU was not to be modified. Instead, by democracy Gorbachev seemed to mean much more open and honest public debate about Soviet history (with no people or topics forbidden to be discussed) and similarly open and honest public discussion about the problems of Soviet society and its future development. All this would be based on much fuller access to the necessary information and data.

The main institutional manifestation of *glasnost* was, in the beginning, the advocacy of contested elections between individuals who would not, however, put forward policies differing from those approved by the party. At first, limited experiments took place with contested elections for factory managers, Komsomol, party officials and for deputies to some soviets. In addition, there were plans for the decentralization of the economy and for giving managers financial responsibility for their own enterprises. The initial reaction of the Soviet people to this was varied and mixed.

There was certainly a burgeoning of free comment and discussion in many circles, but also uncertainty as to how to respond, difficulty in understanding the purpose and procedures of contested elections, scepticism about the permanence of the changes and apprehension as to where they would lead. Gorbachev acknowledged that there was opposition to his reforms at all levels: from conservatives and vested interests but also from working people who objected to his clamp-down on alcohol consumption and to the loss of bonus payments due to the more rigorous rejection of substandard goods by the quality-control commissions. Such uncertainties did not mean that a wholesale rejection of the reform programme, but its pace, extent and depth faced considerable resistance. This struggle became the responsibility of the separate republics after the collapse of the Soviet Union in 1991 (Smith, 1992, pp. 60–7).

## Conclusion

Rapid economic and social change, which characterize the end of the twentieth century, have led to pressures and tensions in both liberal democracies and socialist societies. In the former there has been a loss of confidence in the collectivist policies of social welfare and Keynesian economics, with both left and right putting forward alternatives. During the 1980s the right largely prevailed, with an approach based mainly on earlier individualist, market-orientated liberal values. Neo-liberal policies in the West ran into difficulties, with many rejecting what they alleged to be the inegalitarianism and unsound economics of the New Right. In the Soviet Union Gorbachev advocated a form of democratic openness to past and present lessons as an essential basis for an urgently needed restructuring of the economy. Radicals were impatient with the pace and disorganization of reform, while conservatives impeded and plotted against it; their opposition culminated in the failed coup attempt of 19 August 1991. Finally, *glasnost* and *perestroika* could no longer be controlled and precipitated the breakup of the Soviet Union.

## Questions for Discussion

1   Are individualism and collectivism incompatible?
2   Would you agree that state socialism is inevitably authoritarian?

3  What criteria should be used to decide the level and scope of state intervention in the economy and society?

## Further Reading

Barry, N. (1990), Ideology. In P. Dunleavy, A. Gamble and G. Peele (eds), *Developments in British Politics* 3. Basingstoke, Macmillan, ch. 2, pp. 17–41.

Dunleavy, P. and B. O'Leary (1987), *Theories of the State*. Basingstoke, Macmillan, pp. 1–8, 319–34.

Eccleshall, R., V. Geoghegan, R. Jay and R. Wilford (1984), *Political Ideologies*. London, Hutchinson, ch. 2.

Foley, M. (1991), *American Political Ideas*. Manchester, Manchester University Press, chs 1–4.

Hindess, B. (1987), *Freedom, Equality and the Market*. London, Tavistock, chs 4–6.

King, D.S. (1987), *The New Right*. Basingstoke, Macmillan, ch. 7.

## Further Reading

# Part II

## The Context of Politics

# 9

# Political Stability

## Introduction

In our discussion of analogies and models used in the analysis of politics in chapter 5, we pointed out that a major contemporary analogy is that of the 'system'. We are interested in the reactions of the interdependent parts of the political system to factors entering the system from its environment. This analogy is particularly useful in considering the relative importance of dynamics and stability in the life of the political process. Of course, the real world of politics is not as ordered and regular as the concept of a system implies, nor is it as enclosed as it suggests. But if we are not careful we may allow our thinking to be subtly shaped by the concepts we use. Why is one concept in popular current use rather than another? What prejudices and assumptions does it imply and what meanings does it obscure? Is it accidental that the seventeenth century saw politics as analogous to the human body, while today a model like cybernetics would appear more meaningful to us?

## Stability and Dynamics

The term 'political system' must, therefore be used with due reservation. Like the other concepts we have discussed, it too is relative in its meaning. But, given this reservation, it is always possible to categorize the activities that the system exists to perpetuate. These can be summed up under the general heading of decisions: who takes them, how they are taken and implemented, and why some decisions rather than others are taken. In other words, the central concept for understanding the political system is power – who wields it, how they do so, and what the priorities of the power-holders are.

For the most part, the primary purpose of the decision-making power-holders is that of system stability, which implies both limiting social change and encouraging it in order to maintain the system in a state of more or less stable equilibrium or, one could say, tolerable disequilibrium. Success in this aim means that the existing power-holders are likely to remain in power. It should perhaps be pointed out here that when we refer to changing the power structure we are not referring simply to changes in the governing party (or parties), as sometimes occurs after general elections in liberal democracies; a change in the power structure means a fundamental realignment of social and economic forces within the political system. Parties like the Conservative, Labour and Liberal Democratic parties in Great Britain, and the Democratic and Republican parties in the United States, are not contemplating that sort of change. They aim at most to modify the *existing* system. All systems have this strong conservative tendency – the will and the means to maintain themselves in existence. Paradoxically, stability means continuous change, for it is impossible to maintain an unyielding status quo. For any particular system (or structure of power) to persist, the basic relationships between social and economic groups must not be seriously disturbed, or must change sufficiently slowly or sufficiently rarely so as not to appear threatening to the system's shock-sustaining mechanism. Although the political system is active, constantly changing to some extent, its most notable characteristic is inertia. Most of the time the problem is not the rapid pace of change so much as adapting the system to changes in the economic and social environment. A real collapse of the political system – fundamentally altering the nature of society – is rare.

More common is sustained decay, often lasting decades or even centuries. Examples are eighteenth-century Venice, nineteenth-century Austria-Hungary and twentieth-century Britain. Nevertheless, it is possible for fundamental upheavals to occur. Perhaps the most notable example in post-medieval British history is the struggle between the Crown and gentry in the seventeenth century, while the United States, saw the War of Independence from 1776. Russia was dramatically transformed by the 1917 revolution, and the Soviet Union by the failed *coup d'état* of 1991.

If a final settlement cannot be achieved, even instability itself can be institutionalized. A political system can adapt itself to unstable coalition governments and the existence of strong political groups where no one group is able to break through and achieve dominance over the others. Post-war Italy is a contemporary example of institutionalized instability. Conflict relationships can become the norm, whereby the extent and limits of permissible conflict are understood and those ostensibly seeking a new political order may acquire a vested interest in preserving the unstable status quo. Thus, much political activity is directed towards maintaining the stability of the status quo with as little marginal change as possible.

The question of political stability is a particular problem for new regimes with explicitly revolutionary goals. On the one hand, they wish to push through quickly the changes they see as essential to consolidate their hold on power, while on the other, they are conscious that many people's basic desire is for some certainty and stability in their everyday lives. Therefore, periods of intense revolutionary activity may well be followed by periods of consolidation. No political system can maintain indefinitely the sort of upheavals experienced in the Soviet Union during the collectivization of agriculture in the late 1920s and 1930s, or in China during the Cultural Revolution of 1965–75. Indeed, the horrendous events following the Russian Revolution can be interpreted as the desperate struggle of a huge and complex political regime to restore stability and strengthen its hold on power, in the face of internal social and economic collapse, major disaster in war and internal uprisings aided by foreign powers (Reshetar, 1989, pp. 31–59).

Even in far less cataclysmic situations, such as the General Strike in Britain in 1926, the governmental authorities took firm steps to maintain control of the supplies of essential goods and to preserve law and order. In other words, they attempted to ensure that the prestige and coercive power of the government was sufficient to sustain a level of stability acceptable to the people at large. The then recent events in Russia during and after the revolution, together with a long period of industrial unrest in Britain itself, had made the British government unusually sensitive to what it perceived as threats to the power structure.

Thus we seem to be faced with two different views of where the emphasis of political activity lies and what the overall goal of the political system is. At one level, it seems that governments aim to implement new policies while, at another, they decide to adopt new policies only in order to maintain a basic, overall stability. In the complex and interdependent modern world it has sometimes seemed as if governments are increasingly precluded from taking bold initiatives, whether in domestic, economic or foreign policy, because their time is taken up entirely with crisis management. This suggests that governments do not embark on long-term strategies for change in this or that policy area, but that the press of events means that, like the fire brigade, they are having to respond to emergencies as they arise and hope that they will be able to cope in the event of a large number of simultaneous crises. Significant policy shifts – like that attempted by Gorbachev in the Soviet Union – can be achieved only with enormous effort, while at the same time courting disaster. Because of or despite the pressure to adapt to events and the inertial qualities of political systems, governments can never achieve anything other than a state of 'dynamic conservatism' without risking major disruption.

Some writers hold that the sole function of the political system is to aim at equilibrium, so that political activity involves simply marginal incremental adjustments. Such an interpretation is highly conservative. The system is seen as having no goals or purpose other than maintaining itself in stable existence. This view, closely associated with the work of some behaviouralists and with a school of political philosophy linked to the name of Michael Oakeshott, is difficult to sustain as an explanation in all circumstances, particularly in the light of many examples of systems that are driven by goals arising out of material desire or ideology.

But circumstances can require the dynamics of the political system to go beyond mere adaptation to preserve a basic stability. Challenges to the existing order from within or without can force the system to take on responsibilities it has not hitherto envisaged, like embracing economic affairs within the ambit of state activity as in the United States in the 1930s. It can seek to extend its borders, influence and wealth by incorporating new territory or overseas expansion (imperialism) as Britain did in the nineteenth century. Fundamental changes can be induced or accelerated by external pressures like losses in war, or invasion, as in Russia during the First World War. However, the capacity of the political system to respond to such challenges will depend to a great degree on its institutional sensitivity and on the openness of the prevailing ideas. The dynamism can come from a particular class or elite group driven by exigencies or by the rewarding possibilities that power opens up to them. To realize such aims requires the control of essential institutions, be they the monarchy, parliament, political party, coercive forces like the army and police, or whatever the appropriate vehicles are at a given time. Thus it is probably rash to state that the dynamics of the political system depend on any one particular circumstance, like class conflict. History may not simply be the story of great individuals, but it would be unwise to discount them entirely. Neither can we overlook the force of such facts as ideology (political, nationalistic, religious) and natural disaster.

In the end, the dynamics depend on a consciousness of relative deprivation together with an awareness of possible and viable alternatives. The realistic possibility of material gain may act as the stimulus to action, but equally dynamic are goals defined by ideological principles. It is impossible to ignore the creative dynamism of religious ideas throughout history or the impact in the twentieth century of Marxist and nationalist ideas. Perhaps defined goals are essential to any dynamic political system, whether it be fulfilling the will of God, pursuing material progress, asserting national identity or the achievement of a utopia. Without a certain level of dynamic activity, decline tends to set in and ultimately becomes irreversible. Decline and decay can be a very long-drawn-out process, but its continuation makes the likelihood of revolution or other dramatic change ever greater. Overthrow may then be precipitated from within or from without or by a combination of both (Crouch, 1989, pp. 143–78).

Political institutions often survive by reinterpreting their role. Political activities are redefined. The systems themselves frequently have their internal structure, personnel and functions reorganized, sometimes in ways that are as unrealistic as those they replace. An apparent continuing identity can hide deep changes. Is the House of Commons the same kind of institution that it was was fifty, 100 or 400 years ago? Does the function of voting have the same meaning for electors today as it had at the turn of the century? Or, for that matter, has it the same meaning and significance for any two voters at any time? Names, titles and formal functions can remain the same while the reality hidden by them changes profoundly. With respect to the post-Soviet republics, we may ask how far the CPSU's functions had become largely bureaucratic rather than revolutionary. What were the real political relationships between the CPSU and informal and semi-formal political groups within the Soviet system? How had such relationships changed over time?

## Conclusion

In the political processes of all systems there is an inevitable tension between pressures for change and those for stability. Different groups at different times will want different degrees of both change and stability. Their attitude will depend on the extent of the power that they wield within the existing political structure and processes. It is tempting to think that ruling groups or classes would normally prefer stability and that subordinate groups will be looking for dynamism and change. While this may be the 'normal' state of politics, there are conditions in which the reverse may be true. Certainly, newly established ruling groups will attempt to force through changes that they believe to be necessary before the euphoria surrounding their victory begins to dissipate and, in the case of revolutionary regimes, before the deposed groups or classes have time to prepare a counter-revolution. Equally, there may be occasions when subordinate groups resist changes that they believe to be inimical to their interests and contrary to their traditions, for example the Luddites who smashed new machines in nineteenth-century Britain and the *kulaks* who resisted the enforced collectivization of agriculture in the Soviet Union in the 1930s.

Therefore, the important questions to ask of any political system are: To what extent is it undergoing either relatively superficial institutional or more fundamental structural change? What changes in power relationships are involved? How are these changes coming about? Which sections of society are supporting or opposing them? Do these changes reflect a fundamental stability or instability in the system?

## Questions for Discussion

1   What is the connection between power and political stability?
2   Is political stability inimical to change or vice versa?
3   What is fundamental political change and how do we recognize it?

## Further Reading

Almond, G.A. and S. Verba (1965 edn), *Civic Culture*. Boston, Little, Brown, ch. 13.

Carter, A. (1973), *Direct Action and Liberal Democracy*. London, Routledge & Kegan Paul, ch. 7.

Coates, D. (1984), *The Context of British Politics*. London, Hutchinson, ch. 10.

Crouch, M. (1989), *Revolution and Evolution: Gorbachev and Soviet Politics*. Hemel Hempstead, Philip Allan, ch. 7.

Held, D. (1987), *Models of Democracy*. Cambridge, Polity, ch. 7.

# 10

# History, Tradition and Myth

## History

The meaning and significance of political stability and change for the citizen of a given political system depends partly on socialization and experience, but equally on an understanding of the history, traditions and myths of the political system. History is the remembered experience of a people. It consists partly of recollection of lived experience of the past which, to a greater or lesser degree, affects the present, and partly of perceived lessons and interpretation of the events) handed down by successive generations. These experiences are a legacy which contain fundamental lessons on what to do and what to avoid in political behaviour. For a long time recollection of the English Civil War in the seventeenth century caused political activity to be directed towards avoiding the recurrence of what was seen as a catastrophe. The Labour party has been very suspicious of coalitions since the party lost its leader and most of its members of parliament in the election following the formation of a 'National' government during the economic crisis of 1931. Universal suffrage and parliamentary reform are interpreted as central achievements in the advance towards liberal democracy.

In the Soviet Union the revolution of 1917 was, of course, the great remembered historical event (now undergoing a fundamental reinterpretation), but it does not exclude recollection of the achievements of prerevolutionary figures like Alexander Nevsky or Peter the Great. In the United States the fourth of July is a major annual holiday to celebrate the Declaration of Independence from Britain in 1776. The names and achievements of past presidents deemed to be great are evoked as symbols of the past with which the constitutional structure of today is identified. History, then, is the temporal experience of a political process which helps to put contemporary events into perspective and give them meaning. But history is not a given, constant collection of information to be drawn on. Like everything else, our understanding of it depends on variables such as the availability of information, and its interpretation (or reinterpretation) which is greatly affected by the needs of the present – history is harnessed to support or challenge the power structure of the existing status quo (Nove, 1989, pp. 37–71; Oberländer, 1990, pp. 47–53).

Just as we use models to help us select from a mass of information in studying contemporary politics, so we can observe history through interpretative models geared to our own requirements and need to understand. These needs arise out of our own place in history. The rise of the British Empire, for example, can be interpreted as the carrying out of a noble duty to bring the benefits of a superior civilization and religion to primitive peoples, as an economic enterprise bringing material benefits to both sides or, as the economic exploitation of the colonized by the colonizers. British domestic history has been understood as a steady progression over 300 years towards the full attainment of liberal democracy, in which more and more of the people have been given a participatory role in politics, or, alternatively, as a series of events designed to preserve the essentials of a status quo in which a small elite aimed to enjoy a disproportionate share of the wealth and power. Yet again, it has been analysed as a situation in which class division gives rise to tension between economic classes that are extremely unequal in ownership, privilege and control. Russian and Soviet history is equally susceptible of various interpretations. For example, it has been argued that the Soviet regime was essentially a continuation of the autocracy of the tsars, that an entirely new form of government – totalitarianism – was developed by the Bolsheviks, that the tsars were replaced by the dictatorship of the proletariat as a temporary stage on the way to the establishment of a full communist society, and that the Soviet Union was an industrialized and bureaucratized state, whose characteristics and problems had much in common with other industrialized and bureaucratized states.

Thus our understanding of history requires appropriate concepts and models. Such models will change from time to time as they are felt to provide inadequate or inappropriate understanding. Some of these developments result from real changes, such as the discovery of new sources of information, but historical models may be based as much on a psychological need for reassurance from the past as on a desire for truth. In chapter 5 we saw how the final choice between models of politics is inescapably evaluative, and so it is with historical models. History is called on to give coherence and justification to our views of what political activity in the past has achieved. Therefore, alternative models of historical change will be deployed by different groups with different ends in view. But in all cases an understanding of history is vital to the sustaining of a political identity in the present, whether the group is a class, a race or a nation. That is why history is regarded by politicians as one of the most important subjects in education. The teaching of history was firmly controlled in the former Soviet Union, and even in an open and relatively stable system like Great Britain it gives rise to intensive debate, not least among politicians. In the United States, likewise, there have been demands for the teaching of 'neglected' history, such as that of ethnic minorities, women and gays. An early development in both the black civil rights movement in the United States and the feminist movement there and in Europe was, significantly, a critical re-examination of orthodox history from which blacks and women had been excluded. The implication of modern British history as taught in schools – whose main theme has been the development of the British monarchy and the system of parliamentary government (other institutions like nationalist aspirations or extraparliamentary protest impinging from time to time) – is that the activities of traditional elites are the most significant features of history.

We can take this even further. Although all history is an interpretation of past events, it may be so liberated from events that it becomes simply propaganda, which tells us more about the requirements of the current political orthodoxy than of an understanding of history. For example, Soviet 'history' required that Trotsky and Stalin become non-persons, and when Stalin died Beria, the disgraced head of the secret police, had his entry in the *Great Soviet Encyclopaedia* replaced at the last moment by a lengthy article on the Bering Straits! These may seem rather crude examples of history as propaganda, but all regimes attempt, to some extent, some more subtly than others, to present their preferred interpretation of history, especially in schools.

# Tradition and Myth

The concepts of tradition and myth are closely associated with the concept of history. Briefly, we suggest that 'political tradition' be understood as the accepted form of political behaviour within the political process. Thus the characteristics of the British liberal democratic system, such as free speech, widespread opportunity for limited participation, governmental secrecy, control by pluralistic elites, inhibitions against extralegal or violent behaviour, can be said to make up the tradition of political behaviour.

Given that their elites have traditionally been dominated by people of Anglo-Saxon extraction, it is not surprising that the United States shares some of these traditions of political behaviour. But there are important differences, many of which derive from American scepticism as to the benevolence of central government authorities. One manifestation of this scepticism concerns attitudes to secrecy. The British Official Secrets Acts of 1911 and 1989 are based on the assumption that no citizen has the right to know anything that the state chooses not to reveal. The United States Freedom of Information Acts rest on the opposite assumption: the citizen has the right to examine all records, with certain exceptions, unless the government can convince a court of the need for secrecy. Another difference concerns attitudes to violence. A strong strain of vigilantism runs through American history. In the past the imperfect reach of central government over a large and heterogeneous country bred a strong belief in the virtues of community self-defence against unwanted persons, groups or ideas. It has sometimes supported the aims of central government and at other times contradicted them. This reflects very different attitudes towards central authority from those in Britain and the Soviet Union.

The Soviet Union inherited from tsarist times a tradition of detachment from the government and the state. The people generally did not expect to be involved in government or even in indirectly choosing their leaders. They were expected to trust their rulers whose legitimacy was based once on God's will and later on impeccable party credentials. The citizen was seen not as the partner of government, but as petitioner, drawing the attention of the authorities to needs and grievances and requesting redress – hence the shoals of letters to *Pravda*, the CPSU newspaper, during the period of communist rule, and the practice of directly approaching the authorities in Moscow, which often entailed travelling many miles. Distance and secrecy were thus accepted as natural attributes of government. The government saw its role in relation to the citizens as explaining its policies to them and mobilizing their support. Involvement of the citizens in the non-political administration of society at lower levels was, however, encouraged to a very limited extent.

It can therefore be seen that political history is partly the study of the development of such traditions of behaviour over time. Political myth we take to mean an acceptable interpretation of a nation's political past and present, which acts as a key to understanding; it is closely linked to the accepted paradigm of historical interpretation. For example, we can speak of the myth of liberal democracy, of parliamentary government and of civil liberties. Such myths are an essential link between the individual and the political system itself. They provide a short cut to under-standing for the majority of the citizens who need to relate to the political system but have neither the inclination nor the leisure to study politics in depth. Thus both traditions and myths con-tribute to the significance of the political system, giving it legitimacy and stability in the eyes of the majority.

Such traditions and myths can lose credibility over a shorter or longer period of time. Events and experience tend to overtake the myths and traditions of the political process so that they begin gradually to lose their significance for contemporaries. They may continue to be proclaimed and clung to as the norm or as ideals towards which the political process should be striving, but the greater the divergence between traditions and myths and the real political needs of the people the less they can contribute to the stability and legitimacy of that process. The time will come when they will have to be reassessed or even replaced, but it does not necessarily occur to order. When a political process continues to rely on traditions and myths that are losing their credibility, and before it has found acceptable substitutes, there is likely to be a period of relative instability and loss of confidence – a crisis of legitimacy. Such a crisis occurred during the first half of the nineteenth century in Britain, which saw the campaign for par-liamentary reform and the Chartist movement. The period from the 1950s to the present day has also seen the questioning of myths and traditions as Britain adjusted, first, from being a great imperial power to having a lesser role, and then to being a leading member of the European Community.

In Russia the central myth of the tsarist regime was the auto-cracy – which was considered to be the great unifying institution of the empire – while in the Soviet Union the central myth was that of the revolution, sustaining the dynamic which that enabled society to progress towards the goal of full communism. It has been argued that the central tradition, of centralized, bureau-cratic dictatorship, remained unchanged in substance from that of the tsars, even if it was established on a different economic and social base. This view is debatable, at least in such a simpli-fied form. It may have been nearer to the mark to speak of a new alignment of social and economic forces within an industrialized context giving rise to authoritarian, bureaucratic and centralized government. The myth and tradition showed clear signs of break-ing down from the 1970s, as economic and social difficulties, together with foreign and defence problems, undermined the re-gime. This led to its collapse in 1991. New traditions and myths will have to be developed, or old ones reasserted, and until they are political stability (that is the new power structure) will remain fragile (Hosking, 1992, pp. 35–56).

In the United States there are a series of myths which ultim-ately derive from the belief that every individual has the oppor-tunity to improve his or her material position within society. The main political manifestation of this is the notion of 'log cabin to White House' – anyone can become president (and, indeed, some have!). Closely allied to this is the myth of the 'frontier'. In the nineteenth century the existence of large tracts of land in the west acted as a safety valve for the industrializing East. In similar cir-cumstances in Britain people could not escape the urban slums except by emigrating, but in the United States they could go west and make a new life for themselves. The power of this myth can be seen from the fact that long after the end of the western frontier John F. Kennedy adopted the slogan 'The new frontier' for his administration in 1961.

## Conclusion

History has been defined as the remembered experience of a people which helps them to relate to, and find meaning in, present events. It provides them with a yardstick against which to measure con-temporary issues and personalities. Complete objectivity is no more possible in the study of the past than in that of the present, and all history is seen through interpretative models which are conditioned by the requirements of the present. The student of politics, for example, may well be more interested in different aspects of a nation's past than members of the regime who are concerned mainly with rationalizing current political events rather than with the complex forces and developments that go to make up human political activity.

Traditions are the accepted modes of political behaviour, and myths the acceptable interpretations of the political past and present. It is not important whether traditions and myths are in any sense 'true' or 'false'; that they are widely held to be true or credible is critical to political stability and, equally, if they come to be disbelieved then there is a potential threat to stability.

On the face of it, many of the myths and traditions of British, United States and Russian politics seem quite different, but it is important to consider whether there may be consistent threads that reveal more basic political processes at work in these countries. We should also consider under what conditions apparently stable myths and traditions may change.

## Questions for Discussion

1　Do you consider the influence of history on political systems to be positive or negative?
2　Discuss the uses of history as propaganda.
3　In what sense are myth and tradition invented, and does this matter if they have the effect of reinforcing political unity and stability?

## Further Reading

Barker, R. (1978), *Political Ideas in Modern Britain*. London, Methuen, esp. ch. 2.

Denenburg, R.V. (1992), *Understanding American Politics*, 3rd edn. London, Fontana, ch. 1.

Gamble, A. (1990), The Thatcher decade in perspective. In P. Dunleavy, A. Gamble and G. Peele (eds), *Developments in British Politics* 3. Basingstoke, Macmillan, pp. 221–45.

Kavanagh, D. (1991), Why political science needs history. *Political Studies*, 34 (3), pp. 479–95.

McKay, D. (1989), *American Politics and Society*, 2nd edn. Oxford, Blackwell, ch. 3.

Nove, A. (1989), *Glasnost' in Action*. Boston, Unwin Hyman, chs 2 and 3.

Smith, G.B. (1992), *Soviet Politics: Struggling with Change*, 2nd edn. Basingstoke, Macmillan, ch. 1.

# 11

# The Economic and Social Context of Politics

## Introduction

To conduct a detailed study of the political process, it is necessary to extract it, somewhat arbitrarily, from its economic and social context, in the same way as systems analysis extracts the 'political system' from its 'environment'. It is important to remember that this is an analytical device and that there is continual interaction between the political, the economic and the social. Equally important is that this interaction resembles a two-way flow of cause and effect, not just a one-way flow. So while it may be obvious that not everything that happens in the economy and society is caused by the government and the actions of the political system, it is equally misleading to suggest that every activity of the political process is caused solely by events in the economy or society. In other words, although a large number of political actions can be traced back to events in, say, the economy, the political process itself can have an independent effect on the economy and society. As we would expect, the relative weighting given to these effects varies among analysts, depending on which model (or models) they use.

## The Context of American Politics

The first point to bear in mind may appear rather obvious, but it is very important. The United States of America is very large. Even though it has 'shrunk' with the advent of air transport and modern communications, the country's size has had the greatest historical significance for its politics and is by no means irrelevant today. In Britain substantial cultural differences may be perceived between, say, Scousers (from Liverpool) and Cockneys (from London) who are only 200 miles apart; thus it is not surprising that the differences between, say, natives of the south-western United States and those of the north-east are very significant indeed.

The major manifestation of this in political terms has been the phenomenon known as 'sectionalism'. An example from the nineteenth century demonstrates its importance. The major cause of the American Civil War of 1861–5 was not so much the moral question of slavery *per se*, although that became more important as time went on, but the critical political and economic question of whether slavery could be extended into new territories in the west as they became admitted to the union as full states. The economic structures of the northern and southern states were diverging increasingly by 1860. The North was undergoing the early stages of industrialization under the same basic conditions of capitalism as had transpired in Britain eighty years or so earlier: the free movement of capital and labour. The South, meanwhile, remained stagnant in an agricultural economy dominated by large plantations relying mainly on slave labour. In essence, these economic systems were incompatible, and for several years it had been recognized by politicians of both sides who negotiated a series of compromises which would maintain the balance of power between North and South. Such compromises meant that for every slave state admitted to the union, another free state would be admitted, thus maintaining the tenuous balance of power in Congress. The balance came under increasing strain, not least from the decision of the Supreme Court that no man in a free state could be deprived of his property – that is his slaves – by Congress. It followed, therefore,that there was no legal way in which slavery could be prevented from spreading throughout the United States.

The Civil War between North and South cemented a sectional split in American politics which remained for a century. During that time the South remained solidly Democratic in congressional elections and, together with the industrialized states of the northeast, provided Democratic presidential candidates with the core of their support from the 1930s to the 1960s. Thereafter, when Democratic presidential candidates became clearly identified with the cause of black civil rights, Southerners were increasingly likely to vote Republican in presidential elections, while still voting Democrat in congressional elections. The relative decline of traditional heavy industries in the north and east, the rise of high-technology industries in the southern and western 'sun-belt', and the accompanying population shifts meant that the sectional divides became far less clear-cut.

As the sectional aspects of American politics has become less certain, so too has American economic predominance. In many respects, the average standard of living in the United States is still higher than almost anywhere else, and the influence of the American economy on economic activity in the rest of the developed and less developed world is enormous. But the crucial difference is that the *independent* power of the United States has declined: from its long-standing position as the world's largest creditor nation in 1982, it became the largest debtor by 1986. The massive budget and balance-of-payments deficits have been financed by increasing Japanese penetration of the United States economy (Hogan, 1992, pp. 216–28).

To those of us brought up in the relative comfort of the British welfare state, an apparent paradox of the American economy is that its unparalleled private affluence has gone hand in hand with considerable public squalor. Public-transportation systems have almost ceased to exist in many places, social-security provision is minimal in many states and derisory in some, health care is run mainly on the principle of profit-maximization, and many families suffer irredeemable financial disaster because of the high cost of health care, which in Britain and (in principle) in the Soviet Union and its successor republics is freely available. The reasons for this are complex but its roots are to be found in the American faith in individualism and concomitant distrust of collectivism.

The lure of the United States for many nineteenth-century immigrants was its image as a land of opportunity (unlike the closed, semi-feudal societies of their birth), in which station in life mattered little and anyone could make it to at least a decent standard of living, if not a fortune. Like all myths, it had some substance to it, but the myth has far outlived the reality. Yet debates in the United States over the public provision of welfare and medicine are still dominated by the ethos of individualism and distrust of collectivism (enhanced for most of the twentieth century by the bogey of communism).

Another reason for the public squalor that Europeans are likely to emphasize is the lack of a significant political party committed to socialism, whether in the social democratic or revolutionary tradition. Their influence on the politics of all European countries can be observed; even if they have not actually wielded governmental power they have and do exert considerable leverage on more conservative governments. Various reasons have been put forward for this: for example the impact of the historical absence of feudalism in the United States on the subsequent development of the class structure, and of the existence of large tracts of unpopulated land which provided an alternative for the sector of the population that would otherwise have been forced to live in industrial towns. Furthermore, the United States is the only country where men were integrated into the liberal democratic party system before the process of industrialization developed to the point where socialist ideas could give rise to a specifically socialist political party.

Although class has had an often underrated impact on American politics, other factors have been relatively more important than elsewhere and these have tended to cut across class lines and thus prevented their taking on a European significance. The first of these is ethnicity. In 1860 out of a population of 31.5 million only 4 million were foreign-born and they were mostly white Anglo-Saxons. By 1890 the population had doubled, of which 10 million were immigrants primarily from Germany, Britain, Ireland, Italy, the Balkans, Russia, Scandinavia and even Canada. In the next fifteen years a further 15 million immigrants came, drawn largely from Austria-Hungary, Italy, Russia, Greece, Romania and Turkey, and also from China, Japan and Mexico. And, as tends to be the case, these groups concentrated geographically: Germans in Wisconsin and Michigan, Scandinavians in Minnesota, and Mexicans in Texas, Arizona and California (Lees, 1975, pp. 25–6). Many immigrants congregated in the cities, however, and ethnic groups of 'hyphenated Americans' became a major factor in urban politics. They also came to play an increasingly important part in the politics of the United States as a whole as it became industrialized and urbanized. While many of the immigrants came from countries with growing socialist movements, the splits between various ethnic groups usually proved too strong for the development of class consciousness among the workers. Also, standards of living for many of these groups reached levels that they could only have dreamt of in their own countries and as successive waves of immigration pushed them up the scale of social status they were able to achieve the political power to go with their economic success.

Religion was another factor that tended to cut across class lines. The fact that there is no established religion in the United States, and the guarantee of religious freedom in the Bill of Rights, has meant that religion has impinged on politics in the United States in rather different ways from many European countries. The most significant manifestation of religion in American politics was the involvement, in elections and single-issue campaigns in the 1970s and 1980s, of a variety of fundamentalist groups, often with charismatic leaders, who spent enormous sums of money on political campaigns raised from the faithful through regular television and radio programmes; their support invariably went to conservative candidates. Another was the involvement of Catholics, especially in the pro-life (anti-abortion) movement, while the black churches were active in Jesse Jackson's campaigns for the Democratic Party's nomination as presidential candidate.

The last great division is, of course, that between different races. Historically, white Americans have oppressed and exploited a range of non-whites. Native-Americans, African slaves, Mexican and Asian immigrants have all suffered systematic discrimination and violence. In law, slavery ended with the success of the North in the Civil War, but its failure to reconstruct southern society meant that by 1890 the political and economic subordination of the African-Americans in the southern states was reinstituted. In the first half of the twentieth century they trickled into the industrial towns of the north, but it was the Second World War that was to be a major catalyst of change in this respect. Many more left the south for the north after 1945, and the many incongruities between the American stance on issues in the postwar world and the situation in its own southern states added to the pressure for change.

The attack on the structure of Southern racism between c.1950 and 1970 achieved real but also strictly limited gains. The legal supports of racism were successively removed by a combination of mass protest and governmental action orchestrated from Washington. Thus African-Americans achieved the effective right to vote and to be educated with whites. The result has been a great increase in the number of minority office-holders and legislators in the south. Progress has been far more limited, however, especially as the economy sank into recession in the 1970s, in improvements to the socio-economic position of ethnic minorities. There has been no redistribution of income to poorer minority groups as a whole, although the development of a middle class means that the class structure within the ethnic minority population, which is now pyramidal, resembles that of the population as a whole. The continuing impoverishment of millions of African- and Spanish-Americans, and the racial discrimination they experience, exploded back on to the American political agenda when south-central Los Angeles was devastated in three days of riots in April 1992. Politically, however, the African-Americans have remained the most loyal of all the groups that have supported the Democrats for the past sixty years, and this continued in the 1992 presidential election.

## The Context of British Politics

In considering the impact of economic and social change on the political process, one's perception of events is significantly affected by the model used. For example, capitalism in the West has become more and more humane and has taken on board ideas of people's rights, of health and safety standards, and financial support in cases of unemployment that would have been considered unthinkable 100 years earlier. It has been suggested that these developments were a logical progression, a rational process carried out by people who were gradually convinced by the argument for increased democracy (expressed by extension of suffrage) and government intervention to mitigate some of the worst excesses of the *laissez-faire* economic system – a conversion to new ideas and policies by sound and persistent argument. By an alternative model these events can be seen not in terms of sensible development, but rather as the result of a conflict of interests, with strategic and minimal concessions being made by those in control of the political and economic system, in order to preserve the essentials of the power relationships and privileges that are associated with the economic system. If we follow a Marxist analysis, these nineteenth- and twentieth-century developments were the result of a conflict of class interests in which those controlling the means of production, distribution and exchange conceded as little reform as they could to avoid more fundamental crises like major civil disorder. Other reforms came, it could be argued, not so much in the wake of expressed moral indignation, but as the result of technical innovation which enabled higher productivity to be achieved without such long hours, poor working conditions and low wages.

The interpretation of politics in Britain as a conflict between classes in the twentieth century is certainly more convincing than the idea of rational progress, although it is by no means the whole story. The years up to the General Strike of 1926 were marked by significant industrial unrest, which at times was regarded by the government as sufficiently serious for them to move and prepare troops and ships for use against strikers. The period was also marked by significant reforms which recognized the changed disposition of political forces, for example there were, successively, the National Insurance Act of 1911 and the extension of suffrage. But control of economic resources remained in the hands of much the same economic and financial interests as before. Another notable feature of the period was the open determination of governments to maintain the status quo, epitomized not only by the fierce reaction to strikes but also by the 'Back to normal' slogans at the end of the first World War (by which was meant back to the social and economic disposition of 1914) and a firm adherence to then orthodox economic policies.

In this period of social and political conflict the established authorities were noticeably dominant and kept organized trade-unionism comparatively quiescent for several decades. To achieve this, they were significantly helped by the political arm of the Labour movement, the Labour Party. The party had been formed rather reluctantly by basically conservative-minded trade-unionists, whose attitudes very much favoured integration into the existing political system rather than any more fundamental change. Although the Labour Party has always had a left wing of a greater or lesser degree of radicalism and militancy, its leadership has consistently been loyal to its original purpose: the greater representation of the the interests of working men and women in Parliament. In so far as it envisaged the revolutionary transformation of society, it saw it being achieved by rational argument – the conversion of all classes to socialism by the irrefutable logic of the argument – and taking place within the traditions of the parliamentary representative system which had been created by others but which the Labour movement unquestioningly joined. The energies of the Labour Party leaders in this period were therefore devoted to proving their competence in the parliamentary system rather than in supporting militancy: their lack of enthusiasm for the General Strike is well known.

The Labour Party was simultaneously weakened by the failure of its 1929–31 minority government, together with the defection of its long-standing leader, Ramsay MacDonald, and strengthened by its demonstrable capacity to survive, the continuing loyalty of the trade unions and its ability to retain a sizeable support among the electorate. Its participation in the wartime coalition government and the support and co-operation of the trade unions with that government marked its final acceptance into the parliamentary system. Long-standing ineffectual movements for reform came to a head during the wartime period, and Labour's claim to office was strengthened by the extended period in power of the Conservatives and the drastic failure of their economic policies in the 1930s. The election of the first majority Labour government in 1945 enabled them to implement some significant reforms but they were proposed more in the hope of harmonizing rather than of transforming British capitalism.

Helped by favourable economic circumstances, the British political system avoided the collapse and revolution that characterized the recent history of other major European powers. It gained a reputation for flexibility, resilience and tolerance. The obverse side of this was an inheritance of much dead wood from the past – old, comparatively unreformed institutions, unchallenged attitudes and slowly changing social structures. The political system had become steadily more and more out of line with economic and social realities. The cushioning effect of great economic prosperity based on empire had long postponed recognition of the underlying weaknesses. When these finally began to show in the 1960s, with underinvestment, unemployment and serious errors of planning and administration, the inertia of the political system was revealed. In spite of various royal commissions, inquiries and reports, the structural and psychological difficulties of change appeared insurmountable. Some radical neo-liberal policies in the years of the Thatcher government highlighted the fact that these problems of reform have not yet been decisively tackled – but neither has political and social inertia reached the point of causing the system to collapse. Nevertheless, it can be plausibly argued that the British political system, long praised for its adaptability and stability in a period of favourable economic circumstances, now shows the very opposite characteristic – an inability to change in unfavourable economic and social conditions. A temporary cushion was provided by North Sea oil during the 1980s, but as that runs out the economy may well come under added strain.

But even if we accept that some of the worst effects of British capitalism have been mitigated by working-class pressure, clearly the working class has not developed the revolutionary consciousness of which Marx spoke. The evidence as to whether class as an independent factor in British politics is diminishing is mixed. On the one hand, the study of voting behaviour in the 1970s suggested that it was diminishing. In the 1979 election the Conservative campaign advisers, Saatchi and Saatchi, advised that the Conservatives should direct their campaign particularly to the wives of those classified as C2 in the Registrar-General's occupational ladder, that is wives of the traditionally Labour-voting skilled manual workers. Evidence suggests that this group was indeed vital in providing the Conservatives with the swing necessary to win the 1979 election. In the three subsequent elections Labour failed to recapture this prime part of its voting constituency. In the 1983 general election the picture was further complicated by the formation of the Social Democratic Party which, in alliance with the Liberal Party, succeeded in attracting votes from previous supporters of both the Labour and Conservative parties. In the 1987 election the Alliance lost votes to Labour from among manual workers and the unemployed, but retained its support among the middle classes. Just one-third of the manual working class voted Labour (Crewe, 1987). However, after the election moves to bring about a formal merger of the Liberal and Social Democratic parties precipitated a major split in the latter and the collapse of Alliance support in the opinion polls by the end of 1987. The election of 1992 showed that, in spite of Labour making gains, largely at the expense of the Liberal Democratic Party (the main successor to the Alliance), the Conservative vote held up and was still significantly greater than that for Labour (for details see table 26.1).

Voting patterns aside, class remains an important variable. For example, trade union opposition to government incomes policies in 1973–4 and 1978–9 was a critical factor in the governments concerned losing the subsequent elections, and the length and cost of the miners' battle with the government over pit closures during 1984–5 indicated the importance that both sides gave to the issue. Apart from its effect on voting behaviour, religion has not been of particular importance in twentieth-century British politics except in Northern Ireland, where religious divisions are intimately connected with felt loyalties towards either Ireland or the United Kingdom. In the rest of Britain the remaining vestiges of religious cleavages tend to reinforce those of class, with Catholics rather more likely to vote Labour, Church of England adherents to vote Conservative and Nonconformists to vote Liberal Democrat or Labour. Race has had a sporadic impact on British politics since the Second World War, with race riots in London in the late 1950s and as an issue in some Midlands constituencies in the 1964 and 1966 general elections. It became more salient in the economic decline of the 1970s, with disproportionate numbers of minority groups unemployed and in poor accommodation. The rate of immigration has declined steadily with increasingly restrictive legislation, and ethnic minorities are predominantly concentrated in particular areas of mainly industrial towns. Because of this, their overall impact in voting terms is not likely to be great, but their ability to swing marginal constituencies could make them more important. A few members of ethnic minority groups have now been elected to the House of Commons. Of greater political significance so far has been the occasional eruption of rioting in urban communities. With one exception, these have been aimed not at whites but at the police and, indeed, in some areas (for example Liverpool in 1981) as many white as black youths were involved. Explanations of these riots have proliferated, but probably the most persuasive arguments are those that analyse the extent to which the people concerned find themselves excluded by a combination of poverty and racism from the conventional channels for voicing political grievances (see for example Lea and Young, 1984, pp. 169–97). This question is further examined in chapters 13 and 24.

## The Context of Soviet Politics

Geographical and climatic factors are crucial to understanding the Soviet Union which, in terms of area, could have contained the United States twice over and still have more than 1.3 million square miles to spare. Moscow is geographically nearer New York than its Far Eastern port Vladivostok. The material resources contained in this vast area were considerable, but exploiting them had always been difficult, owing to a combination of factors – hostile weather conditions, especially extremes of cold, the sparseness of population, the enormous distances that had to be covered to transport resources and supplies for the population and, not least, the shortage of outlets to the outside world because of hot and cold deserts and frozen seas. Major preoccupations of all tsarist and Soviet governments had been the internal stability of a far-flung land containing many nationalities, the protection of its considerable land and sea frontier from external attack, and the acquisition of unfrozen ports for trade and military access to the rest of the world. In our consideration of the successor republics, we should not underestimate the continuing influence of these factors and preoccupations on the policies of political leaders.

In 1917 the new Soviet state took over a country that had already begun the process of industrialization, but still had a vast, uneducated peasantry and a restricted elite, both heavily dominated by religion. The new state was committed to abolishing old power relationships and to instituting overall socialist planning. The task was made overwhelmingly difficult by the collapse of the social and economic order, and internal resistance to the new regime aided by foreign powers. To a significant extent, therefore, Lenin and the other leaders were driven to drastic and Draconian measures which were eventually seen to be self-justifying. The primacy of the Communist Party as a leadership vanguard was more and more emphasized and it was eventually dominated by its megalomaniac party secretary, Joseph Stalin. There is no doubt that the period of Stalin's rule, which by the 1930s amounted to a reign of terror, saw stupendous achievements in economic development and the transformation of the social system of the country. The strength and stability of the nation survived the onslaught of the Second World War and remained for a time under the more flexible regime that emerged after the death of Stalin in 1953. But these events are still within the living memory of some and had a profound effect on Soviet attitudes to internal stability and prosperity and to external threat. Their uncertainty on these issues was founded on grim experience.

However, the Soviet Union had at the same time many severe economic and social difficulties to contend with. Economically, compared to the West, the planned socialist society experienced considerable problems of underproduction, low productivity and inability to supply necessary materials and resources in the right places at the right times. The lack of incentive and motivation became very serious. The Soviet Union fell further and further behind the Western world in agricultural and industrial production, technological knowledge, skills and finished products. The achievements of the planned economy must therefore be seen in the light of the problems it created. The General Secretary of the CPSU from 1985 to 1991, Mikhail Gorbachev, attempted to persuade the party and bureaucracy that more openness (*glasnost*) and reconstruction (*perestroika*) were essential to improving the productivity of the Soviet economy. He took a calculated risk that the country was sufficiently stable to embrace these changes without political or social disruption, and was proved wrong (Davies, 1991, pp. 117–37). Socially, there were a number of areas of potential tension. Many social attitudes had been inherited from the past, including religion, which was allowed a limited revival in the Second World War because of its propaganda value as a patriotic institution. Thus it remained a contradiction and anomaly in Soviet society. In spite or because of much persecution, particularly under Stalin and Khrushchev, all religions experienced a speedy resurgence in the atmosphere of *glasnost*. This applied to both Islam and Christianity.

In a country of many nationalities nationalism was always a major potential cause of tension. Although it was dampened under the authoritarian governments before Gorbachev, it soon became the major cause of dissension, disruption and separatism, with the opportunities created by *glasnost*. First, there was a great imbalance in that the Russians made up about half the population of the Soviet Union (far more than any other nationality, but the declining proportion worried the authorities) and were considered to be in a favoured position. In addition, some nationalities had been incorporated into the Soviet Union against their will, while others had grievances against the government over their treatment. Thus various campaigns for justice on behalf of particular nationalities went on prior to the Gorbachev regime. With *glasnost*, they grew to such an extent that eventually every major nationality and many minor ones were proclaiming 'sovereignty' and, after the abortive coup of August 1991, some even declared independence. The fifteen republics became independent in December 1991, but nationalist forces continue to be a very important factor in their politics for the foreseeable future. Violent disturbances have already occurred in the Caucasus and elsewhere. Religion and nationalism are often, though not always, interlinked. Certainly, religion was a factor in the Lithuanian nationalist movement, and it continues to cause serious tension in many areas where Christians and Muslims live side by side (Lane, 1992, pp. 185–249).

Other tensions have been created by characteristics typical of any industrial society. There is a tendency, even where economic classes have been formally abolished, for social class distinctions arising from advantages of wealth, education, social position and career opportunities to be passed on to children. Soviet trade unions did not regard organizing and negotiating in industrial disputes on behalf of the workers to be a major part of their role. Therefore discontent over food shortages, poor working conditions or unfair treatment by the management gave rise to tensions that could be resolved only by petitions to politicians or even strikes, which were officially forbidden. In the years just before Gorbachev's accession to the general secretaryship of the CPSU, and inspired by the Solidarity movement in Poland, there were efforts by some workers to form so-called 'free trade unions' which were prepared to campaign for better pay and conditions as well as workers' rights. The instigators were dealt with by imprisonment or being sent to mental hospitals. Further difficulties were caused by a growing awareness of the greater material affluence in the developed Western world and the lack of opportunity to travel there or to acquire material consumer goods even by those with high incomes.

A consciousness of the relative lack of freedom in the Soviet Union caused more individuals and groups to organize dissenting activity in the hope of influencing the party and government authorities either directly or by pressure of international opinion. Such groups were led mainly by intellectuals – writers, artists and scientists. Some campaigned for stricter observance of the rights guaranteed in the Soviet Constitution or the Helsinki Agreement of 1975; others wished for a return to a purer form of Marxism and communism; while yet others wanted the adoption of liberal democratic principles in place of socialist ones. Groups such as churches, students and pan-Slavists also adopted dissenting attitudes towards the authorities.

It is difficult to gauge the influence exercised by the pre-Gorbachev dissenters. They appear to have existed in most major urban centres and managed to maintain some contact with one another in spite of lack of access to the mass media and other forms of publicity. The authorities took them seriously and arrests, imprisonment and exile were common. Dissenters themselves were weakened by uncertainty as to the severity of the authorities' attitude at any particular time, and by internal disputes. As for the general public, they heard little about dissenters and what they did hear was unfavourable (Hosking, 1992, pp.

402–45). By 1986 there were signs that *glasnost* was producing a number of liberalizations with respect to dissenters, and more open reporting of social unrest. There was a greater willingness to discuss with outsiders events such the disaster at the nuclear power station in Chernobyl which in the past would have been subjected to a complete cloak of silence. It proved impossible to sustain a news black-out over this incident.

As reforms continued, criticism of all aspects of Soviet politics as well as economic and social policy became the norm. The old-style dissenters were replaced by the beginnings of opposition politics. But little progress was made in agreeing on, let alone implementing, the necessary economic and social reforms. On top of this, the Soviet Union undertook a fundamental revision of its foreign and defence policies. This entailed, among other things, the end of the war in Afghanistan and the withdrawal of Soviet troops from Eastern Europe (and the subsequent collapse cf the communist regimes there). The Soviet authorities made it clear that they wished to play a fully co-operative role in international affairs, and to fundamentally revise the security arrangements in the world. While all this substantially reduced international tensions, it caused internal problems, as conservatives in the military, the party and defence industries resisted these moves. The growing economic crisis, together with ever more powerful manifestations of nationalism, led to a conservative coup attempt in August 1991. This effectively ended Gorbachev's hopes of getting the republics to agree to new economic and union treaties. The Soviet Union finally collapsed in 1991. Its fifteen republics became independent and formed very loose organization – the Commonwealth of Independent States (CIS) – to try to agree on economic and security co-operation. It is a very weak body whose prospects of survival are poor (Smith, 1992, introduction).

## Conclusion

The requirement that a political system reflect in its operation fundamental economic and social realities must be understood in the light of the considerable difficulties that every political system has to contend with. First, social and economic developments are by no means entirely under the control of the policy-makers. Policy decisions and their implementation can have profound social and economic effects, but other developments can take place as a result of internal or external pressures that are, to a greater or lesser degree, beyond the control of political forces. In addition, political policy-makers are unable to foresee all the consequences of their decisions or lack of them, so that a very large part of political activity is in fact taken up with coping with the unforeseen and unexpected consequences of previous decisions. Policy, therefore, cannot follow a totally coherent and consistent course, and the process of adjustment to circumstances does not always improve matters. This can happen whether or not the government is firmly committed to official ideological principles. Indeed, it may well be exacerbated by the need to square its actions with the rigidities of an official ideology.

Another difficulty with which any government must contend is the inertia of the social, economic and political structures themselves. Reform is often structurally impossible until it is too late to avoid serious difficulties, because of the weight of vested interests in the perpetuation of existing power relationships. Thus, on the one hand governments have to contend with change that is unanticipated and hence difficult or impossible to control, and on the other with a system's inertia which is very hard to overcome. The relationship of the political to the social and economic system, therefore, cannot be a simply ordered one. Politics is not just a matter of planning but of crisis and difficult choices. From the government's point of view, bad government is when crisis persistently and fundamentally prevails over planned and orderly policy development. From the point of view of those seeking social and economic change, crisis has the positive value of potentially precipitating such changes. This means that the carefully judged creation of crisis to the desired level becomes the tactic of many reformers and revolutionaries, while the effective management and damping of crisis becomes the primary role of government, except when a government feels that the engineering of some crisis would be in its own interest – for example to divert the public's attention from other awkward problems.

## Questions for Discussion

1  Do you consider economic and social policy to be the result of ideological preconceptions or ideology to be a rationalization of economic and social developments?

2 In what sense can governments be said to control rather than be controlled by events?
3 How far has government involvement in economic and social affairs in our three case-studies changed in kind rather than degree during the twentieth century?

## Further Reading

Davies, P.J. and G.A. Waldstein (eds) (1991), *Political Issues in America*. Manchester, Manchester University Press, chs 2–6.

Lane, D. (1992), *Soviet Society under Perestroika*, rev. edn. Boston, Unwin Hyman, ch. 2.

Macauley, M. (ed.) (1983), *The Soviet Union after Brezhnev*. London, Heinemann, chs 3 and 4.

McKay, D. (1989), *American Politics and Society*, 2nd edn. Oxford, Blackwell, ch. 2.

Moran, M. (1989), *Politics and Society in Britain*, 2nd edn. Basingstoke, Macmillan, ch. 1.

Sakwa, R. (1990), *Gorbachev and his Reforms, 1985–1990*. Hemel Hempstead, Philip Allan, ch. 7.

# Part III

## National Politics in Operation

# 12

# Party Politics

## Introduction

In this and the following chapter we discuss the two main types of organization that seek to influence or control national policy: political parties and organized groups (frequently referred to as pressure or interest groups). Parties are usually distinguished from groups by their intention to seek control of the main offices of government. They therefore put forward a wide spectrum of policies to cover all politically significant aspects of national life, as well as foreign affairs. Organized groups, on the other hand, restrict their aims to those that will promote the interests of their members or further particular causes; they do not have a comprehensive political programme, nor do they seek to acquire control of the main offices of government. Their purpose is to influence government to adopt policies favourable to them.

Some difficulties arise, however, from the generally accepted distinction. Not all organizations that claim to be seeking control of the government can realistically be said to be doing so. Parties such as Plaid Cymru or the Green Party in Great Britain have no chance of controlling the government, although they may get members of parliament (MPs) elected and, in certain circumstances, have some say in making the government's life easier or more difficult. At the very most, they can hope for a modest share in a possible coalition government. In other words, for practical purposes their aim must be to influence the government rather than to control it – which is what pressure groups are supposed to do. There is nothing to stop pressure groups putting up candidates at parliamentary elections on specific and limited programmes. There are examples in some countries of such candidates being elected and of pressure-group members of parliament being sufficiently numerous and permanent to share in office and to be regarded as a permanent parliamentary group – in other words, to behave in many ways like a party. The religious parties in Israel are an example of this type of group (the type of electoral system is crucial to this development – see chapter 26).

The position is further complicated by the fact that pressure groups can be closely or even officially associated with parties. The obvious example in the British context is the Labour Party which was, to all intents and purposes, originally the creation of the trade unions. Trade unions and other groups can be officially affiliated to the Labour Party. But unofficial links can be just as significant as more overt official association, as in the close association of business and financial interests with the Conservative Party.

## British and American Parties Contrasted

In comparing of the two liberal democratic party systems of Great Britain and the United States, let us first outline what it is that parties in liberal democracies are said to do. This can be summarized in four main propositions. First, parties facilitate the aggregation of the large number of group and sectional interests that arise and thus present the electorate with a clarified choice of issues; second, they organize and mobilize the electorate; third, they recruit leaders and provide governments; and fourth, they initiate and oversee the implementation of government policy.

That parties are coalitions of interests can be seen in both Britain and the United States and particularly in the latter. The aggregation of interests is necessary due to the large variety and often mutually incompatible nature of the sectional interests that develop in modern industrialized societies. No one interest can have maximum impact on government policies if it campaigns alone. Combining with other interests of broadly similar aims in affiliation to, or support of, a political party significantly strengthens the political clout of a particular group. The British Labour Party combines the interests of the trade unions and other, but not all, working-class, socialist and reforming groups. The Conservative Party today represents the middle classes, small and large business, finance and agriculture. That a large and heterogeneous society like the United States has maintained just two parties for almost its entire history suggests that the job of aggregation has been performed admirably, but it must be remembered that in the United States these interests are really only aggregated once every four years, just long enough for the parties to select their presidential candidates and fight for their election. For the rest of the time the parties are basically loose amalgamations of autonomous state parties.

However, liberal democracy requires a party – an aggregation of interests – to win the support of a mass electorate at frequent intervals. In the sense that these parties have provided the electorate with a clear either-or choice in both countries for many years, they can be said to be doing their job. It is less certain that, apart from the individual politicians standing for election, the choice was necessarily that clear-cut. It has been argued, for example, that in two-party systems the choice, as far as proposed policies are concerned, is frequently blurred, sometimes to the extent that there is no real choice, particularly in the American case. The reason for this is that each party can count on the votes of its committed supporters; what each wants to do is to capture the votes of those perceived as occupying the middle ground between the parties. Therefore, in campaigns a party attempts less to attract these voters than to ensure that they are not repelled by what the party advocates. As can be imagined, this tends to lead to the blurring of stances on issues rather than their clarification.

The organization and mobilization of the electorate in the United States to turn out to vote and to maximize the party's chances of success is probably not carried out as well as it used to be, as is evidenced by the decline in turnout since the 1960s (see table 26.2). The even more rapid decline in the two-party vote in Britain is to some extent compensated for by the increased vote for the smaller parties since the 1970s, but in the United States the proportion of the electorate mobilized by the parties is almost certainly even smaller because of the growing number of single-issue pressure groups in recent years. Their increased involvement in the electoral process has had as much or greater impact upon the mobilization of some small sections of people as has the more generalized appeal of the parties. Another major factor in the apparent reduction of the parties' role here is the effect of television on campaigning. Although there are important differences in the nature of television coverage between the two countries, television provides politicians in both with a direct (but one-way) link to the voter and reduces the traditional role of the party as mediator.

On the face of it, the parties in the United States still perform the job of recruiting personnel for positions in the executive and the legislature, since presidents, senators and representatives are elected, almost without exception, on a Democratic or Republican ticket. But closer examination of the electoral process reveals that party organizations are increasingly captured by outsiders whose party credentials have been, in some cases, rather slim. Jimmy Carter was a prime example of a little-known person capturing the permanent party organization in 1976 for at least the duration of the election. This is in sharp contrast to Britain where progress up the hierarchy of the party is very much a process of starting at the bottom and working up, first to a seat in Parliament and then, possibly, to ministerial office. This process has been short-circuited on occasions by well-known public figures, but it is inconceivable that a person unknown as a national party figure could, within the space of two or three years, become that party's leader as Carter did in the United States.

The people recruited into official positions through the parties tend to be of high social status, predominantly male, white and middle-aged. Although the United States Congress is dominated by lawyers, there is, in fact, a greater heterogeneity of background among congressmen compared to their counterparts in the House of Commons, but this simply reflects the greater cultural heterogeneity in the United States generally. Internal party reforms in recent years have ensured that the delegates to American party conventions are more representative of the population as a whole, with increased numbers of young people, ethnic minorities and women participating. There has been no similar move in the British parties, although Conservative party conferences have always had a high proportion of women delegates. The majority of Conservative MPs are male, public-school educated businessmen or lawyers. In the Labour Party MPs are likely to be male, university-educated and from middle-class professions like teaching or journalism, but with a working-class parental background. The proportion of Labour MPs who are themselves ostensibly working-class has fallen steadily since 1945. When we consider the attainment of higher political office, the trend is for the 'typical' MP to prevail more and more the higher one goes. Thus a higher proportion of cabinet ministers are middle class and university-educated than is the case with backbench MPs.

In the formation of governments which then present a clear policy programme, the performances of British and American parties are quite different, owing to the significant differences between the British parliamentary system of government and the American presidential system. Because of the distortions of the first-past-the-post voting system (which are discussed in chapter 26), elections in Britain have often provided one party with an overall majority in the House of Commons. The leader of this party then chooses the Cabinet from senior members of the party. Most of them will be MPs with seats in the House of Commons, where there is a premium on party loyalty and discipline to ensure that the measures proposed by the Cabinet can be passed into law with the minimum of amendment. Control of Parliament by the executive has never been more complete than in the twentieth century, with compliant MPs loyally following party policy. The nature of the disciplinary sanctions on which the system rests is that the modern MP is heavily reliant on the support of party activists and party finance in order to be elected. It is not so much the whips as the local constituency activists who indirectly but effectively apply sanctions (such as not readopting him or her) to keep the overwhelming majority of MPs toeing the party line, and government control very tight. Then, there is the simple point that MPs would prefer their party in power, no matter what it does, rather than in opposition. We should also note that a contemporary British government relies, like its eighteenth-century predecessors, on patronage. Over a hundred MPs in the House of Commons hold government posts at the present time and even the humblest of them – the parliamentary private secretaries – are almost always forced to resign if they vote against the government or even abstain. Backbench protests and revolts have, however, tended to increase in recent years, reflecting the changing background of MPs, and growing divisions of opinion over policy issues within parties (see Norton, 1985, pp. 23–81).

The contemporary system of party discipline as a means of executive control over Parliament breaks down when the electoral system fails to produce absolute majorities. In October 1974 Labour won only a small majority of seats but that majority had disappeared by 1976, because a number of minor nationalist parties were able to maximize their effect on the electoral system by virtue of their votes being concentrated into a limited number of constituencies, and because by-elections were lost. The situation was exacerbated by two very important and highly contentious issues – joining the European Community and devolution of some political authority to Scotland and Wales – which could not be contained within the rigid division of two-party adversarial politics. These divisions were reflected in the constituencies and so there was a breakdown in party discipline and a resurgence of freedom of action among MPs. What was remarkable about this state of affairs, however, was not the difficulties of parliamentary control that the executive experienced, but its ability, even in those difficult conditions, to get a great deal of legislation passed and to remain in office.

The reasons for this are essentially divide-and-rule and convenience. The government, even in a minority, is more united than an opposition made up of one majority party and a number of minor parties which do not always act in concert. The government, therefore, aims to avoid circumstances that are likely to unite all these opposition forces against it, and here it is helped by the practicalities of the situation. The major opposition party hesitates to launch too many full-scale attacks on the government if they are likely to result in a series of defeats by however small a majority, since this would tend to demoralize their supporters. Then, there is the real possibility that a serious defeat for the government could result in a general election and, under the British system, the opposition, just as much as the government, would prefer this to happen at a time favourable to themselves. The upshot is that incumbent governments tend to remain incumbent even when they have not got things arranged as conveniently as they would like. The House of Commons realizes that government must be carried on and this often mitigates any tendency to be disruptive. It also shows, however, that the rigid system of party discipline, which Britain has become used to in this century, is by no means necessary and essential to effective government. It is simply convenient for governments, which is not the same thing at all.

The presentation of issues and their translation into government policy has always been the blind spot of American parties. Issues are rarely debated, other than superficially during campaigns, and what the President proposes once he is in office bears no necessary relation to the platform on which he and his party ostensibly fought the campaign. The President and his advisers are in a completely different position *vis-à-vis* the legislature compared with the Cabinet in Britain. First, they cannot (by a provision of the constitution) sit as members of the Congress and therefore they lack the direct access that is available to the British Cabinet. Second, the American parties have always seen their primary job as winning elections, and not as governing. They do not have the degree of ideological and policy coherence normally found in British (and other European) parties, and display far less party loyalty in the legislature. (See table 12.1) The Democrat President Carter had great difficulty in getting even his most basic requests through a Congress controlled during 1977–80 by 2:1 Democratic majorities, a failure that was put down to Carter's unwillingness and/or inability to bargain and deal with members of Congress.

**Table 12.1**  Party unity in the United States Congress, 1981–1990

| Congress | Total recorded party unity votes (%) | |
| --- | --- | --- |
| | Senate | House |
| 97th (1981–2) | 45 | 36 |
| 98th (1983–4) | 42 | 52 |
| 99th (1985–6) | 51 | 59 |
| 100th (1987–8) | 47 | 53 |
| 101st (1989–90) | 44 | 52 |

*Note*: *Congressional Quarterly* defines a vote in Congress as a 'party unity' vote where a majority of Democrats votes one way and a majority of Republicans votes the other.

*Source*: *Congressional Quarterly Annual Almanac*, Congressional Quarterly (various dates), Washington, DC.

Party loyalty is by no means an irrelevant factor in explaining and predicting the behaviour of congressmen, but on any issue that they perceive to be contentious within their districts nobody expects a member of Congress to put party before district. Therefore, in order to get his legislative requests on to the statutebook, the President has to rely much more on *ad hoc* coalitions in support of each specific measure. Clearly, in comparison with the British system, much greater energy and frustration will be expended by the President, for there is no guarantee that any proposal he makes will pass at all, let alone free of amendments that he does not want and does not like.

Although, in terms of campaigning, electoral turnout and party identification, it may be said that the two main parties in Britain are less important than they were, Britain still provides us with an example of party government resulting from a party system having considerable independent influence on the political process. But a combination of the characteristic features of American parties today raises the serious question of whether analysis of American politics from the perspective of a party system or party government is at all helpful. In comparison to Europe in general, the Democrats and the Republicans may best be characterized as two among a large number of groups setting out to influence the course of the American political process (we shall examine such groups in chapter 13).

## Party in the Soviet Union

The party system of the Soviet Union provided a striking contrast to both Great Britain and the United States. One party was considered to be sufficient in the Soviet Union because the country officially had one ideology and one goal – communism. No other parties were considered necessary until the advent of Gorbachev and the policies of *glasnost* and *perestroika*. The CPSU could have been considered analogous to a liberal democratic party in some limited respects. It did to some extent aggregate demands and turn them into viable policy issues, and it also acted as a downward channel of communication, explaining and rationalizing government policies in the hope of their greater acceptance by the citizens. But the co-ordinating and overseeing role of the CPSU at all levels of Soviet society, and its bureaucratic control, went far beyond what would be expected in a liberal democracy.

The CPSU was, in most respects, a parallel bureaucracy alongside that of the government, and integrated with it (through party members in the government and vice versa). It had no adversary or coalition relationship with similarly organized parties. It was all-embracing and claimed that it alone spoke authoritatively for the people. Its policies were not tested by debate in the open political arena, but by private discussion among officials, and by public elucidation and explanation throughout the party membership and beyond. Its legitimacy was not based on electoral success but on its revolutionary principles and antecedents. The effective supervision and guidance of the party was officially seen as the key to the ever-improving welfare of the Soviet people. From the liberal democratic point of view, whatever was gained in this system of planned co-ordination and coherence was counterbalanced by the overbureaucratization and lack of incisive public criticism. Democracy in the Western sense was lacking. The CPSU pervaded almost every aspect of political, economic and social life in the Soviet Union. Its organization was hierarchical with, at the top, the General Secretary, the effective political leader of the country. He was responsible to the Politburo, the main party committee which decided all major issues of policy. Under the Politburo was the Central Committee, composed of over 300 of the party's secretaries and other leading figures. Although the Central Committee could be the centre for major political decisions (as when Khrushchev ousted his rivals), it usually met too infrequently and was too unwieldy for major decision-making. The Central Committee Secretariat (or Apparatus), however, had a major role in supplying data and policy options to the Politburo. At intervals of a few years, party congresses were held at which major changes of policy would be announced and new directions set for the future.

This institutional framework was imitated at all but the lowest levels of the party hierarchy. Each republic, region, city and district had its party secretary, its politburo, congresses and conferences. At the bottom were the primary organizations (the primary party organizations, or PPOs), centred on cells in places of work or study, which were the main point of contact with the party for most of the party members – 19 million in the 1980s. Certainly, the CPSU was the initiator and the final arbiter in the policy process. It worked in close co-ordination with the government bureaucracy and with the soviets. Essentially, it had a directing and supervisory role, ensuring that the policies laid down by the Politburo were known and vigorously pursued at all levels. In addition, by the use of the *nomenklatura* (a list of important posts that could not be filled without party approval) it controlled appointments to all significant offices (Lane, 1985, pp. 141–72).

Of course, things did not always go so smoothly. Party members did not always work enthusiastically or have entirely unselfish motives for joining the party – membership could be a great help to career advancement. Corruption could occur or it could prove impossible to induce much positive interest in and enthusiasm for political matters among a population that had no tradition of political involvement and no overt disputation over policies to excite its interest. Like all great bureaucratic organizations, inertia and conservatism could sap the genuine pursuit of the original ideals. The party attempted to renew vigour from time to time by the 'exchange of party cards' – an opportunity to purge the party of unsatisfactory members – or by the replacement of officials. During the Khrushchev era membership of the party was rapidly expanded, and many felt that there was a dilution in the quality of members. His successor pursued a more cautious path but there was a danger that party membership would become too small to maintain satisfactory links with the bulk of the population. In the 1980s membership rose again, until, with the upheaval and questioning created by Gorbachev, members left the party in large numbers.

The problems of political recruitment were also highlighted by the experience of the Soviet Union, where it was possible to categorize certain politically significant types within the Politburo, and the Supreme Soviet. As in Great Britain, a model of the typical party member could be drawn up – male, middle-aged, hailing from a city rather than from the countryside and, increasingly, with advanced educational qualifications. The authorities recognized the tendencies in the system to favour certain social categories, and steps were taken to try to redress the bias by, for example, laying down quotas for membership of certain groups, like women and young people. It is not clear that this had a significant effect.

The party's fortunes varied over the years. Before the 1980s its lowest ebb was probably during the last years of Stalin's life when his private office and the secret police seem to have had more influence than the party. When its predominant position was restored, the party faced new challenges as the increasing interdependence of industrial society made influential groups realize that the party needed them as much as they needed it. Although, officially, the supremacy of the party was firmly maintained, relationships with other significant sectors of society were slowly being realigned as the party realized the need to recognize and adjust to new social and political roles (Benvenuti, 1991, pp. 46–64).

The reaction of the CPSU to Gorbachev's reforms highlighted its weaknesses. He had great difficulty in getting party support for his reforms and, although he showed great political skills, he was never able to overcome the powerful opposition of party-vested interests. In the summer of 1991 he proposed a new party programme which, in effect, would have brought it much closer into line with a social democratic party, competing with others on Western lines. This, together with his proposed union treaty, which opponents saw as a breakup of the Soviet Union, drove conservatives to try to take over control from him by declaring a state of emergency – in effect, a *coup d'etat*. The failure of the coup, together with revelation of the party's close implication in it, led to its collapse and abolition. Post-coup inquiries revealed widespread financial corruption. Nevertheless, party personnel continue to retain control in many areas (such as Central Asia), in parties with changed names (Smith, 1992, pp. 94–128).

During and after the Gorbachev regime many political groups were formed. Some of these, for example the popular fronts in the republics', established themselves as significant features of the political scene. Many others were small, limited in membership and appeal, and often short-lived. Before the collapse of the Soviet Union, there was no sign of effective, nation-wide parties coming into existence. The independent republics do not, for the most part, have firmly established systems of parties competing for office. They have yet to learn the meaning and significance of constitutional political opposition. The extreme social and economic difficulties they faced on independence meant that the emergence of recognizably democratic party politics was by no means certain.

## Conclusion

Political parties are found in virtually all countries in the modern world and are regarded by most commentators as essential modern political organizations. In effect, they are coalitions of interests necessary to create a viable governing group. In the Western liberal democratic world various parties (frequently coalitions of interests) contest for periods of governmental power. Sometimes a party will win a period of office outright; more commonly perhaps two or more parties will share power. These public contests are firmly based on agreement as to the fundamental characteristics of the type of regime and economic system that is required for the country. Thus Western parties are both focuses for unity and vehicles for public contest. They formulate policies acceptable to their supporters and provide options for voters and those more directly involved in government to choose from. As economic circumstances and social conditions change, the parties too must change if they are to retain the confidence of enough voters to achieve office. They do not necessarily find such changes easy, and periods of considerable intra- and interparty uncertainty and upheaval may follow periods of relative stability in the party system. For example, the changes in the British Labour Party have been extensive, and continue, following the loss of four successive general elections between 1979 and 1992.

The CPSU had some characteristics and functions in common with those of Western parties. The major difference was that it did not operate in a context of contest. It had complete control of the Soviet government and of all other significant sectors of Soviet society. Its prestige and pre-eminence were unchallenged until the period *of glasnost* and *perestroika*. This meant that the public disputes and debates over policy that take place openly in the West were in the Soviet Union argued out within the party and in private. To Western eyes this method seemed restricted and undemocratic, but to the Soviets it was considered an orderly method of proceeding compared to the apparent chaos of Western politics.

If Western parties, in spite of the need to win votes, can become inward-looking and out of touch with economic and social realities, the possibility was as great, if not greater, with a party like the CPSU whose hold on government was unchallenged. The dominance of the CPSU appeared unassailable at the start of the 1980s, but by the end of the decade it was in serious trouble. It reluctantly accepted many of Gorbachev's proposed reforms (it had no alternative to offer, apart from more of the policies of the past – and no effective alternative leader), but conservatives with vested interests tried to restore the status quo in the 1991 coup attempt. The failure of the coup revealed how out of touch the party had become with Soviet political realities. Its support had been visibly waning, and it now collapsed and found itself suspended or abolished in the republics. It still retains control, under other names, in Central Asia and other localities, but is a shadow of its former dominant self. The post-Soviet republics are experiencing difficulty in establishing recognizably democratic party systems in the face of severe social and economic crises with no well-established tradition (or memory) of democratic government behind them.

## Questions for Discussion

1　Is the distinction between parties and pressure groups analytically useful?

2  How is the working of the party system likely to affect the shape of policy decisions?
3  Are political parties essential to democracy?

## Further Reading

Lavenstein, D.H. (1992), American political parties. In G. Peele et al. (eds), *Developments in American Politics*. Basingstoke, Macmillan, pp. 63–85.

McKay, D. (1989), *American Politics and Society*, 2nd edn. Oxford, Blackwell, ch. 5.

Moran, M. (1989), *Politics and Society in Britain*, 2nd edn. London, Macmillan, ch. 4.

Peele, G. (1990), Parties, pressure groups and Parliament. In P. Dunleavy, A. Gamble and G. Peele (eds), *Developments in British Politics* 3. Basingstoke, Macmillan, pp. 69–95.

Smith, G.B. (1992), *Soviet Politics: Struggling with Change*, 2nd edn. Basingstoke, Macmillan, ch. 5.

Tolz, V. and E. Teague (1992), Political parties in Russia. *RFE/RL Research Report*, 1 (1), 3 January, pp. 12–14.

# 13

# Group Politics

## Introduction

As we saw in chapters 6 and 7, for pluralists the activities of groups are the central feature of the political process. Whether or not we accept their view, it cannot be denied that groups are always an important part of any developed political system. To begin with, we must distinguish between the terms 'interest', (discussed in chapter 4), and 'group'. Many sections of society have an identifiable 'interest' be it in jobs, profits, more roads or more nuclear power stations. However, such sections (or their representatives) are groups in our sense only if they are organized to pursue that interest by lobbying government officials or seeking the election of particular candidates. This is an important distinction because pluralist models suggest that we can draw conclusions about the influence of different interests only when groups can be observed at work on their behalf in the political process. This is entirely consistent with their view that people's interests are what they say they are, and that interests are of political significance only when people organize to advance or defend them. It may seem naive, for some interests will be better served than others in all societies regardless of overt group pressures. Pluralists do not deny such a possibility, even probability; they simply say that theirs is the pragmatic solution to the difficult methodological problems involved in the analysis of power and interests (discussed in chapters 3 and 4 respectively).

The key aspects of political activity according to the pluralist group model are: all sections of society are capable of influencing policy, especially if they are formally organized; policy represents the outcome of bargaining and compromise between groups, the role of the state being to act as arbitrator of disputes. The process is democratic because in the long run no one group dominates, countervailing groups develop, and no group is denied access to advance its interest. Some of the problems with this model were discussed in chapter 7. We should also note that it is based on certain assumptions, for example it is assumed that those who have some reason to form a pressure group will, in an open society, do so, and that the degree of governmental response will depend on the degree of pressure the group is able to exert, and that this is directly related to the group's importance to the community.

Both assumptions have been questioned and much evidence adduced to show that group politics does not in fact work in this way. First, those who have a political interest to pursue will not in fact always do so, for example consumers, who are numerous but widely distributed, generally have never organized themselves as effectively or as efficiently as producers, who are much fewer in number but already have a business organization able to be adapted for political purposes. Another group often mentioned is agricultural workers, who are thinly scattered across the land and have had great difficulties in forming a union with political and industrial strength. It has been argued by Mancur Olson (1965) that there is often no incentive to go to the expense and trouble of joining a group, especially when the group is large, because it may make no difference to that particular individual. It is frequently not practicable to withhold benefits gained by the organization from non-joiners in the same area of activity (wage increases or better working conditions, for example). With the benefits accruing to him or her whether he or she joins or not, there is no rational reason why any individual should join the pressure group. The larger the group the greater this tendency, argues Olson, and thus it is not surprising that amorphous groups such as consumers, or even economic classes, do not unite in common action to pursue their interests.

However, it is evident that pressure groups are, in fact, often formed on a large scale and some explanation needs to be offered. Olson suggests that these organizations are sometimes artificial creations required by governments to provide them with a representative body they can negotiate with. Alternatively, they are organizations originally created for a non-political purpose (for example the British Medical Association was originally formed to circulate medical and scientific information to doctors) which have acquired political purposes over time. Their political activities may not be perceived as very significant and useful by the bulk of the membership. In some cases, an established group will attempt to increase its influence and power by making membership compulsory for all those sharing the interest. This is the idea behind the closed-shop principle as developed by such groups as lawyers and printers. However, the explanation for joining a group depends on the narrow conception of 'economic man' maximizing the attainment of his self-interest. As has been pointed out, the motivations of 'political man' are not the same and not necessarily as rational as those of 'economic man'. Clearly, more research needs to be done, but the main point is that the assumption that people with common political aims and grievances will definitely form pressure groups within the liberal democratic context is by no means borne out by the evidence.

The assumption that the degree of governmental response will depend on the degree of pressure that the group is able to exert, which is in turn directly related to the group's importance to the community, must also be questioned. Pressure-group activity is only one factor that the government has to take into account in deciding policy, and the group's importance to the government and community is susceptible of various interpretations. Some are important because they supply and service utilities such as gas, electricity and water; others, even though they are small in number, because their production keeps many thousands in employment; and still others, like doctors, nurses and paramedics, because they deal with human emergencies. However, the importance of the group is often measured by the number or helplessness of the people dependent on such services and the degree to which they are affected, for example we can all fall ill and a strike of doctors would affect all classes, rich and poor, young and old alike. A strike of social workers is not only much more limited in its impact, but affects mostly the poor and underprivileged section of the community whose political muscle is very weak and limited anyway, even though the effect of such a strike on particular individuals or families may be very grave indeed.

## Protest and Direct Action

Another factor affecting the impact of political pressure is the degree to which groups are prepared to make their protest felt.

Those whose actions are most likely directly to involve human suffering or even death may hesitate to use their whole political industrial and political muscle for fear of the adverse reaction of public opinion and decision-makers should their action be the cause of some tragedy, such as death. There is, however, a tendency for the public and the government to get used to industrial action and to adapt to it, so inducing groups to become more and more militant in order to sustain the same level of impact. There is no guarantee that the degree of influence on governmental decision-making of a given pressure group will be in line with any particular interpretation of 'importance'. In the complex interlocking economies of the industrialized world, groups not necessarily engaged in traditionally prestigious occupations are, nevertheless, vital to the smooth running of society and the economy. In these circumstances groups utilize what pressure they can, constrained only by the basic tradition of liberal democracy, for example they do not (usually) adopt violent tactics. However, it would be wrong to measure the power of groups simply in terms of their ability to disrupt. On the contrary, it may be argued that the groups that flex their muscles most forcefully and publicly thereby demonstrate their relative weakness. The most influential groups are those with continuous and private relationships with the bureaucracy in which both sides – government and group – control factors (for example money or information) that are valued by the other. The last thing either side wants is a public trial of strength which would probably succeed only in damaging the long-term interests of each.

This highlights a crucial tactical problem for new groups or those whose demands are seen as in some way unconventional. As we shall see in chapter 27, in recent years there seems to have been a greater willingness in the Western liberal democracies to take action outside the normal channels of group and party politics. One major example has been the rise in the number of groups – some more organized than others – representing communities or neighbourhoods, mainly within the context of local politics. There now exist community groups of a greater or lesser degree of militancy which have eschewed political parties as the main vehicle of their demands (although they often have to use them in the later stages of campaigns). These groups are to some extent welcome to the authorities, as they provide obvious and organized bodies with which negotiations and discussions can be held. In some cases, indeed, the authorities have provided the resources for such groups to be formed, for example community councils in Britain.

However, the relationship between action groups of one sort or another and the local and central governmental authorities is by no means always smooth. The difficulty lies in the fact that the governmental authorities, however highly principled and dedicated to the welfare of the citizenry, are essentially a vested interest running an organization which, to a greater or lesser degree, is designed to preserve and promote the continuing control of those same authorities. Any group that acts in such a way as to threaten to disturb the smooth running of the governmental organization is likely to be seen (often rightly) as a challenge to the status quo. Such a status quo includes not only officials in the bureaucracy but also most elected politicians, together with a variety of supporting organizations, such as the churches, professional bodies and the media. Among such conventional bodies there is an understood set of principles and a mode of proceeding which are characterized as fair, balanced, reasonable and sensible – terms that cover, in reality, some very precise judgements as to policy priorities and the relative importance of some individuals and groups as against others.

Where contact with the organized public is necessary or unavoidable, steps are taken to retain the organizational initiative in the hands of the governmental authorities as far as possible, and to associate with people of like attitude rather than with those who are considered to be 'uncooperative', 'militant', 'extremist' for example. From the point of view of more or less militant pressure groups, there are real problems as to what to do in these circumstances. To adopt a militant, uncooperative or obstructive approach may gain publicity, not all of which will be good. The organizers are often faced with the dilemma of whether they should adopt an all-out militant campaign with the risk that in the end all will be lost and nothing gained in spite of the expenditure of a great deal of energy, time and sometimes money; or come to some agreement with the authorities whereby something can be gained, even though it falls far short of the full objectives of the group and will not significantly affect the position of, and relationships between, vested interests. It is perhaps this dilemma that causes most disagreement among protesters and it is therefore the one most effectively used by the governmental authorities to weaken their position. Peace campaigners in the 1980s, and animal-rights and environmental groups in the 1990s, faced this dilemma.

## The Focus of Group Activity

For the groups that eschew unconventional behaviour – and there may be tactical as well as principled reasons for doing so – the focus and target of pressure is likely to be the people who make the laws and policies and/or the people who implement them. The particular emphasis placed on one or other of these depends on a variety of conditions, such as the 'legitimacy' of the group, the nature of the demand, the stage of the decision process reached and the nature of the political process itself. For example, when should a group direct its attention to the legislature? A comparison of the British and American policy-making processes reveals that the Congress is far more likely to amend or reject proposals coming from the executive than the House of Commons.

We would, therefore expect to see much greater lobbying in Congress than in the Commons, and so we do. Indeed, it may be argued that a British group lobbying Parliament demonstrates mainly its lack of access to, or impact on, the core of the policy-making process (ministers and civil servants), unless the lobby is undertaken explicitly for symbolic purposes and in order to attract the attention of the media. However, British members of parliament do have extensive outside interests and many are retained to act on behalf of groups. In general, this reflects the group's belief that a member of parliament can intervene with the bureaucracy on the group's behalf. In terms of legislative proposals, lobbying the assembly is more important in the United States, especially for groups wishing to exercise a negative or veto power to stop a proposal rather than have a new proposal passed. But in both Britain and the United States the most significant activities of groups are those involving close and continuous relationships with the executive branch bureaucracy that is responsible for the detailed implementation of policy. In Britain there are a multitude of consultative committees in which members of organized interests and officials of the bureaucracy discuss both what legislative changes may be made and how legislation can be implemented. This government–group relationship is symbiotic. Instead of resulting from a successful use of pressure by a group on a reluctant government, the relationship derives from the government's need for specialized information which the group possesses and its co-operation in the eventual implementation of policy. From the group's perspective, it desires to be involved where it can influence the final shape of a policy so that it maximizes the benefits and minimizes the losses to its members. One of the manifestations of this relationship can be seen in the nature of the laws made when the state intervenes in a particular area of interest. General 'enabling' laws are passed by Parliament on the prompting of the executive, which lay down certain principles but, even if they are detailed, leave ample room for bargaining when the drafting of regulations for the implementation of the law occurs. The relevant groups in this bargaining are, of course, the permanent representatives of the state – civil servants – and the representatives of the interests affected.

What are essentially bilateral relationships between group and department in Britain have in the United States long become recognized as trilateral relationships of group, department and, because of its far greater role in the substance of legislation, Congress. In practice, of course, a large number of these relationships rarely involve more than a few people. These will be leaders of or permanent Washington-based lobbyists for the group, two or three members of the relevant congressional subcommittee and a few permanent officials in the relevant bureau of the department. The resulting 'subgovernments' (Cater, 1964, pp. 17–22) or 'iron triangles' have been seen as critical to an understanding of what governments actually do or do not do because of their permanence, the secrecy of their operations and the weak party system in the United States. More recently, however, it has been suggested that these subgovernments have been increasingly complemented by the development of what are called 'issue networks'. These are defined by Heclo as 'specialized subcultures composed of highly knowledgeable policy-watchers' (Heclo, 1978, p. 99). They are larger and more diffuse than subgovernments and owe their development to a variety of factors: the rapid growth of federal spending, the growth in private and semi-private organizations which are used to administer many federally funded policies, the growth in 'public interest' organizations and the great increase in the ranks of professional administrators in all fields, for example planning, health, welfare, education and housing. Thus these issue networks provide a kind of intellectual community in specific policy fields which to some extent transcends traditional political boundaries between Congress and the executive and between the layers of government in the American federal system (this is examined in more detail in chapter 16).

A major outstanding question in the relationship between groups and government is, as was suggested in chapter 7, whether the interaction is best analysed by a model of pluralism or one of corporatism. Clearly, neither reflects the totality of the situation in Britain or the United States, and therefore we would agree with Cawson (1978) that it is possible to discern sectors resembling corporatist relationships and sectors resembling pluralist relationships in both contemporary Britain and the United States.

## Group Politics in the Soviet Union

On the face of it, given the dominant place of the CPSU in initiating policy and its penetration of the state administrative apparatus which implemented the policies, there was no room for any manifestation of group politics in the former Soviet Union. But in such a modern industrialized state it was not long before many groups realized that their role in the social and economic system made their co-operation and support essential to the Communist Party. This gave them potential political leverage were their sectional interests to be threatened. The overall guiding role of the party was therefore likely to meet with resistance at some stage and there are signs that this indeed happened increasingly in the post-Stalinist period. It is unwise, however, to give way to the temptation to apply the pluralist model to the Soviet Union on the grounds that 'basically all industrial societies are alike'. Group politics in the Soviet Union was by no means so clearly and permanently organized as in Great Britain or the United States. Organized group politics would have been incompatible with the official position of the party. Pressure-group activity, therefore, tended to occur on an *ad hoc* issue basis rather than be based on a system of permanently structured relationships. This did not imply that interested groups acting in this context could not be effective, as, for example, the resistance to Khrushchev's proposed educational reforms showed.

It is clear that other groups, such as the military, scientists and intellectuals, could exercise influence over the party and modify policy. In addition, there were informal groups based on general policy orientations within the party itself, which were usually divided by the distinction between conservative and liberal policy preferences. But it would be unwise to assume that the advancing industrialization of the Soviet Union was increasingly leading to a form of politics in which organized groups took a more significant part. It has been suggested (White, 1978, p. 101) that if we look at the delivery of key speeches in the Supreme Soviet, for example, there was no evidence that prominent groups were gaining proportionately more influence *vis-à-vis* the party, which may demonstrate that there is no good reason to assume that industrialized societies necessarily develop similar political characteristics. Nevertheless, in changing social and economic circumstances the role of the party *vis-à-vis* groups needed constant adjustment in reality if not officially. The party developed various ploys to maintain its position, like acquiring its own experts and co-opting people with strong group links on to the Politburo. That a form of group politics existed in the Soviet Union is, therefore, indisputable. It was, however, looser, more flexible and far less permanent and structured than in the West. There is no evidence to suggest that it would have developed more closely along Western lines.

The period of *glasnost* and *perestroika* under Gorbachev led to a great burgeoning of group activity throughout the republics. Some of these groups, for example the popular fronts, soon developed overt political aims in opposition to the CPSU. Signs of organized pressure-group activity among, for example, trade unions and environmentalists, became evident. But the lack of a well-established party system in the republics, and the general economic and social crisis, suggested that it would be some time before institutionalized pressure-group systems were operating, if at all. Some republics, like those in Central Asia, were still basically authoritarian systems. In others, like the Baltic republics, democratic traditions had flimsy historical foundations. Thus, the nature and scope of pressure-group politics in the former Soviet republics remain uncertain (Lane, 1992, pp. 107–44).

## Conclusion

The existence of competition between organized groups of people sharing interests, and their peaceful mediation by neutral governments, has been the central argument of those who analyse liberal democracies in terms of the pluralist model. We have suggested that, while competition of this sort does exist, there are serious problems with accepting all the assumptions and propositions associated with pluralism. One important problem has always been the question of how groups operate and to what effect. In other words, why do some groups advancing certain interests enjoy access to centres of government policy where their case may be made peacefully and with apparently good chance of acceptance, while others advancing different interests find access to these forums extremely difficult, if not impossible? The latter have to decide whether to stop trying or to resort to more unconventional methods in the hope that government will be sufficiently embarrassed by the ensuing mayhem to consult them.

Some commentators saw corporatist trends in both Britain and the United States in the 1960s and 1970s. In the 1980s, in principle at least, government drew back from collusion with pressure groups and tried to leave economic market conditions to decide policy. Whatever relationship exists between government and groups, we must raise the question of whether the advancing of organized interests enhances democracy or, at least, provides the only realistic chance of obtaining some democracy in industrialized societies, as the pluralists have argued. On the one hand, does the integration of groups into the bureaucratic structure make them a threat to traditional democratic norms of accountable government? On the other, does the policy of government to leave much decision-making to commercial factors or the market enhance or hinder democracy?

The dramatic change in the political structures of the former Soviet republics raises many questions about the development of group politics in these areas. In the period of *glasnost* and *perestroika* incipient group politics could be observed, but its likely development and its characteristics following the breakup of the Soviet Union remain a matter for speculation. It does not necessarily have to develop along Western lines to remain democratic. New forms of group politics may emerge, depending on the types of democracy or other forms of government that become established.

## Questions for Discussion

1 Is the domination of politics by organized groups inevitable in large industrialized societies?
2 What strategy would you recommend to a group who wanted (a) to defend a threatened economic interest and (b) to advance a moral cause?
3 In what sense are organized groups (a) a manifestation of and/or (b) a threat to democracy?

## Further Reading

Budge, I. and D. McKay (1988), *The Changing British Political System:
Into the 1990s*, 2nd edn. Harlow, Longman, pp. 35–8, 192–4.

Dearlove, J. and P. Saunders (1984), *Introduction to British Politics*
Cambridge, Polity, ch. 3.

Grant, A. (1991), The American Political Process, 4th edn. Aldershot,
Dartmouth, ch. 5.

McKay, D. (1989), *American Politics and Society*, 2nd edn. Oxford,
Blackwell, ch. 11.

Merridale, C. (1991), Perestroika and political pluralism: past and prospects. In C. Merridale and C. Ward (eds), *Perestroika: The Historical Perspective*. London, Edward Arnold, pp. 14–33.

Miliband, R. (1984), *Capitalist Democracy in Britain*. Oxford, Oxford
University Press, ch. 3.

Moran, M. (1989), *Politics and Society in Britain*, 2nd edn. Basingstoke
Macmillan, ch. 5.

Sakwa, R. (1990), *Gorbachev and his Reforms, 1985–1990*. Hemel
Hempstead, Philip Allan, ch. 5.

# 14

# Executives

## Introduction

We began our discussion of the policy-making process by considering the roles of parties and pressure groups as if they were on the outside looking in, so to speak. Now we continue by looking at the inside workings of the process at the national level, beginning with a discussion of executives and assemblies. In this and the following chapter we shall examine their basic workings as institutions in their own right, and in chapter 16 we shall examine their interaction.

There is a good deal of confusion over the use of concepts to analyse the institutions and processes of policy-making. In the past, people have used models of particular institutions carrying out legislative, executive and judicial functions, that is law-making, law-implementation and law-adjudication. This model reflects only certain aspects – some of them myths – of what happens in the world of political decision-making. It is analytically more revealing and significant to identify actors by the roles they play, for example politicians and officials. Then it becomes clear that politicians, for example, can be involved in processes of policy-making, implementation, evaluation and adjudication. Similarly, officials (bureaucrats) can also be involved in all three areas. It is the role people play in political processes, not the job they officially hold, that matters in our analysis.

The growing scale of the bureaucracy, the increasing complexity of its role and the intricacy of its relations with the politicians means that bureaucracy today needs to be studied as a separate institution (see chapter 17). We also prefer the term 'assembly' to 'legislature' because legislation (making the law) is an inadequate definition of the role of modern elected assemblies. Throughout this discussion, therefore, it is important to be aware of the gulf that frequently exists between out-of-date constitutional models and inappropriate concepts (although these are still sometimes invoked by politicians), and the actual practice of policy-making.

## Chief Executives

A certain amount of confusion is often generated by the interchangeable use of such concepts as 'the executive', 'the state' and 'the government', because there are no universally accepted definitions of them. It would, therefore, by helpful to distinguish clearly between them. The state (otherwise often referred to as 'the regime') is the most inclusive of the terms and is usually understood to embrace all the main institutions of the political system, including the judiciary, police and the military (see chapters 18 and 19). 'Government' is often reserved to describe the actions of the 'government of the day'. It refers to a much smaller group of politicians who hold executive office temporarily (following a *coup d'état*, revolution, election or other succession process) as presidential appointees, or members of a majority party, coalition or military junta, and we shall use the concept in this sense. What is the difference between the executive and the government? For our purposes, the executive will be understood to refer to the body of government ministers together with permanent senior officials (bureaucrats) who are involved in the basic decisions over what policy proposals to initiate and pursue and the priority to give them. Compared to states or executives, governments tend to be of short duration – state institutions often remain in existence for long periods and officials in the executive may have lifelong careers, while governments come and go (although some of their personnel may hold office in more than one government).

Executives, at their apex, they may be single or collective. This means that the final decision-making responsibility is either formally concentrated in one person or, alternatively, in a collective body – a committee – like the British Cabinet, or the Communist Party Politburo in the Soviet Union. In reality, it is often much harder to classify actual systems unambiguously than this simple dichotomy would suggest. For example, the United States appears to provide a clear example of a single executive – the President. But, after their experiences, as British colonies, with George III's government, the Americans were wary of putting too much power into the hands of one man and, in 1787, discussed the possibility of having two or three coequal presidents. Ultimately, it was decided to provide checks in other ways. The result is that the United States Congress shares in the performance of some executive tasks, for example the making of treaties and the appointment of federal judges.

The British Cabinet provides a good example of a collective executive in which all decisions must be agreed by the members. A combination of government secrecy and collective responsibility (the notion that an individual member must not disagree publicly with a Cabinet decision) have made it difficult to discover the extent to which cabinets are genuinely collective decision-making bodies, but a succession of leaks and memoirs, such as Richard Crossman's (Crossman, 1975–7), has built up a picture of a committee in which genuine debate tends to be restricted to issues that come to assume major political importance for the government. More typically, it sits to give the final yea or nay to policies generated within the bureaucracy and the network of cabinet committees.

The difficulties inherent in classifying systems according to this criterion are illustrated to some extent by the position of the British Prime Minister. In the nineteenth century and well into the twentieth, the Prime Minister's position *vis-à-vis* the Cabinet was described as *primus inter pares* – the first among equals. Particularly since the Second World War and the advent of television, with its concentration on individuals and the personalization of political issues, it has been argued that the system is becoming increasingly presidential. It is said that the powers of the Prime Minister have developed to such an extent that the traditional constraints are ineffective. Certainly, the collective nature of policy-making in Great Britain depends to some degree on the attitude and personality of the prime minister of the day. While Winston Churchill (in his 1940–5 wartime government) and Margaret Thatcher (1979–90) were very dominant figures in the cabinets they presided over, prime ministers like Clement Attlee (1945–51) and John Major (1990 to date) seem to have run their cabinets on something closer to a collective-decision basis.

In the Soviet Union there was a pattern of swings between

single and collective leadership in the post-Second World War period. When Stalin died in 1953 and his domination of the executive role ended, there was a struggle for power between leading party figures like Malenkov, Khrushchev and Bulgarin. In October 1953 Khrushchev replaced Malenkov at the head of the party, and in 1955 Bulganin took over the chairmanship of the Council of Ministers. Between 1955 and 1958 Khrushchev and Bulganin appeared to rule in tandem until Khrushchev replaced Bulganin as head of the Council of Ministers. Thus single-man rule seemed to have returned, although officially the collective responsibility of the Politburo was proclaimed and the 'cult of personality' denounced (Westwood, 1987, pp. 379–90).

When Khrushchev was removed in 1964, he was replaced by Brezhnev as first secretary of the CPSU and by Kosygin as chairman of the Council of Ministers. For a few years the two seemed more or less equal, but after 1968 Kosygin seemed to be losing authority. Although he remained as chairman of the Council of Ministers his influence waned compared to that of Brezhnev, who eventually became formal head of state in addition to party secretary. He was now easily the most influential person in policy-making. Nevertheless, while Khrushchev, Brezhnev and their successors as general secretary of the Communist Party remained the most prominent figures in the Soviet political process, clearly they did not dominate the Politburo as Stalin did – they had to carry their colleagues with them.

Thus, in spite of the tendency of the Soviet leadership to pass into the hands of one man, the importance of the Politburo, especially since Stalin's time, must not be underestimated. We know some details of the backgrounds of the twenty-two or so party members who made up the Politburo. Increasingly, the career background of members was that of a party official, although in the 1970s major government officials with professional expertise, for example in foreign affairs and defence, were included. All were, of course, party men, but they were not politicians in the British sense of having won a reputation as fighters in the party battle. Essentially, they were administrators, who would have built up a following among other administrators who supported their attitudes and often owed their careers to them. The reputation and prestige on which their position rested, therefore, was an intraparty one rather than one created in the public arena. This again highlights the complexity of real situations which we must bear in mind when applying our over-simple divisions of executive, bureaucracy and assembly.

Gorbachev undermined the position of the Politburo when he transferred executive power to the presidency, advised by the presidential councils. The former Soviet republics have, for the most part, retained a single executive as their preference, based on the American or French model, rather than the collective type of executive found in parliamentary systems of the British model. Such a choice accords with both the political traditions of the area and the perceived need for a strong, decisive executive in a time of economic, social and political turmoil. Nevertheless, the presidents of the new republics have to deal with often volatile parliaments which do not have an established party system. They can be more difficult to manage than even the United States Congress. A considerable learning process is going on and the outcome – democracy, authoritarianism or prolonged instability – is uncertain (Sakwa, 1990, pp. 159–69; Smith, 1992, pp. 129–45).

## What Do Executives Do?

What are the policy issues that executives discuss and decide? In the main, these will be the great financial, economic and social questions, together with internal and external security and relations with other states or international bodies. They will also be concerned with more immediate issues involving the well-being of the party or other organization providing their political base. For example, the British Cabinet has to pay attention to the process of getting its proposed legislation through both houses of Parliament; this means considering the views and anxieties of its supporters in both houses. In the United States the President often has to work hard to create a majority to support his proposed legislation in its passage through Congress. Unlike the government in Britain, the President's party often does not have a majority in Congress. The CPSU Politburo was concerned with both great policy issues (including the affairs of the separate republics) and party matters. As with the British Cabinet, officials who were not members would sometimes be invited to sessions dealing with their particular interests. We know little of how the Politburo reached its decisions – it did not produce a Richard Crossman – although some information has been provided by members in the *glasnost* period (for example it appears that, as in the British Cabinet, formal votes were rarely taken). In many of the successor republics tension and conflict between presidential government and assembly is frequent, as well as public disagreements within the government itself.

As we have seen, the policy process is dynamic and flexible, and it is not possible in the real world to draw a firm distinction between policy initiation and policy implementation. The implementation or administrative process is far too important to be left to its own devices. The executive has always been responsible for, and ultimately in control of, both initiation and implementation. The growth of its domination of policy initiation has come about with growing state intervention in society and the increasing extent and complexity of the policy-making process. Since the beginning of this century the executive has tended to extend its influence *vis-à-vis* the assembly (especially in parliamentary systems) by dominating the parliamentary timetable and making regulations subsidiary to major legislative measures.

But the comment (or complaint) that executives are becoming increasingly dominant is also heard in presidential systems. In the United States, before 1921 each department was free to ask Congress for funds; in that year Congress passed the Budget and Accounting Act which centralized all such requests in the Bureau of the Budget (renamed the Office of Management and Budget in 1970). In Roosevelt's New Deal administration the bureau was brought under closer presidential control and two main effects became apparent: the bureau assisted the President in the difficult job of controlling his own bureaucracy, and the President's programme, cleared and co-ordinated by the bureau, increasingly set the congressional agenda. It is now reckoned that 80 per cent of laws enacted by Congress emanate from the executive – if one were to weight these laws in terms of importance, almost certainly that proportion would be higher. As one House of Representatives committee chairman told the Eisenhower administration in 1953: 'don't expect us to start from scratch on what you people want. That's not the way we do things here – *you* draft the bills and we work them over' (Mullen, 1976, p. 60). We shall look at the executive role in policy implementation when we examine the workings of bureaucracy later.

In the Soviet Union there was a very close association between party and government bureaucracies. Members of the Soviet government (the Council of Ministers) were essentially administrative heads of ministries, but at the same time they were party members, and a few of them may even have been members of the Politburo. Other members of the Politburo were sometimes heads (secretaries) of sections of the Party Secretariat. Thus in the Soviet system there was far less separation of position and responsibility between executive and bureaucracy than is found in liberal democratic systems. During and following the Gorbachev era there were numerous complaints about the tendency of presidents to arrogate more power to themselves on the grounds that it was a temporary measure to deal with the extremely serious economic and social situation facing the republics. For example, it is argued that former communist officials in the Russian provinces continue to wield much power and are in a position to render executive decisions ineffective. Thus strong powers are needed by the centre to enforce decisions. Opponents fear that 'temporary' powers all too easily become permanent and that the idea of renewing or rejecting governmental authority in regular elections is not fully understood.

## The Replacement of Executives

One of the crucial questions to be discussed here concerns the way in which executives are replaced. Generally speaking, there are three main ways in which governments are succeeded by others – election, elite (backstairs) intrigue and force – the last being both older and more prevalent. In the Soviet Union before the advent of Gorbachev succession was a struggle within the ruling elite, for example there were prolonged struggles after the death of Lenin in 1924 and of Stalin in 1953, the main difference between the two episodes being that the losers in the 1950s escaped with their lives whereas those in the 1920s did not. The period of succession in regimes with no constitutional provision for it often tends to be a time of unrest. Sometimes elites succeed in confining the struggle; sometimes, as in China after the death of Mao Zedong, the masses may play a role by becoming mobilized on behalf of this or that elite faction. In the Soviet Union successions to the general secretaryship after Stalin were achieved in a relatively orderly fashion but entirely as an internal party matter with no element of public choice. The element of backstairs intrigue is, of course, also present to some extent in Western liberal democratic states, especially when the head of a parliamentary executive (like the British one) is replaced between elections (for example John Major's succession of Margaret Thatcher in 1990).

Struggles between elites may be conducted in various ways. One of the most common is the military method. There has been a high incidence of political succession by means of military *coups d'état*. Elites representing different religious, ethnic, tribal and ideological beliefs and different views on the desirability and pace of industrialization frequently seem to engage in a highly dangerous form of musical chairs. Other forms of backstairs succession may be more peaceful but do not indicate much greater governmental stability. Italy, for example, has avoided a military coup since 1945 but still has on average a new government every year. Relatively few of these governments have been formed following elections; most have been created by means of negotiation between the main parties and personalities in order to establish the distribution of offices between parties.

Elections provide a more stable method of succession, especially in liberal democracies. These may be fixed or variable. In the old Soviet Union the timing of elections was fixed – but the elections under that system did not decide succession anyway. The new republics are likely to settle for fixed times for elections, following the American model. In the United States the President is elected every four years and, according to the constitution since President Eisenhower, no president is constitutionally eligible to remain in office for more than two successive four-year terms. In Britain elections to the House of Commons, from which the government is formed, must be held at least every five years (until Parliament says otherwise) but may be held at any time during the five years, for example there were only eight months between elections in 1974 and the average length of a parliament is around four years. Under conditions of a clear parliamentary majority, the choice of when to hold an election lies with the Prime Minister. It has long been argued that this gives great advantage to the ruling party because of its ability to manipulate the economy for the desired results on election day. During the 1970s, however, doubt was cast on this idea. The miscalculations of Wilson in 1970, Heath in February 1974, Callaghan in 1978–9 and the patent inability of government to manipulate the flagging economy of the 1970s culminated in 1979 with the minority Labour government suffering the indignity of being forced to call an election when defeated on a motion of 'no confidence' by the combination of all parties in opposition in the House of Commons – the first time this had happened since 1924. The general election of 1992 also had to be called by a Conservative government at a time of unfavourable economic circumstances because of the approaching legal time-limit before which an election had to be called. Nevertheless, the ability of a British prime minister to decide the timing of a general election must still be considered a significant political advantage over opponents.

Another form of executive succession, which has received little attention until recently, is impeachment. In the American presidential system, with fixed elections the executive is virtually immune from removal by the legislature. The exception is impeachment by which an official may be charged by the House of Representatives and tried by the Senate. Such a procedure was well advanced against President Richard Nixon in 1974 for the variety of criminal offences known collectively as 'Watergate', when he pre-empted the process by resigning – the first American president to do so.

## Conclusion

A full conclusion must await our further consideration of the interaction of executives and assemblies in chapter 16. The major questions are how governments achieve executive power, what they do and how they may be removed. It is clear that the relationships between executive, assembly and bureaucracy are crucial and these can be varied, from a separation of powers to close integration. These relationships will be discussed in chapters 16 and 17.

## Questions for Discussion

1  Is there a more useful distinction than that between single and collective executives, and if so what do you consider it to be?
2  Why has executive power tended to increase in the twentieth century?
3  Is a smooth, legitimate executive succession more desirable than a popular one, however it is achieved?

## Further Reading

Campbell, C. (1992), Presidential leadership. In G. Peele et al. (eds), *Developments in American Politics* Basingstoke, Macmillan, pp. 88–114.

Dunleavy, P. (1990), Government at the centre. In P. Dunleavy, A. Gamble and G. Peele (eds), *Developments in British Politics 3* Basingstoke, Macmillan, pp. 96–125.

McKay, D. (1989), *American Politics and Society*, 2nd edn. Oxford, Blackwell, ch. 9.

Rahr, A. (1991), Yeltsin sets up a new system for governing Russia. *Report on the USSR (RFE/RL Research Institute)*, 3 (34), 23 August, pp. 9–12.

Sakwa, R. (1990), *Gorbachev and his Reforms, 1985–1990*. Hemel Hempstead, Philip Allan, pp. 142–51.

Smith, G.B. (1992), *Soviet Politics: Struggling with Change*, 2nd edn. Basingstoke, Macmillan, pp. 136–45.

Willerton, J.P. Jr. (1992), Executive power and political leadership. In S. White, A. Pravda and Z. Gitelman (eds), *Developments in Soviet and Post-Soviet Politics*, 2nd edn. Basingstoke, Macmillan, pp. 44–67.

# 15

# Assemblies

## Introduction

Parliamentary assemblies are essentially meetings of elected representatives of the people whose purposes include considering
the policy proposals put before them by the executive, sometimes
(though to a much lesser extent) initiating policy proposals of
their own, examining and calling to account those responsible for
the initiation and implementation of policy, and giving approval
and legitimacy to the actions of the executive and bureaucracy.
Assemblies in Western liberal democracies are either unicameral
or bicameral, that is they consist of one chamber or two. Even if
there are two chambers, however, they are not necessarily equal
in power. Great Britain, for example, has two chambers – the
House of Commons and the House of Lords, but the power of
the House of Lords is restricted to the possibility of delaying
legislation passed by the Commons for a short period and trying
to make amendments to bills, if the government is prepared to
accept them. It is argued that the Lords provides an important
opportunity for more careful consideration of legislation that has
been steamrollered through the Commons, and that it provides
high-class debates. On the latter point it is possible for the public
to judge since proceedings in both houses of Parliament are
now televised. It may however, be questioned, whether this role
should be performed by a mixture of hereditary and life peers
who make up the Lords' membership or, indeed, whether there

is an important role here at all. Is it not the case, as was pointed out at the time of the French Revolution by the Abbé Sieyes, that if the second chamber agrees with the first it is superfluous and if it disagrees it is mischievous? The countries that have only one chamber – for example New Zealand, Denmark and Finland – are, indeed, quite small, but their twin features of cultural homogeneity and lack of federal structures suggest that the model could be adopted in Britain with little upset.

The United States provides a good example of a bicameral system in which the two chambers are more or less equal. The Senate is smaller (100 senators, two elected from each of the fifty states), and generally more prestigious. It has greater power in certain areas than the House of Representatives, for example the Senate can vet all major presidential appointments to the executive and the judiciary and must concur in any treaties negotiated by the President. The House of Representatives is larger (435 representatives elected on the basis of population). The most populous state, California, has nearly fifty representatives while the smallest states have only one. Perhaps the single greatest function of the house concerns money: the house takes the initiative in dealing with the President's requests for appropriations and revenue-raising suggestions and the Senate acts on what the house produces. The budget still represents one of the major sources of executive–assembly controversy. Congress tried to reassert some control over the budget process in 1974, specifically to prevent President Nixon from refusing to spend (impounding) money appropriated by Congress. Ten years later its concern had switched to the massive budget deficits being run up by the Reagan administration. On taking office in 1980 Reagan promised to eliminate the deficit by 1984, but actually set new record deficits by increasing military spending while refusing to countenance tax increases. The Gramm-Rudman-Hollings Act passed in 1985 mandated the federal government to balance the budget by 1991 and allowed for the sequestration of funds if President and Congress failed to reach agreement. However, by making use of various creative accounting techniques, for example treating expenditure as 'off-budget', the Act failed and was replaced in 1990 by the Budget Enforcement Act which formalizes 'zero-sum' budgeting until 1995. During the period, apart from emergencies, any additional funding must come from existing programmes (Collender, 1992, 280–93).

# What Do Assemblies Do?

A brief comparison of British and American assemblies demonstrates the importance of the question: who or what do representatives represent and how do they set about it? In Britain the traditional role of the MP was enunciated by Edmund Burke in the late eighteenth century: it is the duty of the MP, he said, to represent the national interest, not the interest of some section of the community. In reality, in Britain today MPs represent primarily their party. The extent of party unity in the Commons is very high and very rarely do any substantial number of MPs stray from the fold. Of course, in a hung parliament (where no one party has an absolute majority), such as that dissolved in April 1979, even one or two defections can be critical.

In the United States Congress the picture is rather more complex. The party affiliation of the member is still the best single indicator of how he or she is likely to vote on a given bill, but party unity is very much less than in the British House of Commons. On a measure which, if applied to the Commons, would produce 100 per cent party unity, the figure for Congress fluctuates normally between 30 and 60 per cent (see table 12.1). A major factor accounting for this difference is that American parties are much looser organizations than British ones, geared traditionally to winning elections rather than to implementing coherent policy programmes (see chapter 12). If members of Congress wish to explain why they will not support their party's position on any given policy, they usually do so in terms of the interests of their state or district. As table 12.1 shows, there has been an increase in party unity in the last ten years in the house, but not in Senate.

The major difference in the way the British and American assemblies operate concerns the role of committees. To all intents and purposes, congressional committees are Congress. The fate of any bill, whether initiated by the President or by a member, is effectively decided by the committee to which it is allocated on its introduction to Congress. Most bills never re-emerge from committee; those that do may be altered beyond recognition, and during floor debate, on those lucky enough to get that far, changes are not usually made that go against the wishes of the relevant committee. This whole process is carried on within the context of the legislative norms of expertise and reciprocity. Individual members gain influence by becoming acknowledged experts in a particular sphere of government and on other issues will tend to accept the cues provided by their colleagues who are experts in that particular policy area. Recent efforts to increase the general policy expertise among members have resulted in more amending activity during floor debate (Bailey, 1992, p. 132).

In the late 1960s the House of Commons experimented with some special committees modelled very loosely on the American pattern but they did not last long. Continuing frustration among backbench MPs at their treatment by the executive and the non-accountability of civil servants revived interest in the idea. In December 1979 a new set of twelve select committees was introduced into the House of Commons, one to cover each major government spending department, and all with a majority of government party members reflecting the position in the house overall, although some of the chairs are opposition MPs. They have achieved notable publicity in some areas, such as the issues of deaths occurring in police custody and government economic strategy, but there is no possibility that they could achieve a significance equal to that of the United States congressional committees. British backbenchers may cast envious glances at their American counterparts who both have a greater impact on executive-initiated legislation and conduct more thorough investigations of the bureaucracy, but the problem remains of how to transfer political institutions from one political system to another. As we can see, the British parliamentary and the American presidential systems work in very different ways.

In contrast to the United States, executive control of the House of Commons via party loyalty has become so thorough that such committees can operate only within a context defined by the executive. Another, more specific, factor inhibiting the Commons committees concerns staff. In Congress, in addition to large personal staffs of members, the senior Democratic and Republican members of each committee may hire their own committee staff, and the recruits tend to be bright and ambitious postgraduates, especially lawyers. In the Commons, by contrast, committee members do not hire and fire committee staff and will not usually have more than one personal staff assistant.

The Supreme Soviet of the USSR was another Soviet institution that was often misleadingly dismissed as a meaningless formality by Western observers. Such a conclusion was not entirely correct.

The Supreme Soviet was bicameral, consisting of the Council of the Union and the Council of the Nationalities, each consisting of 750 deputies elected for five years. Two striking differences from British and American assemblies were noticeable: top government officials were not disbarred from being deputies, the deputies were all part-timers who held another full-time job. The Supreme Soviet usually met for two sessions of a few days each year. A high proportion of the deputies (over 40 per cent) were ordinary workers, but the membership also included all important party and government figures. Sessions of the Supreme Soviet and of its standing commissions were dominated by these important figures, a domination reinforced by the fact that the more humble deputies were not usually elected for a second term. This gave them little time to develop influence where it mattered, but also meant that the Supreme Soviet had a body of deputies holding important jobs who were in a position to be influential (Lane, 1985, pp. 177–81).

Although (until its last days) all votes in both houses of the Supreme Soviet were unanimously in favour of government proposals, both specific and general policy criticisms were made in speeches and it seems certain that these were sometimes seriously considered by party and government in formulating future policy. While the Supreme Soviet was not sitting, its functions were carried out by the Praesidium, a committee of Supreme Soviet officials and other members. More interestingly, where involvement in policy-making was concerned, was the activity of the standing commissions of the Supreme Soviet, on which over 70 per cent of the deputies served. The standing commissions usually met twice a year to examine relevant sections of the Five Year Plan, the budget and any laws pertaining to their area of interest. Before the formal meetings, preparatory groups examined in detail the matters before the standing commissions. It is difficult to assess the real impact of these activities on actual policy formulation, but it seems clear that the activities of the preparatory committees at least were thorough and significant, and to some extent taken seriously by the party and government (Lane, 1985, pp. 188–90).

We may conclude that, as with other Soviet institutions, the public side of the old Supreme Soviet was used to display unbroken unity in a way uncharacteristic of Western assemblies. However, the formality of its public proceedings – merely ratifying decisions taken elsewhere – was in effect analogous to much activity in the British Parliament which is also usually effectively controlled by the executive. In the Supreme Soviet standing commissions and their preparatory committees, however, limited serious examination of policies took place. If there is a point of similarity and comparison between the assemblies of these three countries, it may be in the influence and growing importance of their committee systems.

Dramatic changes occurred under Gorbachev, who was anxious that genuine discussion of public issues should take place in the Soviet Union. Even before his reforms the old Supreme Soviet had begun to assert itself. His new parliament took into account the vast size of the Soviet Union. A Congress of People's Deputies was elected from the whole country, but it contained too many deputies to be an effective parliamentary assembly. It therefore elected a Supreme Soviet consisting of two smaller chambers from among its members (the Soviet of the Union and the Soviet of the Nationalities). Deputies were elected both on a constituency basis and as representatives of official bodies like the Academy of Sciences, the trade unions and so on. Powers were divided between the Congress of People's Deputies and the Supreme Soviet, but it was the Supreme Soviet that met and conducted business for about eight months of the year. In most respects, it was a real parliament and often gave government ministers, collectively and individually, a hard time (Schneider, 1990, pp. 30–9; Smith, 1992, pp. 132–6). As time went on, however, it became less assertive in the face of the growing political and economic crisis in the country. President Gorbachev demanded and got more and more personal power, although he was hardly able to use it effectively. With the collapse of the Soviet Union, the Congress of People's Deputies and the Supreme Soviet ceased to function, but the newly independent republics have all inherited active parliaments from the Gorbachev period (only Russia – the largest – had a Congress of People's Deputies too). It is now their individual responsibility to decide the constitutional powers of these assemblies and to see how democratic parliaments may be established in the presidential systems they have adopted. There is little or no tradition of democratic government in these new states and the influence of Western liberal democratic traditions is not always likely to be great. In manyof them assertive political leaders are trying to enhance their power. The grave social and political crises that they all face will prove a severe test for their new, untried assemblies.

# Conclusion

We need to know who the members of assemblies actually represent and to what extent they are able to investigate and influence executive actions. These issues will be discussed further in chapters 16 (executive–assembly relations) and 26 and 27 (representation and elections).

# Questions for Discussion

1 Discuss the adequacy of assemblies as *representative* institutions. How may they be improved?
2 Should assemblies be merely institutions reacting to the initiatives of the executive? What other roles *vis-à-vis* the executive can they play?
3 Discuss the practical problems facing assemblies operating in a modern industrialized society.

# Further Reading

Bailey, C.J. (1992), Congress and legislative activism. In G. Peele et al. (eds), *Developments in American Politics*. Basingstoke, Macmillan, pp. 115–37.
Dearlove, J. and P. Saunders (1984), *Introduction to British Politics*. Cambridge, Polity, ch. 4.
Hough, J.F. and M. Fainsod (1979), *How the Soviet Union is Governed*. Cambridge, Mass., Harvard University Press, pp. 363–80.
McKay, D. (1989), *American Politics and Society*, 2nd edn. Oxford, Blackwell, chs 7 and 8.
Merkl, P. (1977), *Modern Comparative Politics*, 2nd edn. Hinsdale, Ill. Dryden, pp. 133–44.
Sakwa, R. (1989), *Soviet Politics: An Introduction*. London, Routledge, pp. 106–10.
Sherrill, R. (1979), *Why They Call It Politics*, 3rd edn. New York, Harcourt Brace Jovanovich, ch. 4.

# 16

# Executive–Assembly Relations

## Introduction

In the day-to-day operation of the political system the relationship between policy-making executive and elected assembly is of central importance. The two dominant models in discussion of the relationship are the presidential and the parliamentary. In the first there is a significant degree of independence between the assembly and the executive; basically, neither is able easily (if at all) to remove or dissolve the other. In the second there is a high degree of mutual dependence between the assembly and the executive, and each is able to dismiss or dissolve the other. Theoretically, in parliamentary systems the assembly embodies the sovereignty of the people and is therefore the source of authority for the executive. In practice, the executive frequently comes to dominate the assembly, as in Britain.

The Soviet Union could not be easily categorized as either presidential or parliamentary. Formally, it was parliamentary and the approval of the Supreme Soviet was needed for all significant laws and appointments. In reality, the party and government leaders were in no way dependent on the assembly; parliamentary approval was formal and automatic. The Supreme Soviet could at best exercise only a marginal influence on policy, laws and appointments since it was closely controlled by the executive (see chapter 15). The successor republics have all adopted presidential-type systems, although the degree of power and authority inhering in the executive president varies from republic to republic and according to prevailing political conditions.

As an example of a presidential system, the American system is often said to embody the separation of powers. (Subscribers to the 'cock-up' theory of history will be interested to learn that the framers of the American constitution were much impressed by Montesquieu's idea that it was the *separation* of powers in Britain that had enabled the British to maintain their freedom from tyranny. On the contrary, it was the *fusion* of executive and legislative power that was at the heart of the eighteenth-century British constitution!) In fact, the American constitution has been more accurately described as one of 'separated institutions sharing powers' (Neustadt, 1976, p. 101). This model reflects more clearly the fact that in the United States no person can be a member of both executive and assembly simultaneously while the executive and assembly share many powers, for example legislation (normally), treaties and many official appointments must be approved by both institutions.

There are, as always, certain complications to this simple dichotomy. First, that a system is headed by a president does not mean that the system is presidential! Often a president is simply a head of state with few, if any, powers (like the British monarch) and the system of government is, in fact, parliamentary. Ireland and Germany are two examples among many of this type. Second, France under the Fifth Republic, that is since 1958, has an amalgam of the two systems. Compared to the Fourth Republic (1945–58), which was truly parliamentary, the President in the Fifth Republic has important powers in emergencies, foreign affairs and the appointment of governments, as well as being head of state. But he must appoint a premier (prime minister) who is acceptable to the assembly and the assembly can, subject to restrictions, remove the government. Third, in the old Soviet Union arrangements varied. The position of formal head of state was sometimes, but not always, held by the politically most powerful figure – the Party Secretaries Brezhnev and Gorbachev did in fact hold both posts. Among his many far-reaching reforms, Gorbachev effected a transfer of power from Communist Party to executive presidency. Thus in its latter years the Soviet Union was constitutionally a mainstream presidential system.

One of the prime differences between the systems is in the practicalities of succession. Elections in the United States take place every two years (more frequently if one includes state and local elections) and, as part of the checks and balances built into the process by the constitution, different institutions are elected for different tenures. The President is elected for four years, but members of the House of Representatives have to face election every two years, while a senator is elected for six years. At each two-yearly election one-third of the Senate comes up for re-election. In parliamentary systems the formal head of state may be a hereditary post (as in monarchies), or chosen by popular election or by a vote of members of the assembly. Assemblies are usually elected – by popular election for both houses or by popular election for the lower house and restricted election (or appointment) for the upper house. The British House of Lords is anomalous in that part of its membership is by government appointment and part hereditary.

Electing the executive and assembly for different periods and for different constituencies in a presidential system can have important consequences for the ability of the former to control the latter. In the United States, because this system is aggravated by a relatively weak party system, there is no guarantee that the President will be of the same party as the majority in Congress. Indeed, Eisenhower (Republican, 1953–60) for six of his eight years and Nixon (Republican, 1969–74) for all of his years faced Democratic majorities in Congress. Reagan, elected in 1980, had a Republican-controlled Senate but a Democrat-controlled House of Representatives until 1986 when the Democrats recaptured the Senate. President Bush (Republican) also had to deal with Democratic Party majorities in Congress. (However, even a president with a majority of his own party in Congress – for example Clinton – is by no means guaranteed an easy ride.)

While the CPSU dominated Soviet politics it did not have to worry about majorities in the Supreme Soviet. All deputies were either party members or carefully vetted non-party people. In the last years of the Soviet Union Gorbachev usually had the clear, if anxious, support of the assembly, but on occasion he still had to use considerable political skill to deflect criticism. Likewise, the presidents of at least some of the successor republics cannot rely on firm support from their assemblies on all issues.

Since the composition of the government in parliamentary systems is determined by the composition of the legislature, such a situation could not last for long. If there is a party with an absolute majority in the lower house it will form the government. Complications arise as soon as there is no clear majority party in the lower house. In such cases the composition of the government will rest as much on negotiations conducted between the parties as on the elections *per se*. The governments that result, either a minority party governing with the consent of other parties, or a coalition of two or more parties, tend to last for a shorter period than one-party governments but the difference disappears if re-shuffles of ministerial posts within single-party governments are taken into account (Blondel, 1990, p. 271).

## The Cabinet

The 'cabinet' is a term whose meaning differs according to the political system being considered. It is not used in the Soviet or post-Soviet systems, where the term 'council' is more usually employed. An important indicator of the difference in executive–assembly relations between the American and post-Soviet presidential and the British parliamentary systems is the position of the respective cabinets or councils. The British Cabinet is chosen by the leader of the majority party subject to constraints imposed by factionalism within the party. Its members will be drawn mainly from the Commons (the lower elected house), a few will be from the same party in the Lords (the non-elected upper house) and, although they remain in Parliament as MPs or peers, their role is very much as members of the executive, aiming to steer their programme through the assembly with as few complications or delays as possible. The people chosen will be acknowledged generally as the senior members of the party and there will be few surprises when the Cabinet is announced. If a coalition government is necessary, Cabinet and lesser government posts will be allocated after negotiation with coalition partners.

The Cabinet in the American system is quite different. It used to be the case that a successful president would choose some of his Cabinet members from his party's ranks in Congress; this still happens, but relatively infrequently. Many of his cabinet members will have been nominal party people rather than loyal servants over many years, as would be the case in Britain. The biggest single difference between the two Cabinets is that the American version is not a collective policy-making body of any significance. Although most presidents promise, on taking office, that they intend to re-establish the cabinet as a decision-making body, few seriously try. Carter made greater use of it than most but Reagan went even further. In 1981 there were thirty-seven meetings of his Cabinet and during the first term the flow of routine domestic-policy business was routed through seven cabinet committees. During his second term changes in key advisers, the Iran–Contra scandal and Reagan's growing inattention to his job all contributed to a less coherent administration. Bush retained similar formal structures, but his greater personal involvement in decisions and preference for informal meetings with advisers resulted in a less structured and sometimes indecisive White House (Campbell, 1992, pp. 93–113).

Heads of United States government departments usually end up playing one of two roles. They may act as presidential emissaries to the largely autonomous empires of the bureaucracy and try to instil some loyalty to the programme of the President in their department. Alternatively, their loyalty may be captured by the career staff in their departments so that they become primarily spokespersons for, and defenders of, department policies against encroachments from elsewhere. Something of this split may also be observed in Britain but to a lesser extent because of the collective responsibility of the Cabinet and party control of the assembly.

Interestingly, something similar seems to have occurred in the Soviet Union after the death of Stalin. It has been argued that the demise of rule by terror led the leaders of sectional elites to become more assertive and supportive of the interests they represented even against those to whom they owed their appointment (Ross, 1980, pp. 262–3). Nevertheless, overall, the party Politburo acted in effect as a cabinet – that is as a committee type of government, with the Party Secretary as chairman. The Party Secretary, like a British prime minister, could have great influence and authority, but in the last resort he was essentially *primus inter pares* – first among equals – and had to carry his colleagues with him. Various arrangements were tried when Gorbachev established a presidential system in the late 1980s. At first he was advised by a Presidential Council, consisting of representatives of the government and community, and a Council of the Federation, representing the major nationalities. Later, the Presidential Council (which was politically ineffective) was replaced by a Security Council (responsible for internal law and order and external security), while the Federation Council was given enhanced powers to meet the demands of the republics. In the face of growing crisis, Gorbachev tried to get more and more power transferred to himself in order to rule by decree. But as the system disintegrated his decrees were increasingly ignored. The successor republics have systems analogous to the American system, with government ministers and committees of advisers. The Russian Federation for a time revived the old tsarist name of 'State Council' for the main advisory body to the President (Rahr, 1991, pp. 9–12).

## The Power of the Executive

If executive–assembly relations are seen as basically a struggle for influence over the policy-making process, what are the weapons available to each side in the struggle? The essential condition of executive dominance in the British system is party loyalty. It is not the case that high degrees of party unity are displayed in the House of Commons because the whips (those members of the government responsible for the passage of government legislation through both houses) mercilessly compel members to betray their consciences and constituencies in the cause of party dogma. A member is more likely to be in trouble with his constituency if he fails to support his party on all (or most) occasions. Moreover, members believe that having their party in office, whatever be-trayals it may perpetrate on its supporters in the country, is better than having the opposition take over. From this basic fact arise the other manifestations of executive dominance, for example their control over the agenda of the chamber, membership of committees and the time to be allowed for committee delibera-tion and floor debate.

The force of party loyalty is not nearly so strong in the American Congress but it does exist (see table 12.1). The difference boils down to the fact that the Member of Parliament in Britain is expected by all concerned – his leaders, whips and colleagues – to owe his primary loyalty to the party. In the United States that is not so; it is acknowledged that the multitude of pressures (some real, some imagined) that converge on a member from his constituents and from vested interests may make the call of the party electorally disastrous.

Another weapon of considerable strength that resides in the hands of the executive is information because 'information is power'. Executives tend to monopolize the information that as-semblies need to do their job. An inevitable by-product of all that the executive branch as a whole does is a vast amount of infor-mation, which assemblies need if they are to carry out their roles of law ratification and oversight of the bureaucracy. A combination of tradition, statute and powerlessness on the part of the assembly ensures that the control of information in Britain is almost entirely in executive hands. Apart from anything else, this gives the executive enormous power in determining what is and what is not debatable – and therefore over the limits of the assembly's power. There has been modest improvement in this situation as a result of the establishment of select committees but secrecy is still a significant feature of the British executive, especially compared to the American. In 1992 the Prime Minister, John Major, indicated that his government would release more information, but it is still the executive that decides what is and is not released.

Again, in the United States executive dominance is less strong. There is a constant battle over the question of access to information that is generated primarily by the executive, but the Congress can point to some significant successes in recent years. These have been mainly the result of executive excesses, for example in the field of intelligence-gathering and the operation of such bodies as the Central Intelligence Agency (CIA) and the Federal Bureau of Investigation (FBI). For many years these agencies operated free of any congressional oversight and, while many members of Congress clearly preferred not to know what they were doing, any attempts that were made to find out were firmly rebuffed. But the death of J. Edgar Hoover in 1972, the subsequent involvement of the FBI in the Watergate scandal which led to President Nixon's resignation, and the revelation of CIA plots to assassinate foreign leader culminated in 1975–6 with unprecedentedly thorough congressional investigations of these institutions.

To date, the only remote equivalent to this in Britain has been the inquiry carried out by the House of Commons Select Committee on Home Affairs into police special branches in 1984–5. However, the committee, which eventually divided on party lines, defined its terms of reference at the outset so narrowly that it effectively ruled out any possibility of discovering the truth or otherwise of the allegations of malpractice that had been made against the police. In general, the Commons has had less success than the Congress in either developing its own sources of information or in forcing information out of the executive.

In the Soviet Union executive power was virtually supreme until Gorbachev came into office. The confusion of constitutional change amid economic and social crisis left the executive and assembly struggling to establish their range of control and influence

*vis-à-vis* each other. In the first flush of *glasnost* much information was made available and deputies often asserted themselves
aggressively. As time went on, however, the executive began to
gain more control over the situation. This came about partly
because of the executive's inherent advantages, as outlined above,
and partly because tradition and crisis seemed to point to the need
for a strong executive. Similar struggles have gone on in many of
the successor republics (some are still firmly authoritarian) and
the nature of the executive–assembly relations that will finally be
established is uncertain.

## The Power of the Assembly

These main weapons that an assembly may have against the executive are: involvement in appointment or recall of personnel,
investigation and approval of policy proposals by the executive
(especially of the government's taxing and spending proposals),
and rights of investigation and oversight of executive and government activity. Theoretically, the British Parliament freely approves
the Cabinet chosen by the Prime Minister, but in practice support
is maintained by party discipline and loyalty. Again, constitutional theory maintains that ministers are both collectively and
individually responsible to Parliament for their actions. It is now
over thirty years since an individual minister was forced by the
House of Commons to resign. More commonly, the minister under
attack is shielded by collective responsibility and the decision as
to whether he or she goes or stays is one for the Prime Minister,
based on the criteria of the extent to which he or she has become
a liability to the government.

The United States Congress retains more power over executive
personnel. Those nominated by the President to high executive
and judicial office must be accepted by the Senate. As a general
rule, the belief that a president is entitled to pick his own team
overrides criticisms of the nominee, but presidential choices are
subject to more scrutiny by the legislature than are British prime-
ministerial ones. Similarly, in the Soviet Union assembly approval
for presidential appointments was required under Gorbachev's
presidential system and is still required in some of the successor
republics. As in the United States, although criticism of proposed
appointments may sometimes be vigorously expressed, presidents
usually get the appointees they want.

As we have seen, in the case of both policies and budgets, the initiative has passed to the executive. In terms of the disposition of the executive's programmes, however, the Congress retains great influence over whether a president gets the legislation he is after and in what form it will become law. In the post-Soviet republics strong figures like Boris Yeltsin in Russia have a firm hold on the assembly but not one that is unchallenged. Often, conservative ex-communists, impatient radicals or politicians seeking to capitalize on popular discontent can give presidents a hard ride. Examples of resignations of prime ministers have occurred (for example in Lithuania and Estonia) when their policy proposals have been rejected by majorities in their assemblies.

Until 1974 the British House of Commons had virtually given up all but the slightest influence in the disposition of executive proposals. The only amendments to government proposals that would pass in the house could be those that the government could be persuaded to accept: nothing would be passed against their will. Between 1974 and 1979, however, backbench power enjoyed something of a resurgence. With the Labour government unable to control a majority of seats in the Commons, it was occasionally vulnerable to policy defeats on the occasions when the other parties were able to unite or when its own backbenchers staged guerilla attacks. Even under the firmly established Conservative government of Margaret Thatcher, backbenchers showed a degree of independence that would have seemed remarkable thirty years earlier. Some argue that a large government majority (such as Thatcher's government had) can also encourage backbenchers to assert themselves, confident that they will not be endangering the government by doing so.

As assemblies have in general diminished in influence and executives have asserted more control, it has been argued by some that assemblies must change their role and become much more concerned with overseeing the work of the ever-growing bureaucracy. The committee system, the greater resources of staff and money available to members, and the relatively weak calls of party loyalty have combined to suggest that this role can most successfully be performed by the United States Congress. Indeed, one can point to notable successes such as the investigations of the intelligence agencies (see above), but the sheer size of the federal bureaucracy means that oversight can at best be random and episodic. Still, that is more than is managed by the House of Commons in Britain. The twelve select committees established by the Commons in December 1979 seem to have attracted enough criticism from the executive to suggest that they have been asking some pertinent questions, but their overall impact on policy has so far been slight. However, pressure for more effective investigatory powers by the committees of the Commons and Lords continue. The former Soviet republics are still trying to sort out the relative powers of executive and assembly.

## Conclusion

In the twentieth century there has been a steady drift of power from assemblies to executives in Western liberal democracies, and this is as true of Britain as of the United States, although to different extents. There are many reasons for this, two important ones being the generally greater degree of government intervention in society and the increased predominance of foreign and military affairs in a century that has seen two world wars and the development of nuclear weapons. As a result, much of the work of contemporary assemblies should be viewed in the context of institutions struggling to adapt to massively changed social and world conditions and to impose some check upon the burgeoning executive bureaucracies.

However, it would be wrong to view assemblies as no more than talking-shops. The United States Congress, in particular, may exercise very real political power if only because, were its formal weapons against the executive to be blunted there would be the important so-called 'law of anticipated reactions' to consider. This means simply that there are actions that the executive will not take because it knows that the assembly will make a huge fuss. This is clearly one of those exercises of power that take place very subtly, but it is no less real for that. Of course, a critical factor in this 'law' becoming a real check on executives is the extent to which they can operate in secrecy. It is far easier for the British than for the American executive to do this.

Under the old Soviet system executive power was as strong as it is ever likely to be. The new presidential system established by Gorbachev was never able to consolidate its authority and relationships with the assembly effectively. There was too little time and too great a crisis. Attempts to establish such relations firmly in the successor republics are still going on, but the crisis inherent in contemporary political conditions is likely to result in strong executives.

Thus an important question in analysing executive–assembly

relations is: does the assembly have the ability and/or the political will to oversee the executive branch effectively? This in turn raises subsidiary questions such as the recruitment and length of tenure of members of the executive and the assembly, their formal and informal sources of power with respect to each other, and wider issues such as political traditions, especially those of the party system. In an essentially two-party system like the British one, for example, the main opposition party contending for office may not wish to fight too hard to curtail the power of an executive they may soon have control of themselves. In weak party systems politicians may have to give considerable weight to popular opinion and pressures from vested interest. Perhaps the fundamental question is: can assemblies in contemporary politics convincingly fulfil their traditional role of representing the people?

## Questions for Discussion

1  Is the control of information the key to executive power?
2  Discuss the pros and cons of separation rather than fusion of powers in the policy-making process.
3  What can the ex-Soviet republics learn from Western liberal democracies as they try to establish effective executive–assembly relations?

## Further Reading

Burch, M., J. Gardner and D. Jaenicke (eds) (1985), *Three Political Systems: A Reader in British, Soviet and American Politics*. Manchester, Manchester University Press, chs 1.7–1.13.

Fiorina, M.P. (1992), An era of divided government. In G. Peele et al. (eds), *Developments in American Politics*. Basingstoke, Macmillan, pp. 324–54.

Friedgut, T.H. (1979), *Political Participation in the USSR*. Princeton, Princeton University Press, pp. 188–200.

Hahn, J.W. (1992), State institutions in transition. In S. White, A. Pravda and Z. Gitelman (eds), *Developments in Soviet and Post-Soviet Politics*, 2nd edn. Basingstoke, Macmillan, pp. 88–106.

Mayer, L.C. and J.H. Burnett (1977), *Politics in Industrial Societies*. New York, Wiley, pp. 165–215.

Sherrill, R. (1979), *Why They Call It Politics*, 3rd edn. New York, Harcourt Brace Jovanovich, chs 1 and 2.

# 17

# Bureaucracies

## Introduction

As we have seen, the formal liberal democratic theory of bureaucracies was that officials (sometimes called bureaucrats or civil servants) simply implement the policies that their political masters – the representatives of the people – present to them in the form of laws and regulations. This view of bureaucracy is based primarily on a model of nineteenth-century developments, one important aspect of which was the growing scandal over the inefficiencies of administration. The situation in many systems was typified by the American slogan 'To the victor the spoils'. In other words, the party in power was expected to reward its supporters with paid government positions, many of which were relatively undemanding. Reformers came to believe that many of the problems of government could be solved by the application to public administration of management techniques being developed in the private sector by large firms. In addition, they were convinced that if only administration could be removed from the hands of often corrupt politicians and given a semi-autonomous status, social improvements could be made.

The notion of bureaucracy as a neutral technical instrument with which industrialized nations must be administered received its clearest statement by Max Weber, the German political sociologist. Weber's name tends to be most commonly associated with the 'ideal type' bureaucracy which is neutral, hierarchically organized, efficient and inevitable in contemporary society. In fact, Weber argued that bureaucracies were seldom so in practice.

Bureaucracies do not simply enter the policy-making process at the stage of implementation. The policy process is dynamic, with inputs, conversion, outputs and feedback forming a continuous chain. Bureaucracies are involved to some extent in the input and conversion processes as they are in the output phase. The bureaucracy, at least at its lower levels, is the part of the government that comes into most frequent contact with the public and thus receives feedback – positive and negative – on the policies being pursued by government. In the nature of things, much of this feedback will go no further than the local office, but senior bureaucrats are much involved in the preparation of new policies for politicians and it would be strange indeed if such feedback never featured in new recommendations.

Relatively ignorant, inexperienced and amateur politicians may find themselves at the mercy of the bureaucracies, which possess knowledge, experience and technical expertise. Frequently, all that they will have to guide them through the recommendations of officials will be their own political common sense; this may well be adequate for a strong minister, but others may find it hard to change the bureaucracy's course. Even in the implementation of policy the bureaucracy maintains its own preferences and there are infinite opportunities at this stage for manipulation. Indeed, it would be wrong to distinguish too sharply between policy formulation and policy implementation. The implementation of any policy requires the official to exercise discretion – even if it were possible to prepare a rule-book catering for every eventuality it would probably be undesirable – and on each of these occasions he or she is 'making' policy. Nor is this unimportant compared to the 'major' policy decisions made by the Cabinet or an assembly. 'What people get from government is what administrators do about their problems rather than the promise of statutes, constitutions or oratory' (Edelman, 1964, p. 193).

## The Responsiveness of Bureaucracy

One way of examining bureaucracies is to ask the question: to whom are they responsive? Liberal democratic theory would answer that, of course, the bureaucracy should be responsive to the elected politicians and, through them, to the people. However, it is important to examine the realities more closely. The first possibility is that the bureaucracy is responsive primarily to itself – that is to its own interests and priorities. Certainly this is likely to be the case in all bureaucracies to some extent. If there is any iron law of bureaucracy it must be that such organizations will not willingly do anything that may be against the organization's perceived long-term interests and that, on occasions, this will lead the organization to ignore its nominal masters. But, apart from the basic concern of the bureaucracy for its own interests as an organization, it is also likely to develop specific policy interests of its own. As the administration of industrialized societies becomes more complex and the number of technicians required increases, bureaucracy is bound to develop very sophisticated views on how things must be done, and indeed, what, if anything, should be done.

Furthermore, there is the possibility that a bureaucracy will be more responsive to the needs of a particular social or economic class than to those of the government. According to the Marxist view of bureaucracy, this is indeed the case in capitalist systems. If the state is perceived as an instrument of class rule, so are the 'servants of the state'. But it is not only Marxists who argue that bureaucracies may owe their primary allegiance to a particular class. Weber's criticism of the Prussian bureaucracy, for example, was that it acted as an instrument for the preservation of the dominance of the *Junker*, or aristocratic, class (Beetham, 1974, p. 66).

This may become an especially acute problem for a newly installed revolutionary regime, for example the Soviet Union. Five years after the revolution Lenin complained that the Communist Party had good political control only over the top echelons of the vast bureaucracy: 'Down below, however, there are hundreds of thousands of old officials who came to us from the Tsar and from bourgeois society and who, sometimes consciously and sometimes unconsciously, work against us' (quoted in Merkl, 1977, pp. 166–7). This was clearly another example of prior loyalty to a class, but problems of loyalty may also afflict systems in which the change is between party governments, not regimes. When Nixon was forced to resign from the American presidency in 1974, his administration was embarked on an attempt to improve the responsiveness of the American bureaucracy which, while not illegal, led to cries of outrage from his liberal enemies.

The greatest periods of peacetime growth in the American bureaucracy were the New Deal in the 1930s and the Great Society programme of the 1960s. They were both periods when

the presidency was in the hands of the Democrats and the programmes necessitating large growth in the bureaucracy were social-
welfare policies of the type embraced by liberals. Therefore, the
sort of person attracted to work in the bureaucracy on the implementation of such programmes was likely to be sympathetic to
them and their commitment to the programmes was likely to
grow rather than diminish with time. Nixon entered the White
House in 1969 committed to budgetary restraint and reducing
spending on welfare programmes. While all presidents have testified
to the difficulty of shifting the course of the bureaucracy, the task
was made even more difficult for Nixon by the direct clash between the political philosophy of his administration and that
prevailing in the bureaucracy, particularly the social-services
agencies. Throughout his first term in office there was a series of
battles between his political appointees and career bureaucrats.
At the beginning of his second term he started to deal with the
problem by introducing people loyal to the administration at
strategic levels throughout the departments. What enraged the
liberals was that this involved placing political appointees at much
lower levels of the hierarchies than had been usual, to increase
the positive responsiveness of the bureaucracy to his policies.

Similar complaints about party bias have been heard in Britain,
especially from Labour ministers, for example Richard Crossman
(1975-7). Such actions are harder to prove in Britain, partly
because of the notorious secrecy maintained by the Civil Service,
but civil servants are certainly not political eunuchs, whatever the
impression they may like to encourage. One aspect of the argument
concerns the process of recruitment to the top policy-making
positions within the Civil Service. Criticism of the recruitment
policies of the Civil Service, institutionalized in the division of the
Civil Service into different grades, each with its own entry requirements, came to a head in the Report of the Fulton Committee in 1969. It strongly condemned, among other things, the
narrowness of the social and educational background of those
recruited, and the neglect of qualified specialists as opposed to
generalist administrators educated in the humanities. In spite of
official acceptance of the suggested reforms by both government
and the Civil Service, various examinations into the implementation of the proposals suggest that they have had very little real
effect. This is due not so much to positive resistance on the part
of the incumbent civil servants, as to their preconceptions of
what makes a suitable candidate for the higher Civil Service. It is

to be expected that the criteria by which those in authority decide between the various candidates will be those that they see and most approve of in themselves. In this way the self-perpetuating mechanisms work in order to supply 'suitable' occupants of Civil Service posts, that is similar in outlook and qualities to the existing incumbents. Attempts to attract candidates without this bias are very difficult to make successfully, especially as much of the self-selection process will have taken place by social conditioning in homes, schools and colleges, long before the Civil Service Commission enters into the reckoning.

The second aspect of the argument concerns the attitude taken by senior civil servants to the policy-making process. Whether individual civil servants have party preferences is not the crucial issue, as Tony Benn observes: 'The issue is not their personal political views nor their preferences for particular government. The problem arises from the fact that the Civil Service sees itself as being above the party battle, with a political position of its own to defend' (Benn, 1980, p. 9). The Civil Service view is that what is best for the country is a continuation of the centrist and consensual policies that have been developed and sold to party politicians over many years. Responsibility for the replacement of parliamentary rule by bureaucratic dominance, Benn argues further, must be shared by the successive prime ministers; they encouraged it in order to maximize their personal power within their administrations. He also criticizes other ministers and Parliament in general who failed to speak out against these developments. Needless to say, his views are not shared by all observers of the policy-making process and, given the strong tradition of secrecy in Britain, obtaining evidence one way or the other is difficult.

The ability of Margaret Thatcher's government to carry through the radical departure from 'consensus' economic policies in the 1980s was not inhibited by civil service power, although there were titanic struggles and some officials were replaced by others more sympathetic to the government's policies. In both the United States and Great Britain during this time the New Right provided its own answer to the problem of bureaucratic responsiveness, or lack of it – the market. Processes of hiving-off, privatization and contracting out are all based on the belief that 'public' services will be provided more efficiently if those providing them have control of their own budgets and compete for contracts. Actual organizational changes along these lines went further under

Thatcher in Great Britain than they did under Reagan in the United States, but both constituted a significant attack on the status of public bureaucracies.

If the position regarding bureaucratic independence versus party control is uncertain in Britain, it was less so in the Soviet Union. No secret was made of the fact that the government bureaucracy was guided in everything it did by the CPSU bureaucracy, the Secretariat: 'The CPSU, and particularly its full time staff, monopolizes the processes of generating and controlling political power in the USSR, transmitting its binding decisions to elites in state and public organizations through its territorial party committees and primary organizations' (Barghoorn and Remington, 1986, p. 305). Bodies with an ostensibly overseeing role, like the People's Control Commissions, were half-hearted in operation and often effectively controlled by the people they were supposed to be investigating. As Barghoorn and Remington go on to point out, however, this did not mean that the government bureaucrats could not influence decisions and occasionally obstruct their implementation. There was bound to be some tension between the governmental bureaucracy and that of the CPSU. The period of *perestroika* under Gorbachev revealed widespread criticism of the lack of control and supervision over the party and government bureaucracies, together with resentment at their ostentatious privileges. Boris Yeltsin built his early popular reputation on his castigating of bureaucratic privilege while he was secretary of the Communist Party in Moscow (Józsa, 1990, pp. 23–9).

Whatever system we are discussing, it is neither necessary nor helpful to subscribe to conspiracy theories of the behind-the-scenes influence exercised by civil servants. It is more important to study the structural relationships maintained by bureaucrats, and the potential power coming to them from their control over much of the information required for the administration of a modern state. How, with respect to what, and for and against whom they use that power are what we should be investigating.

One important structural relationship is that between bureaucracies and groups that represent particular interests. This essentially symbiotic relationship has already been discussed in chapter 13. But what of the responsiveness of bureaucracies to people in general? In the Soviet Union criticism of the bureaucracy was voiced primarily through letters to the press, especially to *Pravda*, then the newspaper of the CPSU. It is difficult to assess how effective such channels were, but the publicizing of grievances can be enough to lead to some bureaucratic adjustments. Clearly, such adjustments were likely to be restricted to relatively low levels of the bureaucracy because of the greater centralization of control at the upper echelons, but this probably applies to other systems as well.

In Britain, while the ability of an MP to gain access to the bureaucracy and publicity for a cause may amount to some protection for the public, it is hardly adequate, given the size of the bureaucracy and the number of MPs. Partly to overcome such problems, the office of ombudsman (Parliamentary Commissioner for Administration) was instituted in the 1960s. Similar offices were established for other bodies, such as the National Health Service. While the ombudsman has revealed the occasional bureaucratic horror story, he or she lacks some of the powers of his or her opposite number in other systems. Perhaps the greatest restrictions are that he or she can act only on the request of an MP and the only weapon available is to publicize the misdeeds. The ombudsman has no power to order compensation for example.

Essentially, the prospects for court action against the administration in Britain are limited to allegations of actions taken that are *ultra vires*, that is beyond the powers delegated to the institution by Parliament, or where a minister acts 'unreasonably'. In the United States a number of factors have combined to render the bureaucracy more open to public scrutiny. First, the Freedom of Information Acts give an individual a right to information possessed by the government about him or her and the government may have to justify non-disclosure in court. This is in sharp contrast to Britain's Official Secrets Act, and the one-sided relationship between citizen and bureaucrat in the Soviet Union. Second, having obtained the information, the American citizen has greater possibilities for action, inasmuch as the existence of the constitution and the Bill of Rights enables government action to be tested in the courts against that standard (see chapter 18). By such methods, considerable progress has been made in certain respects by women's, environmental and minority groups.

## Conclusion

As we have seen, Max Weber himself appreciated the large gulf existing between the ideal position of permanent bureaucratic officials and their real position *vis-à-vis* party politicians. Clearly, modern officials in the higher echelons of bureaucracy are involved in all stages of the policy-making process rather than just that of implementation. But even if they were involved only with implementation, they would still be extremely powerful because of the importance of administration in determining exactly what people get from government.

It has been suggested that most of the major problems in the analysis of modern bureaucracies concerns the degree of responsiveness they display in adjusting their behaviour to the wants of the public they are supposed to serve. First, there is the possibility that restrictive recruitment policies provide the context for the development over time of a separate bureaucratic 'view'. This may consist either of views as to the proper policy-making procedures – the way things are to be done – or of particular sets of policies that are perceived to be in the best interests of the nation. Second, there is the possibility which, according to the Marxist model of capitalist liberal democracies, will become a certainty) that the bureaucracy will be responsive primarily to the interests of a particular class in society. The third possibility, and one more in tune with an elitist model of the process, is that bureaucrats will see their accountability as being primarily towards the organized interests in society that succeed by one means or another in obtaining regular access to the policy-making process.

Lastly, there is the question of the extent to which the bureaucracy is responsive to citizens in general. Acceptance of any of the patterns of responsiveness outlined above will suggest that the bureaucracy is not likely to be particularly responsive to a largely unorganized 'general public' and, in most contemporary forms of democracy much will depend on the ability of the people's representatives to publicize their grievances. Whether citizens' charters on the model of those introduced in Great Britain from 1991 onwards amount to more than a symbolic empowerment of consumer-citizens remains to be seen. The ability of any group to hold decision-makers accountable must depend on their access to information as to what and how decisions are being made. While information is not exactly power itself, it is always a condition of the exercise of power. Certainly, it is important to study bureaucracies as institutions in their own right, even if we would not go as far as the poet Alexander Pope who wrote:

> For forms of government let fools contest;
> Whate'er is best administer'd is best.

# Questions for Discussion

1  Is it fair to argue, as Edelman (1964) does, that what administrators do is more important than other aspects of the policy process?
2  What are the relative advantages and disadvantages of placing a substantial number of political appointees at the head of each department when a new government assumes power?
3  What are likely to be the most effective methods by which bureaucracies can be made democratically responsible?

# Further Reading

Barghoorn, F.C. and T.F. Remington (1986), *Politics in the USSR*, 3rd edn. Boston, Little, Brown, ch. 8.

Blondel, J. (1982), *The Discipline of Politics*. Harmondsworth, Penguin, ch. 3.

Cawson, A. (1978), Pluralism, corporatism and the role of the state. *Government and Opposition*, 13 (spring), pp. 178–98.

Denenberg, R.V. (1992), *Understanding American Politics*, 3rd edn. London, Fontana, ch. 7.

Dunleavy, P. (1990), Government at the centre. In P. Dunleavy, A. Gamble and G. Peele (eds), *Developments in British Politics 3*. Basingstoke, Macmillan, pp. 96–125.

Hough, J.F. and M. Fainsod (1979), *How the Soviet Union is Governed*. Cambridge, Mass., Harvard University Press, pp. 380–91, 409–48.

McKay, D. (1989), *American Politics and Society*, 2nd edn. Oxford, Blackwell, ch. 10.

Sakwa, R. (1989), *Soviet Politics: An Introduction*. London, Routledge, pp. 228–35.

Sakwa, R. (1990), *Gorbachev and his Reforms*, 1985–1990. Hemel Hempstead, Philip Allan, pp. 357–68.

# 18

# Law, Courts and Judges

## Introduction

In this chapter we propose to consider the political relevance of the law, the courts and the judges within the context of the making and implementation of policy in the political process. It is important to do this explicitly since there were, at one time, frequent assertions to the effect that the law is quite distinct from or, indeed, above politics. While not wishing to deny that there are differences in the ways executives, bureaucracies and assemblies operate compared with law courts, we suggest that the politics of any system cannot be understood without some awareness of the crucial part played by law in its operations.

At the outset, let us distinguish the different types of disputes, dealt with by the courts that have greater or lesser political relevance. First, there are disputes between private individuals or organizations. The rights and duties of individuals towards each other are together known as private law which in Anglo-Saxon countries, such as Britain and the United States, tends to derive from custom as incorporated by judges through time in what is known in Britain as the common law. Nowadays such law is increasingly replaced or augmented by statutes (parliament-made laws). Second, there are disputes between the individual and the state. Some of the law will also originate in customs but is more likely to be statutory. The main manifestation of this is, of course, the criminal law in which the state (since Norman times in Britain) takes the initiative in enforcing certain standards of behaviour on the people. Also in this category is the area of administrative law that deals with the mass of relationships involved in the administration of the interventionist state. Generally, the area concerned with administration is known as public or administrative law. A third type of dispute that is likely to be of particular interest to students of politics is that between separate branches of government. This is part of public law but tends to go under the name of constitutional law.

How are these disputes settled? In essence, they are settled by the application of legal principles and rules to the particular facts of the case as it is presented to the judge (and, in some cases, a jury). Legal principles tend to reflect the basic values that the legal system is committed to uphold. In most countries these are enshrined in a written constitution, as in the United States and the Soviet Union, and now its successor republics, while in Britain, unusually, they are not; rather, they are found in a variety of sources – custom, statutes and conventions. In addition, other legal principles are laid down by the decisions of judges over time, or proclaimed in legislation. In the Soviet Union there was a code of legal principles in line with the European (Napoleonic) codes, augmented and supplemented by laws and decrees (of the Presidium of the Supreme Soviet) and decrees (of the Council of Ministers); the new republics have adopted similar systems. However, even when legal principles are committed to one constitutional document, set out in legal codes or reiterated by judges over time, they tend to remain highly ambiguous and not worth the paper they are printed on until somebody – the judiciary – interprets and defers to them in their judgments, and somebody else – the executive – enforces those judgments.

Legal rules are the more detailed regulations applicable in practice, and derive from a variety of sources. In Britain parliamentary statutes and the subsequent mass of secondary legislation called statutory instruments (or the equivalent in the United States) are the main source of rules today. In the Soviet Union the party and government bureaucracies issued a mass of rules and regulations – so many, in fact, that sometimes ways had to be found to circumvent them so that the system would not grind to a halt. The process by which legal principles are established is pre-eminently political. The particular set of values that comes to be enshrined in a constitution or code reflects the preferences of the groups in power at the time of their drawing up. This can be seen most clearly in a comparison of the attitudes towards private property enshrined in the United States constitution with those in the constitution of the old Soviet Union. The Fifth Amendment to the United States constitution provides a clear echo of the words of John Locke quoted above: 'No person shall be . . . deprived of life, liberty or property, without due process of law; nor shall private property be taken for public use, without just compensation.' On the other hand, Article 10 of the 1977 Soviet constitution stated: 'The foundation of the economic system of the USSR is socialist ownership of the means of the production in the form of state property (belonging to all the people) and collective farm and cooperative property.' The clash in underlying values between Britain and the United States on the one hand and the former Soviet Union on the other, is illustrated by the fact that an act of financial speculation – which has not only led to the accumulation of great wealth but has also occasionally received public honour in Britain and the United States – might have earned the perpetrator the death sentence in the Soviet Union.

But, of course, writing something into a constitution does not necessarily mean that it will be honoured in practice. For example, Article 25 of the Soviet constitution not only guaranteed citizens freedom of speech, press, assembly and demonstration, but also stated that printing-presses, paper, buildings, streets and communications facilities would be put at the disposal of the people for the exercise of these rights. Whether control of these facilities by the CPSU fulfilled this requirement is debatable, but before we jump to the conclusion that we could not have expected anything else from the Soviet system, consider the chequered history of the First Amendment to the United States constitution, which reads *inter alia*: 'congress shall make no law . . . abridging the freedom of speech.' Now that sounds fairly unambiguous, but in 1940 Congress passed the Smith Act which, at a time of fear of subversion, made it an offence 'to advocate the overthrow of the United States Government'. After the Second World War, as the Cold War was approaching its height, Eugene Dennis, a member of the American Communist Party, was indicted and convicted under the Smith Act. His appeal to the Supreme Court that the Smith Act was unconstitutional because of the First Amendment was rejected. The court was quite prepared to introduce its own qualifications to the First Amendment.

The lack of a single authoritative constitutional document means that it is relatively difficult to point to breaches of the constitution by British governments, although it is by no means impossible, as we shall see below in cases involving national security. But, of course, executive control of Parliament and Parliament's supremacy over the courts mean that the constitution may become simply what Her Majesty's Government says it is. There will be great political problems for any government tampering with the more fundamental principles or institutions of the constitution, but the extent of such tampering will depend entirely on the political condition of the time. However, political issues of a constitutional character – like joining the European Community, devolving power to a Scottish assembly and reform of the voting system – are usually given extended consideration (and possibly even a referendum) in recognition of their special nature (Norton, 1991, pp. 475–98).

The Dennis case in the United States provides us with a hint as to how departures from constitutional principle may be explained. In the first and last resort, the law, and therefore all courts and judges, are committed to upholding the prevailing social, economic and political order and they will not countenance activities that threaten that order. This applies equally to the United States, Britain and the old Soviet Union and its successor republics. However, within the context of their common aim of legitimating and preserving the political system, there are significant differences between these systems. In the Soviet Union the gulf between constitutional principle and political practice was explained by the central role of the CPSU. This central role was not made explicit in the 1936 constitution but is in Article 6 of that promulgated in 1977: 'the Communist Party of the Soviet Union is the leading and guiding force of Soviet society and the nucleus of its political system, *of all state and public organizations*' (our emphasis). Thus the courts were clearly subservient to the commands of the Communist Party, although it should be noted that the degree of independence available to the courts has varied over time: in the 1930s it was minimal, but after 1956 it became greater. Nevertheless, the idea of judicial independence in the sense of politicians not directly interfering with the activities of the courts was not a principle upheld in the Soviet Union. In the West the principle of the priority of the individual is emphasized. In the Soviet Union the emphasis on 'socialist legality' meant that the interests of particular individuals had to give way to the interests of society as a whole as interpreted by the party and government. Still, it should be pointed out that the average Soviet citizen's contact with the courts was likely to be as unpolitical as that of his or her Western counterpart, and he or she was no more likely to be dealt with unjustly in the run-of-the-mill case (Lane, 1985, pp. 192–7).

In the United States the courts exercise a good deal of influence quite independently of the other branches of government. At certain times the Supreme Court, in deciding the constitutionality of cases brought before it, has pursued policies directly at odds with those of the President and the Congress. Between 1934 and 1937 it invalidated a string of measures initiated by President Roosevelt and passed by Congress to attempt to deal with the economic depression, while between 1954 and 1963 it made a series of decisions regarding the rights of blacks far in advance of anything that could obtain strong presidential and congressional support. It is at such times that the independence of the Supreme Court is at its greatest, but they are rather untypical. More often, the court is in step with the other branches and, in emergencies such as war, will quite explicitly defer to them, particularly to the executive.

On a scale of judicial independence the British courts would be somewhere between those of the United States and the former Soviet Union, but rather closer to the former than the latter. The highest court in Britain is the House of Lords, but when they sit as a court the Lords consist only of a panel of members who have long judicial experience and who have been appointed as Law Lords. Parliamentary supremacy means that in Britain the courts cannot invalidate legislation (except when it conflicts with European Community legislation, when EC law prevails). In the United States the obvious involvement in the political process of the Supreme Court is due to the court having laid claim early in the nineteenth century to the power of judicial review, that is the right to review the constitutionality of executive and legislative acts. The House of Lords has no such power.

However, the British courts are not even now totally subservient to the executive and Parliament. As we have seen elsewhere, the wording of statutes tends to be general and is therefore frequently ambiguous;  thus when a case revolves around what a statute actually says, judges have a good deal of discretion which they will exercise according to their view of what the law requires. There are rules of interpretation which judges are said to follow and which prevent arbitrariness in the process, but in fact there are so many conflicting rules that judges are effectively free to choose which to follow. Growth in the interventionism of British judges has been noted since the 1960s and is now encapsulated in specific procedures for judicial review. However, this is only on procedural grounds and not, as in the United States, on the merits of the decision, that is on whether it conforms to the judicial view of what the constitution requires. Thus in Britain the grounds for review are summarized as illegality, irrationality or procedural impropriety by the public agency being challenged. In practice, the difference between procedure and substance can be very narrow; for example, in *Bromley* v. *Greater London Council* (1981) the House of Lords decided that the council's 'Fares fair' policy for public transport was in breach of its 'fiduciary duty' to ratepayers and London Transport's duty to run its operations on ordinary business principles. This decision depended on highly loaded definitions of contested terms such as 'economic' and appeared to substitute judicial for electoral decisions as to the proper balance between the interests of ratepayers and public-transport users (Griffith, 1991, pp. 128–36).

'The independence of the judiciary' is a much used phrase in the United States and Britain, but there are strict limits on this independence. In matters of 'national security' – a phrase that can cover a multitude of sins – the judiciary in Britain is very reluctant to question executive action. In a number of cases since the 1960s, which have involved a variety of circumstances (demonstrations, deportations and publications), judges in the United Kingdom have refused to accept that 'national security' can mean anything other than what the government of the day says it means. Such judicial deference to the executive can be contrasted to the recent grilling on the subject experienced by Sir Robert Armstrong, head of the British Civil Service, in an Australian courtroom at the end of 1986 during the *Spycatcher* trial over the alleged revelation of state secrets.

## Judicial Recruitment

Generally speaking, there are two main patterns of judicial recruitment – the European and the Anglo-Saxon. In the former, becoming a judge is a matter of electing one career path over another; having trained as a lawyer, one may select the path of the judge or that of the advocate. This is also the pattern in the republics of the former Soviet Union. In Britain and the United States judges are selected from lawyers, usually only after many years in practice, in Britain as an advocate, and in the United States as an advocate or in a legal post within the government. There are several modes of appointment. In the United States state judges (that is judges sitting in state courts and administering, in the main, state laws) may be recruited via election or appointment by the Governor. In recent years an increasing number of states have been attempting to remove the appointment of the judges from the partisan political process and to ensure minimum standards of efficiency and ability on the part of judges. Their success has, on the whole, been variable to date.

The federal judiciary in the United States is nominated by the President and appointed with the consent of the Senate. Presidents usually nominate persons of the same political party as themselves, but at the lower levels of the federal judiciary a critical factor in the President's choice is the views of the senators of the state in which the appointee is to serve. The President is most concerned with nominations to fill vacancies on the Supreme Court, since it is the Supreme Court's decisions that are most likely to affect the policies of his administration. Therefore, he is likely to nominate those whose views seem most in line with his own, although there is no way a president can guarantee the direction of a justice's decision and it is estimated that the President's choices have backfired in a quarter of appointments. The Senate's discussion of the nomination frequently depends as much on wider political concerns as on the suitability of the nominee himself or herself. Generally, senators assume that the President has the right to make the nominations and they will block them only if they feel that the nominees are particularly weak and the President needs teaching a lesson. This occurred when two successive nominations by President Reagan failed in 1987: the first was rejected by the Senate for his extremely conservative views, the second withdrew his nomination when he admitted to having smoked 'pot' years earlier.

Partisan nomination of senior judges used to be the rule in Britain but has not really been so since the 1920s. Technically, appointments are made by the Prime Minister but, in practice, they are recommended by the Lord Chancellor after discussions with the senior judiciary. The Lord Chancellor's position is significant. He is head of the judiciary, but he is also a politician and a member of the Cabinet. There are other law officers who are politicians and members of the government, all of whom are expected to act impartially in their legal functions, but there is obviously scope for ambiguity and interpretation here. But if direct partisan considerations are largely absent from the process, wider concerns of suitability are not. For example, in 1975 a man was appointed to the High Court at the relatively late age of 62. It was suggested that one of the reasons for this was that his main work as an advocate had been on behalf of trade unions, and on one occasion he had walked out of the National Industrial Relations Court in protest at the judge. Such behaviour would not normally be a recommendation to the High Court bench, but it was less of a problem for the Labour Lord Chancellor who appointed him in 1975. At the lower levels of the British judicial system are the magistrates' courts which deal with the overwhelming majority of criminal cases. Magistrates are not trained lawyers, although they do have available the advice of legally trained clerks, and are appointed with a specific political criterion in mind. Specially, appointment to the bench should achieve some overall balance as between the nominees of the main political parties in the area. Some of the main urban areas also have stipendiary (professional, paid) magistrates.

What senior British and American judges have in common is their high social status. In both systems the vast majority of professional judges come from upper-class and upper-middle-class backgrounds; the United States Supreme Court has one black member and one woman; the British Law Lords in the House of Lords have had neither. At lower levels in Britain and the United States, however, a few women can now be found. The elite educational background of the British judiciary is often cited as a major factor in their apparent ignorance of affairs in the world outside the courtroom. About three-quarters of the judges are educated at public schools and Oxford or Cambridge, but there are also other factors that reinforce their exclusiveness: their socialization into the legal life via their training as barristers (that is those entitled to appear in the higher courts) and the need to demonstrate professional competence in order to 'take silk', that is become a Queen's Counsel and thus gain themselves a place among the elite of barristers from whom judges are chosen. This is further compounded by the peculiarities of the judges' work situation: they live almost exclusively among other judges and senior barristers and, as one new judge put it, 'you have to watch your invitations' (*Sunday Times*, 5 October 1975). The important question at this stage is, of course, how this affects their decision-making.

## Judicial Decision-Making

It has traditionally been argued, particularly by judges, that they do not make decisions, but, instead, they simply apply the known law to new facts or declare what the law is in cases of uncertainty. Such an argument bears little examination, however, when one considers the role, particularly, of appeal courts. That the view of the judge's role as declaratory is inadequate can be seen if one considers that the reason many cases come to court (which are only a minority of the cases that are actually started) is because there is genuine doubt as to what the law is. This may be because the facts of the dispute are unique or that statutes and previous decisions are capable of more than one interpretation as to their meaning; Some of the words that pepper these documents, for example 'reasonable', are inherently ambiguous and judges must decide between the competitive interpretations of what the law is as argued by lawyers.

Social scientists proceed differently from lawyers in explaining why particular decisions are made. Lawyers rely primarily on close analysis of the wording contained within the judgment to seek out the *ratio decidendi* (reason for deciding). We would argue that this does not give a clear explanation of the decision because the judgment is an after-the-event rationalization of the decision and does not necessarily give the real reasons for it. A judge or judges may reach a decision for a variety of reasons but the judgment must be presented in a form that is acceptable to the legal profession and thus it is cast in the form of a discussion of previous similar cases and relevant statutes. Part of the problem we have in the analysis of the British judiciary, however, is the shortage of hard evidence on the intrusion of the other, hidden, decision-making variables into the process. This is due partly to the great unwillingness of the legal profession to submit itself to scrutiny and a general lack of scholarly interest in the subject until recently. Therefore, much of what follows may more accurately be characterized as hypotheses of British judicial behaviour derived deductively from research into decision-making in other judiciaries and/or in non-judicial settings.

First, the class, religious and ethnic backgrounds of judges are likely to have an impact on their general attitudes, which in turn may be translated into particular views on certain legal issues. Data on the class background of both British and senior American judges show clearly the dominance of the upper classes. The differences between judges will decline to some extent as they share a common socialization within the legal profession. In Britain this is reinforced by such practices as attending a number of dinners a term in the Inns of Court while they are students for the Bar; in both Britain and the United States there is the shared experience of dealing with problems from a legal perspective and extensive contact with other lawyers. Second, there is the question of the extent to which the personal values and attitudes of judges intrude on their making of legal decisions. In the United States it has been clearly demonstrated that they do. A variety of statistical techniques have been employed to relate the attitudes of judges on general political issues, such as the desirability of government intervention and the importance of individual as opposed to governmental rights, to their decisions in substantive cases. It this way the decisions of courts may frequently be predicted. This has not been demonstrated in Britain; first, because of the lack of judicial review of statutes in Britain, policy issues (politics) are often not as self-evidently present as they are in the United States and, second, in the Court of Appeal and the House of Lords where more than one judge sits, panels of judges change, whereas in the United States Supreme Court the same panel of nine judges hears all cases.

Thus the British courts are less amenable to the study techniques applied in the United States. It has further been argued that in Britain one finds less variety of opinion among judges than in the United States. Certainly, Supreme Court judges are likely to have had a much wider variety of governmental and legal experience than their counterparts in Britain where the rather narrow process of socialization into the law and recruitment process seems to ensure less variation. It has been argued that in Britain, on every major social issue has come before the courts during the last thirty years, the judges have supported 'the conventional, established and settled interest [and] have reacted strongly against challenges to those interests' (Griffith, 1991, p. 325).

Another factor in judicial decisions is the interaction within the court itself. This can have two main dimensions: first, that between the judge and the other participants in the process – lawyers, witnesses, police, juries; second, in the courts where more than one judge sits, that among the judges themselves. Clearly, a large part of the job of a person making a submission to the court is to 'know' the judge, to try to predict what the judge does and does not want to hear and so on. Interaction between judges is probably more significant in the United States with the stable membership on the Supreme Court, but even in Britain the phenomenon of 'opinion deference', whereby one or more judges defers to the opinion of another because he or she is acknowledged to be an expert or to have seniority, is not unknown.

Finally, there is the highly significant question of the relation between the court itself and other political institutions, especially executives and assemblies. In Britain and the United States this relationship is described by the phrase 'the independence of the judiciary' which, as we have seen, fails to convey the complexity of the relations between courts, executives and assemblies. Overall, the most fruitful way to examine the interaction of courts, executives and assemblies is to see them all as engaged in a continuous process by which the law and rights are constantly being defined and redefined. This may be seen even in Britain, where the courts are formally subordinate to Parliament but are not powerless to affect the intention of Parliament by means of legal definitions because of the inevitable ambiguity of statutes. The clearest example in Britain concerns trade union rights in which this process of redefinition has continued for about 150 years and shows no signs of abating.

In the United States a most dramatic contemporary example of this process is the abortion issue. Although it is not stated explicitly in the constitution, in 1965 the Supreme Court decided that there was a constitutional right to personal privacy, and in *Roe* v. *Wade* (1973) it ruled that this included a woman's decision regarding abortion. The decision was opposed by many, including some who were pro-choice (in favour of women deciding for themselves), on the grounds that the court's decision was apparently based more on a balancing of policy interests than on specifically legal argument, and it had the effect of stimulating the anti-abortion movement which in turn became a major part of the New Right. The effect of the decision was to give women the choice of an abortion during the first six months of pregnancy if they could find a doctor to carry it out, and it came to have enormous symbolic importance for feminists. The pro-life (anti-abortion) campaign, which has attempted to overthrow *Roe*, has included proposals for constitutional amendments, none of which has succeeded, and proposals for new state and congressional laws to challenge *Roe*, many of which have been passed and have become subject to subsequent decision by the Supreme Court. The campaign has also sought to influence the appointment of federal judges opposed to *Roe*, a highly successful tactic during the Reagan and Bush presidencies, and to present stronger arguments to the courts via *amicus curiae* ('friend of the court') briefs. Finally, there has been a great deal of direct action, from the blockading of clinics by groups like Operation Rescue to prevent women from gaining access, to the bombings of clinics in the mid-1980s by groups like the Army of God.

In cases considered since *Roe*, the Supreme Court has generally shown more deference to congressional restrictions than to the states' attempts to overturn *Roe*, for example it ruled that public funds may not be used for abortions whether therapeutic or non-therapeutic (*Harris* v. *McRae* 1980). The appointment of new and conservative judges in the later 1980s was seen as posing a threat to the basic rights enunciated in *Roe*, yet in *Webster* v. *Reproductive Health Services* (1989) and *Planned Parenthood of Southeastern Pennsylvania* v. *Casey* (1992) the court condoned further restrictions being placed by the states on the circumstances under which women could obtain abortions, while refusing to decide directly to reverse the principles in *Roe*. So the process continues: pro-choice members of Congress hoped to pass legislation incorporating clearer statutory rights to abortion. In part this was intended to embarrass President Bush into having to choose whether or not to veto the legislation before the 1992 election, since abortion is an issue on which he was seen as vulnerable among women who would otherwise vote Republican. Other state legislation is set to come before the Supreme Court in 1992–3, including measures that outlaw abortion except where the woman's life is endangered, which would make it very difficult for the justices to avoid considering the continuing validity of the *Roe* decision (McKeever, 1993, pp. 82–127; *Guardian*, 30 June 1992, p. 24).

In the Soviet Union the judicial process developed along European lines. In contrast to the Western system, there was no power in the Supreme Court to question or set aside legislation passed or decreed by the government. There also tended to be a strong presumption that a person brought before the court was guilty. Thus there was less pressure on the prosecution to have to prove guilt beyond reasonable doubt and, although acquittals did occur, they were comparatively few in number. Some lawyers in the Soviet Union advocated the adoption of the Western principle that the accused is presumed innocent until proved guilty, but met with little success until the Gorbachev period.

Of course, it can be argued that the theoretical presumption of innocence in the West is frequently negated by the pressure, particularly in the lower courts, to 'plea bargain', that is agree to plead guilty to a relatively minor charge and receive a relatively light sentence, rather than plead not guilty, endure a long wait for a trial (possibly in custody) and, if found guilty, receive a heavier sentence, although there always remains the chance of acquittal. It is said that in the United States the overload of cases and the dominance of the system by plea bargaining mean that the theoretical presumption of innocence is replaced by an actual presumption of guilt in which the costs to the defendant of contesting his or her innocence are frequently overpowering. The system in Britain is not as dominated by plea bargaining, but it is certainly present.

Soviet cases with political implications were given a great deal of publicity in the West, but there is little reason to believe that the great majority of cases in the Soviet Union were dealt with any less fairly than elsewhere. Since the death of Stalin there seems to have been a conscious attempt to ensure that legal principles are adhered to and even the KGB appeared to make efforts to observe legality (Hough and Fainsod, 1979, pp. 278–84). For example, their practice of reiterated warnings to an individual of the wrongfulness of his or her words or actions may have been to ensure that he or she did not plead ignorance of wrongdoing, which could have been an acceptable defence in the courts. All in all, the Soviet people came, through bitter experience of arbitrary justice in Stalin's time, to appreciate the value of an impartial, consistent and reliable judicial system. This became evident in their attitude to the comrades' courts. There had developed since Khrushchev's time policies to involve the populace more in low-level administrative activities on a voluntary basis. One manifestation of this was the comrades' courts. As described by Friedgut (1979, pp. 249–56), these were an attempt to give social norms the force of law and to make citizens accountable to each other. Their role became educational, preventative and mediatory, although they could impose minor sanctions and deal with lesser cases. Such courts continued to function under the supervision of a volunteer council made up largely of lawyers, which could review their decisions. But they were not always popular among the citizens because they were suspected of arbitrariness and personal bias. People preferred the more formalized and anonymous procedures of the law courts.

Where political cases were concerned, the Soviet courts were not subject to the Western principle of legality – of the supremacy of the law. Instead, they observed the principle of socialist legality – the idea that the best interests of a socialist society must override even the principle and letter of the law. The guardian and interpreter of socialist legality was the CPSU and it was in this role that the party justified its intervention in the course of justice in cases where the interest and security of the state were thought to be involved. As we have seen, the area of 'national security' is also where British and American courts have demonstrated their independence least. One of the potentially most significant developments in the period of *glasnost* and *perestroika* was the setting up of a constitutional review committee which could comment on the constitutional legality of legislation passed by the Congress of People's Deputies or the Supreme Soviet and decrees issued by the President. They certainly exercised this power, but their ability to enforce their decisions appeared to be weak. Although this was a far cry from the power and authority of a body like the United States Supreme Court, it nevertheless could be seen as the beginning of a practical appreciation of the concept of constitutionality as understood in the West. A similar committee now exists in the Russian Federation (Smith, 1992, pp. 202–32; Schmid, 1990, pp. 54–60).

## Conclusion

We have argued that the law must be studied as part of the political process. This is particularly evident at the time of the establishment of new constitutions. Frequently, after a revolution a new set of politico-legal principles have to be established reflecting the interests and ideals of the new power-holders. Thus a major feature of the 1787 American Constitution was to maximize the freedom of (property-owning) individuals and to disperse the power of governmental institutions (checks and balances) to minimize the chances of a new tyranny developing. Equally, the basic legal principles enshrined in various Soviet constitutions since 1917 reflected the dominance of the principles of Marxism-Leninism. The constitutions of the post-Soviet republics are likely to be notable for the absence of Marxist-Leninist principles and rhetoric.

It is, of course, one of the aims of a new regime to have its preferred political principles regarded as 'the law', that is seen to be self-evidently 'right', in a similar fashion to the way in which ideology is assimilated by the new nation (see chapter 4). Thus, if what were yesterday hot political disputes can today be channelled into the 'legal process', operating with new principles and procedures, and an apparent indifference to 'political' questions, then so much the better for those in power. But even if we accept that there is a significant difference between the 'legal' and 'political' processes in the way in which decisions are reached, they would both still come firmly within the definition of power we adopted in part I, that is the ability to get others to do what you want them to, assuming this is different from what they would have done anyway, with the use or threat of sanctions if necessary. Clearly, this idea of modifying the behaviour of others is central to the operation of law, both private and public, as is the existence of sanctions.

The study of the legal process of any society can reveal much about the distribution of power in that society, for example how and by whom any Bill of Rights is interpreted and enforced, how and from which groups and classes in society judges are recruited, and how decisions are reached. All these questions are a matter of judgement, priorities and vested interest in the exercise of power. The overt intrusion of politics into the courtroom varies widely from one system to another, but at root the legal process is a major way in which the 'who gets what' choices are made in any society, however different the process by which these choices are made appears to be. An individual's attitude to the question of the political context in which the legal system operates will depend on whether he or she takes a supportive attitude to the political status quo or wishes to challenge it.

## Questions for Discussion

1  Discuss the relevance of politics to the different types of legal conflicts.
2  In what senses is the 'judicial' method of making decisions different from the 'political' method?

3 Discuss the arguments for and against the adoption of a Bill of Rights in Great Britain.

## Further Reading

Butler, W.E. (1992), The rule of law and the legal system. In S. White, A. Pravda and Z. Gitelman (eds), *Developments in Soviet and Post-Soviet Politics*, 2nd edn. Basingstoke, Macmillan, pp. 107–21.

Elliott, M.J. (1986), The role of law. In H. Drucker, P. Dunleavy, A. Gamble and G. Peele (eds), *Developments in British Politics 2* Basingstoke, Macmillan, pp. 266–78.

Foley, M. (1991), *American Political Ideas*. Manchester, Manchester University Press, ch. 10.

Griffith, J.A.G. (1991), *The Politics of the Judiciary*, 4th edn. London, Fontana, chs 1, 8 and 9.

Hodder-Williams, R. (1992), Constitutional legitimacy and the Supreme Court. In G. Peele et al. (eds), *Developments in American Politics*. Basingstoke, Macmillan, pp. 138–64.

Robertson, G. (1989), *Freedom, The Individual and the Law*, 6th edn. Harmondsworth, Penguin, ch. 12.

Simpson, A.W.B. (1988), *Invitation to Law*. Oxford, Blackwell, ch. 1.

Smith, G.B. (1992), *Soviet Politics: Struggling with Change*, 2nd edn. Basingstoke, Macmillan, ch. 9.

# 19

# The Police and the Military

## The Police

The term 'police' here refers to the organization employed by the state on a day-to-day basis to enforce its laws, with coercion if necessary. The most usual sense in which the police has previously been discussed in the context of politics is as a secret force repressing dissent in totalitarian societies. Thus 'the Soviet police' tended to conjure up the KGB. However, all societies make use of such security police and we shall consider it later. Most of this chapter is concerned with the activities and political relevance of the ordinary police, and with the associated question of the significance of the intervention of the military in politics.

We believe that this is important because a study of police forces and the way in which they make decisions is essential to an understanding of the role of the law and rights and thus of the distribution of power in societies. For many years the official view of the position of the police in liberal democracies like Britain was that it acted merely as an administrative agent to enforce the law. The police should not, the argument continued, be permitted to exercise discretionary power because it would amount to an unconstitutional delegation of authority and would, in any case, increase the possibilities of discrimination and corruption. A moment's reflection will reveal just how unreal this model of police behaviour is. It implies that the police fully enforces every law against the citizen. Whether such a policy would be desirable is debatable, but certainly no society has been willing to divert the necessary resources to the police in order to come anywhere near such a policy.

Thus the use of discretionary authority is inherent in police activity. In one sense this means that police organizations are comparable to bureaucracies in general, but there are important differences. The police bureaucracy is also organized hierarchically, but the paramilitary aspect of its role means that the hierarchy is far more disciplined and rigid than in a civilian bureaucracy. Discretionary power and the opportunity to exercise it exist at all levels of police organizations. At the highest level, decisions must be made as to the allocation of resources to the different areas of crime and, indeed, can be based on quite contrary notions of policing. In Britain, for example, since the late 1960s policing, rather like the National Health Service, has fallen prey to the belief in the 'technological fix'. At a time of poor recruitment, the introduction of personal radios, computerized command-and-control systems and the increased use of vehicles produced, by the late 1970s, police forces whose main tactic was rapid response to incidents, known as 'reactive' or 'fire brigade' policing. One major lesson drawn from the 1981 riots in Britain by the authorities was that this style of policing had led to a growing gulf between the police and the communities in which it worked. Therefore, efforts have been made since 1981 to put more police officers back in touch with their communities, for example by increasing foot patrols. Nevertheless, these efforts have not obviously reversed the dominant thrust of reactive policing. Currently, the other police strategy aimed at preventing crime is 'multi-agency' policing, in which the police combines with social welfare and other local authority agencies to co-ordinate measures against crime, measures that are both physical (for example designing housing estates) and social (for example deciding the appropriate regime for offenders).

Another important area of discretionary power arises in the setting up of special squads - fraud, obscene publications, robbery and so on - to concentrate on particular crimes. Generally, arrests are not made by such squads for conduct that is deemed less serious than that in which they are mainly interested. Such a generalization is likely to apply to all police concentrating on a particular crime. The most extensive area of discretion, however, is that with which we are most likely to come into contact: police officers on the beat. In dealing with drivers, domestic disputes, drunks and juveniles, whether or not informal cautions are delivered, or arrests made, depends a great deal more on the negotiation between police and citizen, and ultimately on the exercise of discretion by the police, than on any objective notion of the law.

The use of police resources, and the relations of the police with the community, raise profound political questions, even though they are not always immediately identifiable as such. In another area, however, the political importance of the role of the police is clearer, that is in dealing with public disorder. The United States and most European countries have a specialized riot police force, sometimes referred to as a 'third force', which takes over when the ordinary police cannot cope, and provides the state with another option before calling in the military. In Great Britain there is no such force, and the gap has been filled in recent years by a militarization of the police force. In the past twenty years the planning, organization and equipment of order-maintenance has been steadily updated and centralized, so that the police now has the potential to mobilize thousands of riot-trained and equipped police officers. This was seen most recently during the miners' strike in 1984–5. While there were enough differences between police tactics in separate areas to demonstrate that individual police officers retained some control over police operations, the strong overall impression was of a police force subject to central direction by senior chief constables and Home Office officials along lines determined by the Cabinet.

It is very difficult to generalize about the American police because, with the exception of the nationally organized FBI, there are 40,000 police departments at state, county and municipal levels. Moreover, almost everyone already has a firm mental picture of the American police that has been acquired from a lifetime's film- and television-viewing. The quality of state police forces varies widely and, although attempts have been made to nationalize standards and training in the past fifteen years or so, the differences may still be considerable. Historically, the American police has almost certainly been more violent and corrupt than its British counterpart. The violence largely reflects the fact that American society has in general been more violent than British society. The lingering of the 'frontier' myth and the easy availability of firearms have led the police often to shoot first and make enquiries second. The most negative aspects of American policing – its violence and racism – came together in the beating of Rodney King in Los Angeles in 1991, which was followed by rioting when the white policemen responsible were acquitted in April 1992. The corruption also indicates the degree to which the

American political process itself has been more prone to corruption. Traditionally, the connection between the police and the party in power locally has been very close, and the susceptibility of the former to the wishes of the latter has been much greater than in Britain.

In the former Soviet Union the duties of the ordinary police (called the militia) were similar to those in Britain or the United States, for example. It was supplemented to some extent by the *druzhinii* (volunteer popular detachments), formed in 1959. This was part of the policy of attempting to involve the people in minor administrative activities which was implemented after the death of Stalin. They were more than the part-time special constables in the British tradition, in that they were seen as having a social role in the context of an individual's responsibility to his or her community. They patrolled the streets and aimed to prevent, by their presence, the committing of petty offences or minor disorder. Thus social order was apparently being maintained by one's fellow citizens within one's own community. It was hoped by this means to produce an acceptable social order without the overt use of force. Community policing in Britain is inspired by similar hopes. Such initiatives tended to be overcome in time by inertia and indifference. The general demoralization of Soviet society during the Brezhnev period affected the militia also and by the 1980s widespread corruption was reported. In the last years of the Soviet Union and in the new republics the militia found itself dealing with a level of public demonstration – and sometimes disorder – of which it had no previous experience, and it did not always deal efficiently with them. The situation was complicated by the existence of armed troops of the Interior Ministry (MVD) and of the KGB which were also used to maintain internal order.

In both Britain and the United States there has been a great deal of debate on the question of police accountability. The debate arises from the obvious difficulty of avoiding two types of police relationships in the community, each of which is undesirable for different reasons. The first is the position found in most large American cities for much of their history, where the police was highly accountable to the community in the sense that it was controlled directly by the mayor via the police commissioner and acted primarily in the interests of the party in power. The second is the position apparently preferred by the police itself: where it is not subject to the whims of party politics and can develop what it considers to be the best safeguard for the community – the professionalization of the police force, in other words, it wants to be regarded as a profession and, like the medical and legal professions, to be left to do its job according to its own discretion. As the police in both countries in recent years have relied increasingly on notions of professionalism to defend themselves against political attack, so police organizations have asserted themselves more publicly to promote not only their own organization, but also particular policies regarding law and order which they deem to be necessary. Thus in Britain, for example, each of the police organizations – Police Federation, Superintendents' Association and Association of Chief Police Officers – will 'go on record' not only on matters relating directly to the police, but also on more general questions of law and order in society.

## Political Police

There are, clearly, contradictory elements in the relationship of the ordinary police to politics. Many of its tasks – such as the directing of traffic and acting as emergency social services – have only the slightest political connotations, but at other times it is involved in politics in its role as defender of public order. The importance of this role is likely to be greater in times of economic decline. There is in many police forces a group or section whose role is entirely and explicitly political.

In Britain this is the Special Branch, which is formally part of the Criminal Investigation Department (CID) but actually has considerable independence. There are 1,250 officers in the branch in England and Wales, 30 per cent of them in the Metropolitan Police in London. All forces have at least some officers in the branch but the largest contingents are in the urban forces and, because of potential 'terrorist' activity, those with ports serving Ireland, for example Merseyside. Their duties are various: guarding foreign embassies, protecting prominent public figures, carrying out immigration and nationality enquiries, and dealing with Official Secrets Act and election-law infringements.

In addition, and more controversially, it is the job of the branch to 'gather information about threats to public order' and to assist the Security Service in protecting the state against 'terrorism' and 'subversion' (Home Office, 1984). The first of these has meant that systematic surveillance is carried out by the branch over organizations that regularly organize demonstrations and marches or are involved in industrial disputes. Since what the police regards as an entirely proper task of 'threat assessment' means the surveillance of what is entirely legitimate political activity by peace or trade union organizations, it is not surprising that such actions have given rise to concern. With respect to the second of these jobs, terms like 'subversion' often have such elastic definitions that, again, they can frequently provide the pretext for the surveillance of legitimate political activity. In Britain 'subversive activities' are defined as 'those which threaten the safety or well being of the State, and which are intended to undermine or overthrow Parliamentary democracy by political, industrial or violent means' (Home Office, 1984). Such a definition, or a public-order-threat assessment, provides the justification for wide-ranging and controversial police practices. Electronic surveillance (bugging), telephone tapping, infiltration of political organizations and squats, photographing demonstrations, the maintenance of files on perhaps 2 million political activists and (in London) the systematic recording of all public meetings and demonstrations, including the names and addresses of speakers and chairpersons, are all practices that have been admitted by the police or have emerged in the course of court hearings.

The House of Commons Select Committee on Home Affairs carried out an inquiry into the branch during 1984–5 and concluded: 'We are satisfied, *on the basis of the evidence which we have received*, that the special branches of the police service in England and Wales do not justify public anxiety' (House of Commons, 1985, p. x; our emphasis). The minority of Labour members on the committee did not agree with this and issued their own minority report, but the most significant point about the conclusion is that the majority on the committee excluded at the outset the possibility of obtaining the evidence they would need to judge properly whether there was any abuse of power. They refused to examine particular complaints or cases, did not examine branch files and did not interview rank-and-file officers; in other words, they did none of the things that would have had to be done to get at the truth.

In Australia, Canada and the United States during the 1970s inquiries into the political police and internal-security agencies demonstrated clearly that reliance on interviews with chief constables and general assertions of good faith by all concerned would be inadequate. After 1986 parliamentary concern shifted towards the security service or MI5, particularly because of allegations that it had been involved in attempts to smear elected politicians during the 1970s. If some oversight were to be established there, then much greater attention would need to be paid to foreign experience. Clearly, the work of such agencies cannot be conducted in the full glare of the political process, but there are enormous risks also in leaving such agencies uncontrolled and unaccountable, as is graphically illustrated by reference to the recent history of the FBI.

After the Second World War, the FBI built a position of bureaucratic autonomy which lasted until the death in 1972 of J. Edgar Hoover, its director for almost fifty years. Then the bureau became embroiled in the Watergate affair and between 1973 and 1976 it was subjected to unprecedented investigation which revealed the full extent of its post-war activities and the dangers inherent in unchecked police bureaucracies. The illegal activities of the bureau included counter-intelligence programmes which were designed to 'disrupt' groups and 'neutralize' individuals deemed to be threats to national security. This involved the opening of mail, bugging and telephone-tapping subject only occasionally to external check, the dissemination of information thus obtained to favoured politicians and break-ins to install bugs or obtain documents. Hoover's consummate skill as an exponent of the art of bureaucratic politics reinforced the impregnability of the bureau, but its initial immunity was based essentially on its role *vis-à-vis* internal security. The bureau's reputation in the 1920s and 1930s was based on its exploits during and after prohibition, much advanced by Hoover's keen nose for public relations. During the 1940s internal security – first against Nazism and then against communism – became its dominant concern. The strength of the bureau then became founded on two basic propositions: first, that communism posed a serious threat to the United States and, secondly, that the FBI afforded the United States unique protection against that threat. This enabled all attempts at inquiry into the FBI to be squashed, on the ground that they would inhibit or endanger the vital operations of the bureau. Any persistent critics could be dismissed as, at best, dupes of communists or, at worst, communists themselves. It is interesting to note that, the exposure and greater control of FBI activities do not appear to have placed the United States at the mercy of subversives.

A major factor which underlies much of this discussion, and explains why such legislative investigations of the police as occurred between 1973 and 1976 in the United States are still resisted in Britain, is the different attitudes in the two political systems to the dissemination of official information. The assumptions in the two systems are almost diametrically opposed. In Britain the assumption is that citizens have no right to official information, and receive only what the government chooses to tell them. In the United States it is assumed that citizens have the right to know and it is up to the government to prove in court that certain types of information should not be disclosed. Of course, this reflects the very different role of the American courts *vis-à-vis* other governmental institutions but, as we saw in the discussion of courts and rights (chapter 18), if one has no right to information it becomes extremely difficult to exercise all manner of other rights.

The political police in the Soviet Union had a long history stretching back to tsarist times. It was an important vehicle of terror in the Stalinist period and, by the time of Stalin's death, had come to occupy a place in the state machinery which in some ways undermined the position of the Communist Party itself; everyone came under suspicion. Stalin's successors were determined to reduce this role and one of their first acts was to have the head of the KGB, Beria, arrested and executed (it was the last execution of a major political figure in the Soviet Union). The KGB was now much more firmly under party control and there was evidence to suggest that it was required, outwardly at least, to abide by the legal rules. As with security and intelligence organizations in other countries, the KGB was involved in widespread operations abroad, but a major part of its concern was with Soviet citizens themselves. It saw itself in a paternalistic role in relation to them, seeking to persuade wrongdoers of the error of their ways and guiding them back to the right paths. Soviet citizens, however, retained a healthy dislike and suspicion of being involved with the KGB in any way. It was a large organization, estimated by some to involve 40,000 personnel, and relied additionally on a vast network of informers.

In the days of *glasnost* and *perestroika* the KGB came under public scrutiny for the first time, much of it hostile. It tried to improve its image (even to the extent of holding a 'Miss KGB' contest!). There was growing evidence of a split in the KGB between those who supported reform and those who did not. Up to the end, the KGB had under its surveillance even Yeltsin and Gorbachev. Its downfall came with the failed *coup d'état* of August

1991 when it was clear that its head, Vladimir Kryuchkov, was one of the instigators of the coup. Its weakness was revealed when middle-ranking officers defied orders to attack the Russian Parliament Building (the 'White House') because of the likelihood of many civilian casualties. The refusal ensured the collapse of the coup. Russia and the other republics seem to be developing security organizations more analogous to those in the West, with a clear distinction between internal and external security. It is too early to say how much the experience of the past will influence future developments (von Borcke, 1990, pp. 61–6).

It may be questioned whether such elaborate surveillance (engaged in not only by the KGB but to a greater or lesser extent by other security organizations) is really necessary or produces results commensurate with the time, energy and expense involved in the operations. There seems to be a tendency to build up security organizations on the basis of 'worst-case' arguments (such as the possible increase in terrorism), which leads to serious encroachment on the liberties of citizens and to increasing paranoia.

## The Military

The military consists of the armed forces (land, sea and air) whose primary function is to defend the state against external enemies or to enforce the will of the state against other states. They can sometimes be used internally, where the police cannot handle a situation. Any political activity by the military tends to be discussed in terms of 'intervention' because of the widespread belief in liberal democracies that the military should remain outside politics. There is, in fact, a wider spectrum along which political activity by the military may range. At the very least, political action by a military organization will include acting as a pressure group within the policy-making process on questions of weapons procurement; at the other end of the spectrum there is full-scale military intervention as manifested in a *coup d'état*, in which the military, or a part of it, overthrows the government and assumes governing power itself.

Blondel (1973, pp. 142–4) suggests that there are four main variables affecting the propensity of a military organization to intervene in the political process. First, there is the degree to which the military is isolated from the rest of society. The greater the isolation the greater the military's aversion to civilian ways of life is likely to be and its willingness to attempt to supplant them. Clearly, in modern times a volunteer army is likely to be more isolated than a conscript army, and any process of 'professionalization' is likely to remove the norms and values of soldiers further from their civilian origins. Contemporary attempts by the military in liberal democracies to see itself as professionalized, like similar movements among police forces, may be explained by the military's desire, on the one hand, to avoid attacks on its competence or political attitudes and, on the other, to provide a basis from which to claim superiority for its expert views on policy matters from weapons procurement to military strategy.

Second, there is the question of the legitimacy of the political process. Military involvement is likely to increase as legitimacy decreases. The political legitimacy of military regimes is frequently suspect and originates in their exclusiveness and monopoly of force. Having achieved power in certain situations, the military has great difficulty in maintaining it without the support of other important groups in society. Support can be coerced for only so long, after which an acceptable degree of legitimacy must be developed in some form. Thus the question of legitimacy is crucial, and particularly the levels of support enjoyed by the civil political process as a whole compared with those enjoyed by the military.

Third, there is the question of the military's political attitude. The military is frequently characterized as conservative if not reactionary, and certainly on a majority of occasions it is seen to support stability and the status quo. To the extent that it benefits from the status quo, this is hardly surprising. There are cases, however, where the military has seen itself as a force for modernization, particularly in societies perceived to be ruled by traditional elites, and where the military may become imbued with the norms of Western processes of industrialization to the extent that it seeks to impose them on society.

Fourth, there is the question of the political, social and economic complexity of a society. As a general rule, the more complex a society becomes the less often military intervention is likely to occur. In other words, there have been more military coups in underdeveloped than in developed countries. This may be so, but the employment of the ultimate form of intervention – the coup – as the yardstick may be rather misleading. It would be more helpful to consider various types of intervention, and the contexts in which they are most likely to occur. For example, military pressure-group activity and other involvement in policy-making in liberal democracies may well seem less drastic than mounting a coup, but the implications of less overt forms of military intervention may sometimes be almost as great as a coup for the political process.

In the United States the economic impact of the size of the post-war military establishment and budget has been tremendous. The Defense Department employs nearly 80 per cent of the civilian and military personnel who work for the federal government and, in 1978, was paying over 5 million incomes to military personnel and civilian employees past and present. Many of the largest United States corporations, such as Boeing, depend almost entirely for their existence on federal military contracts. In other words, the military budget in the United States is of enormous significance for any government's economic policy and this gives the military tremendous leverage in terms of obtaining new weapons in an age of high technology, especially in conjunction with fears of the enemy's growing strength. It has been argued that the American economy is dependent for its survival on the maintenance of high levels of military spending. Whether or not this is so, the importance of the military is clear and so is the reason for its close consultation on policy for both strategic and economic reasons. For C. Wright Mills, the dominant group among the three that made up the 'power elite' which, he argued, dominated the American political process after the Second World War was that of the new military leaders (Mills, 1956, pp. 198–224). These 'warlords' were the new leaders who, with the 'corporate rich' and the 'political directorate', provided the post-war American power elite. How this structure will react to the end of the Cold War remains unclear.

If the centrality of the military is clear in the relatively open policy-making process of the United States, it is less so in Britain and the old Soviet Union (and now Russia), whose continued high spending levels on the military make it clear that the military will be no less active if and when it perceives its interests threatened. Certainly, in the Soviet Union the military-industrial complex (that is the massive defence industry and military organization) was a major opponent of many of the reforms of *perestroika*. The army, in particular, was very aggrieved by the failure of the war in Afghanistan and the wholesale withdrawal from Eastern Europe. In addition, it found itself not only with inadequate facilities and accommodation at home but also facing strong public criticism, which it was unused to. Refusal to do military service was rife, especially among non-Russian nationalities. The Defence Chief, Dimitri Yazov, and others connected with the military-industrial complex were, not surprisingly, heavily involved in the coup attempt.

In addition to the role of the military in the policy-making process, we should also consider its importance as an executor of policy. Obviously, this occurs mainly in times of war between nations, but the military is also sometimes employed in the maintenance of public order within nations. In general, this role is usually performed by the police or, failing that, by some third force such as the United States National Guard or the French CRS. However, there have been situations in which troops have been used, the most frequent being industrial disputes and antistate violence beyond the powers of the police to control. Troops have been used fairly regularly in Britain in the course of industrial disputes, in the years before 1914, in the General Strike of 1926 and, more recently, during the Glasgow dustmen's strike in April 1975 and the firemen's strike in the winter of 1977–8. It is not clear that military involvement in such disputes is always undertaken willingly and, indeed, the military's own attitude in any given situation may crucially affect the ability of the government to pursue its policy. For example, in May 1974 the Protestant Ulster Workers' Council called a successful strike in protest at the Sunningdale proposals for power-sharing between Catholics and Protestants in Northern Ireland. A major reason for its success was the extreme reluctance of the army to run the power stations, largely because it did not believe that it could break the strike (Ackroyd et al., 1977, pp. 64–6). With the recent growth of political violence directed against the state in the United Kingdom and elsewhere, the military has assumed greater prominence as enforcer of public order. The police is still seen as the first line of defence, but in recent years there has been increased co-operation between the police and the military, as in the joint exercises conducted at Heathrow in preparation for possible terrorist incidents. There has also been direct military involvement, in Northern Ireland since 1969 and in London in 1980 with the spectacular lifting of the siege at the Iranian embassy by the Special Air Service (SAS).

The military in the Soviet Union tended to be shrouded in even more secrecy than most other Soviet institutions. Like the military in other countries, it was of political importance because of extremely heavy defence expenditure and also because, in the last resort, the survival of the regime depended on its loyalty, for it had control of the nation's weaponry. Clearly, the military could and did act as a very powerful interest group and had the support of the heavy industrial interest, which was dependent on the manufacture of armaments. There were various features of the role of the military in Soviet politics that are striking to the Western observer. One was its involvement in politics in a direct sense which would be frowned on in the West. Most military personnel were members of the CPSU or Komsomol, and military figures appeared at high levels in party organizations. In this sense, the military was seen as simply part of the nation's organizational structure under party control and direction, like everyone else. There was evidence to suggest that party (civilian) control was real in policy decisions and appointments, in spite of the significant influence the military must have had. The Ministry of Defence was a typical government ministry in the Soviet Union, except that it was much larger than most. Another striking feature was the existence of the Main Political Administration which was responsible for the political education and consciousness of the military. Political officers would be attached to units who worked in close co-operation with line officers. Evidence does not suggest much tension between them, and the line officers invariably had higher status (and usually higher rank) than the political officers. Thus there was much more overt politico-military co-operation and integration in the Soviet Union than in the West. The military did not always get its own way but it was in a strong position. It had expertise, powerful allies in the heavy-industry complex and could play on powerful emotions and fears within the Soviet Union.

The Gorbachev reforms caused much tension in the military over the question of internal order and security. Another feature of the Soviet situation unusual from a Western point of view was that, in addition to the Soviet army, both the Interior Ministry and the KGB maintained armed troops, which were most likely to be used in maintaining internal law and order. The use of the Soviet army for this purpose (for example in the Nagorno-Karabakh region of Azerbaijan) gave rise to much dissatisfaction among the troops themselves, who did not see action against Soviet citizens as part of their role. At first, there was an attempt to maintain the unity of the Soviet army after the collapse of the Soviet Union, but differences between the republics (especially

Russia and Ukraine) in the Commonwealth of Independent States has meant that only nuclear weapons remain under joint control. The future defence and security arrangements for the region are uncertain (Smith, 1992, pp. 318–23).

## Conclusion

In this chapter we have been concerned with the sharp end of the political process – with the institutions on which rests the job of maintaining order and of enforcing the decisions of the political process, however reached, on any citizens or foreign persons who do not voluntarily accept them. This may seem a strange way of looking at it, since we are used to viewing the police and the military as our protectors; but we cannot avoid the conclusion that, ultimately, the police and the military maintain sufficient force to implement the decisions of the state.

Of course, both police and military prefer to achieve their ends without the use of coercion, and some succeed in this far more than others. Thus, the policing of a community by means of a consensus is always easier and therefore more desirable than a policy of coercion, which relies simply on greater strength. But this is where important questions are raised concerning the police in society. How is the force organized and how extensive is its discretionary power? Given that there is no universal consensus on the ideal police – community relationship, what sort of policing policies does a community need, and who is to decide this? Then there is probably the thorniest problem of all: does the community trust in the professionalism of the police or does it insist on some greater say in its actions?

One sort of policing which, almost by definition, is likely to remain beyond any form of democratic control is that concerned with the survival of the state itself. Every state – whether it is liberal democratic or socialist – employs some form of political police whose sole job is to protect the state against its 'enemies'. Who are defined as enemies and what action is taken against them varies from country to country and from time to time.

With regard to the military and the political process, we should ask, not when it intervenes, but rather how it intervenes, since all military organizations can be observed to intervene in politics at some point. What is important is whether the intervention is in support of or against the state, how it is manifested and what its impact is. In Britain, the United States and the old Soviet Union the most significant intervention has been relatively undramatic but highly significant in terms of its impact on the economic systems of all three countries, not to mention its impact on international politics, which is discussed in part IV. If history is any guide, then future military involvement in the domestic politics of these countries will depend to a large extent on their economic fortunes and the ability of police and other paramilitary forces to maintain order.

## Questions for Discussion

1   What is meant by political control of the police in a liberal democracy?
2   Does the 'political police' defend or threaten democracy?
3   Why does the military often intervene in some political systems and not in others?

## Further Reading

Ball, A.R. (1988), *Modern Politics and Government*, 4th edn. Basingstoke, Macmillan, ch. 12.

Borcke, A. von (1990), The KGB and *perestroika*. In Federal Institute for Soviet and International Studies, Cologne (ed.), *The Soviet Union, 1987–1989: Perestroika in Crisis?*. London, Longman, pp. 61–6.

Budge, I. and D. McKay (1988), *The Changing British Political System: Into the 1990s*, 2nd edn. London, Longman, pp. 184–98.

Burch, M., J. Gardner and D. Jaenicke (eds) (1985), *Three Political Systems: A Reader in British, American and Soviet Politics*. Manchester, Manchester University Press, chs 2.5 and 2.6.

Gill, P. (1993), *Policing Politics*. London, Frank Cass, chs 1, 2 and 7.

Poveda, T.G. (1990), *Lawlessness and Reform*. Pacific Grove, Brooks/Cole, chs 1 and 11.

Reiner, R. (1992), *The Politics of the Police*, 2nd edn. Hemel Hempstead, Harvester Wheatsheaf, chs 6 and 7.

Robertson, G. (1989), *Freedom, the Individual and the Law*, 6th edn. Harmondsworth, Penguin, chs 1 and 2.

Sakwa, R. (1989), *Soviet Politics: An Introduction*. London, Routledge, pp. 113–20.

Smith, G.B. (1992), *Soviet Politics: Struggling with Change*, 2nd edn. Basingstoke, Macmillan, pp. 318–23.

# Part IV

## Supranational and Subnational Politics

# 20

# Global Politics (1): Approaches to Analysis

## Introduction

Politics at the global level has traditionally been regarded as separate from, and only intermittently of concern to, the domestic politics of states. Unless war threatened, or there was a dramatic increase in the price of petrol, the national level remained the principal focus of political attention for both public and elites. While this remains largely true, there is growing awareness, not confined to elite groups, that decision-makers at the national level are unable to solve pressing domestic problems. This is particularly the case in relation to economic policy. The domestic economies of the CIS, Great Britain and the United States are, to differing degrees, experiencing problems whose solution is widely acknowledged to lie beyond national competence.

Environmental issues, too, promote public awareness of the need for global solutions, both to the immediate dangers arising from atmospheric ozone depletion and to the longer-term threats associated with global warming. The often passionate commitment of small children to the protection of distant forests attests to the widespread awareness of the global scope of this issue. Less evident, however, is extensive consciousness of its essentially political nature, involving conflict over control of scarce resources between North and South, that is between affluent and less developed regions of the world.

The issue of the tropical rain forests illustrates some of the central debates of global politics today. The relationship between the sources of pollution, primarily in affluent, developed regions, and the 'sinks' for absorption of pollutants, provided by the rain forests, demonstrates essential interconnections – between disparate regions and between domestic and global issues. It also highlights concerns about the continuing ability of individual nation-states, however affluent or powerful they may be, to provide for the well-being of their citizens.

Despite the importance of economic and environmental issues, however, the continuing prominence of military security cannot be denied. For many political scientists involved in the study of global politics, issues of peace and war remain the principal focus of analysis, a priority with which the peoples of war-torn former Yugoslavia or the post-Soviet Caucasus may well concur.

These debates are associated with different approaches to the analysis of global politics. As in the study of domestic politics, political scientists use models as aids to understanding. Indeed, the vast scope and complexity of politics at the global level makes the use of models essential. Nevertheless, the degree of abstraction required in their formulation, in order to reduce the global to the manageable, leaves considerable scope for criticism. Criticism and debate are to be welcomed, however, and should not be confined to academic circles. Perhaps even more than is usual in the social sciences, theory is closely related to practice. The worldview of politicians, who address the same complex issues, shares many common features with the models developed by political scientists. Whether we choose to focus on military security or protection of the environment, the policy relevance of our research is evident.

In order to give an indication of the range of models applied to global politics, the two dominant approaches to analysis will be outlined and a critique of each advanced. These approaches, political realism and liberal pluralism, will be examined in relation to the following four questions about the nature of global politics:

1 Should nation-states be regarded as the principal actors in the global political system?
2 To what extent can global politics be separated from domestic politics?
3 How can order be maintained in the global political system?
4 Are issues of war and peace the central concerns of global politics?

## Political Realism

Political realism is the oldest, and potentially the most influential, approach to global politics, having its origins in the wars between the city-states of ancient Greece and claiming among its antecedents the writings of Machiavelli and Thomas Hobbes. Philosophically, realism is related to conservatism, and is thus founded on a pessimistic view of human nature and of the potential for social progress. Indeed, the term 'realism' reflects its self-proclaimed basis of historical 'reality', which is seen as demonstrating the inevitability of conflict between states. Above all else, realism privileges the role of the state, both as central actor and as the source of virtue.

In domestic society the authority of the state guarantees order in the face of the human potential for evil. The supreme jurisdiction, or sovereignty, of the state means that no higher authority can exist. Hence, for realists, global politics essentially comprises the interaction of sovereign states in a situation of anarchy – the global system approximating the 'state of nature' of the Hobbesian parable. The state has a duty to protect its citizens from external enemies, and this can best be achieved by maximizing its power *vis-à-vis* other states. Indeed, this is the principal imperative of state action and should be energetically yet pragmatically pursued, based on rational calculation of the policies most likely to enhance or protect power and prestige internationally. This conduct is considered to be common to all states, irrespective of their domestic political arrangements. Foreign policy is, or should be, entirely distinct from the domestic political process – a distinction justifying, in practice, particularly high levels of secrecy concerning its conduct. The moral or ideological considerations that inform domestic politics provide an inappropriate basis for action, whether in relation to Vietnam in the 1960s and 1970s or Yugoslavia in the 1990s – particularly when a positive outcome in terms of power and prestige cannot be assured. Conversely, British action over the Falkland Islands in 1982 was, for realists, very much a matter of international prestige, while the Gulf War of 1991 involved control of oil resources essential to the security of the participants.

Reduced to its simplest form, political realism has been characterized as the 'billiard ball' model. This analogy represents the global political system as a vast billiard-table on which the actors, the nation-states, are the billiard-balls: self-contained sealed units whose interaction is limited to superficial clashes. This representation, while pleasingly graphic, and certainly economical, requires elaboration if the central concepts of realism are to be understood. Two of these – the concepts of state power and national security – are briefly examined here.

Despite the centrality of state power to the realist model, its conceptualization is surprisingly unsophisticated. One of the most influential twentieth-century exponents of realism, Hans J. Morgenthau, provides extensive discussion of the 'elements of state power', cautioning against the reduction of power to a single factor. Nevertheless, Morgenthau's various 'elements' essentially comprise the physical and psychological resources deemed necessary to the successful prosecution of warfare (Morgenthau, 1978). For realists, power is ultimately reducible to coercion. The realist view of power has been particularly influential in the United States among theorists and foreign-policy practitioners alike. Hence the confusion evident in situations where superior military might has little utility – the economic challenge of Japan, the European Community's recalcitrance in negotiations over the General Agreement on Tariffs and Trade (GATT) or attempts to agree global policy on environmental issues at the June 1992 Earth Summit.

The concept of power is closely related, in realist analysis, to the concept of national security. Here the separation of domestic and foreign policy allows realists to avoid consideration of conflicts arising from a lack of compatibility between state and nation, that is a people identified with a territory seeking political self-determination. For realists, nation and state are deemed to be synonymous, and national security is a matter of protecting the state's core values from the depredations of other states. In a situation of international anarchy, constant war is avoided by maintenance of a balance of power, based on a system of military alliances whose purpose is to prevent the domination of a single-power. Contemporary realists, however, have countenanced single-power domination, or hegemony, by the United States, whose role, when appropriately exercised, is to maintain global stability.

States cannot entirely depend on such measures, however, and must make provision for their own defence. Herein lies a central dilemma. Investment in the military by a state enhances its security only at the expense of its neighbours. According to the conflictual, realist world-view, national security is unattainable.

This dilemma has been exacerbated as a result of the development of thermonuclear weapons and other weapons of mass destruction and is associated with the nuclear arms race between the Soviet Union and the United States during the Cold War from the 1940s to the 1980s. Since the end of the Cold War, there have been attempts to reassess the concept of national security, for example by Barry Buzan, whose analysis addresses the contradictions frequently existing between state security and the security of individuals and groups within the state. In addition, he seeks to broaden the notion of threat to encompass political, economic and environmental, as well as military, threats (Buzan, 1991). While this is an interesting and productive attempt to reformulate realist conceptualizations, it does not answer fundamental criticisms originating outside the realist tradition.

## The Feminist Critique of Realism

While realism is criticized from a number of perspectives, and feminist theorists are critical of all the traditional approaches to global politics, the feminist critique of realism is particularly challenging. The Hobbesian analogy is considered to be partial and gender-biased. Just as women are excluded from the 'state of nature', so they are ignored by the precepts of political realism. Thus the conflictual, state-centric model, with its privileging of military security issues, is an essentially masculine representation, in which the separation of domestic and global politics precludes acknowledgement of the social processes constitutive of gender divisions, analysis of which is essential to understanding the role of the state – in particular its military capacity. An interesting discussion of the social manipulations of gender in the promotion of military values is provided by Cynthia Enloe (1988).

The realist privileging of the military is challenged both in the approach to security and in the conceptualization of state power. Thus the notion of security requires reformulation in terms of satisfaction of human needs: weapons cannot meet the threat of starvation. The realist approach to power, in terms of coercion or domination, is essentially masculine. Female conceptualizations of power emphasize its co-operative aspects in terms of alliance-building and problem-solving – that is power as 'energy, capacity, potential . . . the ability to act in concert' (Tickner, 1991).

Thus gender bias is built into the principles of realism, providing a partial and distorted world-view and having considerable implications for the practice of politics at the global level. Here it is appropriate to note the singular absence of women from foreign-policy elites, the higher ranks of the military and senior positions within international organizations such as the United Nations. At the same time, the 'high politics' focus of realist analysis excludes issues that fundamentally, and often disproportionately, affect women's lives. These include global inequality, human-rights abuses and environmental degradation.

## Liberal Pluralism

Unlike realism, liberal pluralism is not based on a single set of ideas developed over time, but embraces a variety of approaches. The first of these is idealism. Idealism has its roots in the writings of the eighteenth-century philosopher Immanuel Kant, who saw in universal adherence to the rule of law the possibility of global peace. Contemporary idealism, however, dates from the period following the First World War when, partly as a reaction to the horrors of the war, it briefly achieved prominence as an approach to global politics, influencing academics and politicians. The American President Woodrow Wilson was a prominent exponent of idealism.

The establishment and maintenance of peace was the primary aim of idealists, and this was to be achieved through the spread of liberal democracy and through international law, administered by a newly created international organization, the League of Nations. The league was charged also with responsibility for collective security, so that individual states could embark on a programme of disarmament. Idealism, then, is an optimistic approach, based on belief in the essential rationality of human nature and the potential for progress. It is also a liberal view, emphasizing the significance of individual participation to the conduct of global politics, and hence the links between domestic and global systems. Thus wars result from authoritarian government, while the peaceful conduct of foreign affairs is a function of liberal democracy – for if the people are properly informed on foreign-policy issues they will choose peace over war. The liberalism of idealists extended also to economic policy. States should abandon national economic protectionism in favour of international free trade, for unimpeded operation of the market, it was claimed, was the key to global prosperity and hence conducive to peace.

Idealism was deeply discredited by the failure to prevent the outbreak of the Second World War. The lack of military prepared-ness of the European democracies and the policy of appeasement left a legacy which has frequently been invoked – for example following Iraq's invasion of Kuwait in August 1990. Neverthe-less, the ending of the Cold War gave new impetus to idealism. The rhetoric of politicians was littered with idealistic assump-tions, from the 'new thinking' of President Gorbachev to Prime Minister Margaret Thatcher's assertion that 'democracies don't go to war with each other'. Meanwhile, policy-orientated aca-demics in the United States began to discuss 'Idealpolitik' on the grounds that idealism had become realistic (Kober, 1990).

While the Cold War period was dominated by realism, liberal approaches continued to be developed. The 'world society' per-spective of John Burton built on the rationalist assumptions of idealism to develop a highly pluralistic model of the global polit-ical system. The world-society model emphasized the linkages between vast numbers of international and transnational actors. It included religious and social movements (like the Catholic Church and the international women's movement), large business corporations (like Coca-Cola, Ford, McDonald's), communica-tions and media links, and even individuals holidaying abroad. The complex pattern of linkages that emerged was labelled by Burton the 'cobweb model'. This model de-emphasized geo-graphical boundaries in general, and the role of the state in particu-lar, and was deliberately juxtaposed against the realist billiard-ball model (Burton, 1972).

While it has the virtue of indicating vast new areas worthy of study, this model suffers from a failure to identify the relative significance of its many components. The problem is, to some extent, addressed by models of interdependence. Models of inter-dependence focus on interstate relations but challenge the realist view of states as independent actors. Interdependence refers to the situation of mutual vulnerability that exists between states (and societies) linked by complex economic and other ties. The vagaries of currency exchange rates provide a good example of interdependence – given the tendency for changes in value of the American dollar or the German mark to provoke a sterling crisis in Great Britain. A useful feature of models of interdependence is their ability to encompass new forms of co-operation between states, such as the development of the European Community. Here the 'complex interdependence' model of Keohane and Nye (1977) is particularly useful. Complex interdependence has the following three principal characteristics:

1   States and societies are linked by multiple channels of communication, both governmental and non-governmental.
2   The agenda of interstate relations is increasingly complex and is not necessarily dominated by security issues. According to circumstances, other issues, from agricultural policy to international crime, may predominate.
3   In conditions of complex interdependence, military force will have no utility.

## The Structuralist Critique of Liberal Pluralism

As with the realist model, it is possible to identify a number of criticisms of liberal pluralism. This model, too, is silent on gender issues, although it leaves more space for their inclusion. Perhaps the most fundamental critique is that provided by theorists emphasizing the global structure of economic and political power. While realists see liberal pluralism as naive in de-emphasizing the role of military might, neo-Marxists and dependency theorists regard it as insidious in obscuring the role of economic power. For them, international free trade and reliance on market mechanisms for resource allocation are not conducive to global prosperity, as liberals claim, but lead to increased economic inequality. Moreover, in their view, this inequality is not random, but is structured by the needs of international capital.

Dependency theory provides a 'Southern perspective' which tends to be overlooked in other theoretical explanations. It employs a core–periphery model which emphasizes the persistence of ties of domination and dependence linking the developed, capitalist states (the core) and their former colonies (the periphery). These ties have had the effect, not only of ensuring that the peripheral economies serve the needs of the core – principally through provision of cheap raw materials – but also of impeding and distorting political, social and cultural developments at the periphery. Hence dependence, not interdependence, characterizes the relationship of the South to the North. In recent years, however, there has been rapid economic development in parts of the South, notably in South-East Asia, while core economies, including those of the United States and Great Britain, have suffered recession. Increasingly, the core–periphery model fails to capture the diversity, in terms of economic performance, of both the periphery and the core. Consequently, it has largely been supplanted by neo-Marxist analysis.

Neo-Marxists emphasize the globalization of capitalist production and the associated creation of a global division of labour. This is a result of the operations of huge, transnational (that is operating across national boundaries) business corporations, the scale and scope of whose organization is such that they are able to transcend or defy the jurisdiction of states. According to this perspective, interdependence between states is less significant than the dependence of all states, to a greater or lesser extent, on the investment decisions of transnational capital. In Great Britain, for example, the future production strategies of the Ford Motor Company are a matter of national concern.

## Conclusion

This chapter has examined a variety of approaches to analysing global politics, in order to demonstrate the diversity of approaches to analysis and to highlight some of their limitations. The complexity and scope of the subject-matter makes such limitations inevitable but they are, nevertheless, significant, because of the close links between theory and policy and the salience of the issues under discussion. Questions of peace and war, global distributive justice, gender and racial inequality, and environmental degradation concern us all. We need to understand the assumptions and models that inform the world-view of those, from politicians to United Nations officials, who attempt to address them.

Returning to the four questions posed in the introduction to this chapter, the answers provided by the two dominant models of global politics are summarized as follows:

|  | *Realism* | *Liberal pluralism* |
| --- | --- | --- |
| Principal actors | States, foreign-policy elites | Plurality of actors: states, social movements, business corporations, international organizations |

| Relationship between global and domestic politics | Separate | Linked |
|---|---|---|
| Source of order | Balance of power, hegemony | Actors' mutual interest in co-operation |
| Agenda of global politics | High politics, especially security issues | Low politics, welfare issues as well as high-politics issues |

In assessing the relative merits of realist and liberal pluralist analyses, the criticisms of feminists and neo-Marxists should not be overlooked, since they highlight important omissions. They also remind us that models are associated with ideologies, and hence with interests and, ultimately, with the exercise of power.

## Questions for Discussion

1　Does the ending of the Cold War cast doubt on the continuing relevance of the realist perspective?
2　How may inclusion of gender analysis affect the subject-matter of global politics?
3　Is it true that liberal democracies 'don't go to war with one another'? Can you give reasons for your answer?
4　How widely can the concept of interdependence be applied? Does it have relevance beyond the interaction of developed capitalist states?

## Further Reading

Burton, J.W. (1972), *World Society*. Cambridge, Cambridge University Press.

Buzan, B. (1991), *People, States and Fear: An Agenda for International Security Studies in the Post-Cold War Era*. Hemel Hempstead, Harvester Wheatsheaf.

Enloe, C. (1988), *Does Khaki Become You? The Militarization of Women's Lives*. London, Pandora.

Hoogveld, A.M.M. (1982), *The Third World in Global Development*. London, Macmillan.

Keohane, R.O. and J.S. Nye (1977), *Power and Interdependence: World Politics in Transition*. Boston, Little, Brown, chs 1 and 2.

Kober, S. (1990), Idealpolitik. *Foreign Policy*, 79, pp. 3–24.

Morgenthau, H.J. (1978), *Politics among Nations: The Struggle for Power and Peace*, 5th edn. New York, Knopf, ch. 3.

Tickner, J.A. (1991), Hans Morgenthau's principles of political realism: a feminist reformulation. In R. Grant and K. Newland (eds), *Gender and International Relations*. Buckingham, Open University Press, pp. 27–40.

# 21

# Global Politics (2): Processes of Change

## Introduction

Political scientists attempting to understand and analyse the processes of change in global politics in the post-Cold War era are having to reassess the utility of conceptual frameworks developed in the past. In particular, we need to assess the relevance of realism and liberal pluralism (outlined in chapter 20) to three key processes identifiable in contemporary global politics – globalization, integration and fragmentation. Globalization is the overarching process, linked in different ways to both integration and fragmentation. All three have different implications for the central question addressed by this chapter: to what extent will the nation-state remain the principal unit of political organization and focus of allegiance in the twenty-first century?

Analysis of contemporary processes, however, necessitates consideration of the past, in particular the Cold War era. The end of the Second World War heralded major changes in the conduct of politics at the global level. Much of the post-war period was dominated by two highly significant sets of events, the Cold War between East and West and the dissolution of the European colonial empires. To a lesser extent, the creation and development of the European Community generated considerable interest as a unique experiment in regional economic and political integration. Nevertheless, the defining characteristic of this period was undoubtedly the Cold War. In the early post-war years the consolidation of Soviet power in Eastern Europe stimulated fears of communist expansion and generated support, in the United States, for the maintenance of a high level of military preparedness.

Despite the significance of the nuclear arms race, the mutual hostility and rivalry that developed between the superpowers (the Soviet Union and the United States) and their allies was not primarily a military conflict, but was founded on the mutual incompatibility of socialist and capitalist economic systems. The Cold War was also a global phenomenon, involving the consolidation of military alliances in Europe – NATO and the Warsaw Treaty Organization (WTO) – and attempts by the superpowers to influence the policies, and gain the allegiance of, states world-wide.

The Cold War was thus complex and multifaceted. Avoiding direct superpower military confrontation, it was fought through intense propaganda, which deeply penetrated the domestic societies of both the United States and the Soviet Union, and through proxy wars in South-East Asia, Central and South America, and Afghanistan.

Decolonization was associated with independence movements invoking strongly nationalistic, anti-imperialist sentiments, and the subsequent creation of a number of new, formally sovereign and independent states. The rapid increase in the number and diversity of states has had long-term consequences for global politics. Membership of the United Nations has more than quadrupled since 1945, greatly complicating international negotiations, while a fundamental conflict of interest between developed and less developed states introduced a North–South dimension to global politics.

The coincidence of the decolonization process with the development of Cold War antagonism ensured, however, that the immediate impact was experienced primarily in terms of superpower competition for influence in the newly independent states. Frequently, this competition involved provision of military equipment to potential allies – an aspect of Cold War rivalry that has contributed to conflict in Ethiopia, Somalia and the Middle East. The creation of the Non-Aligned Movement in 1961 represented an attempt to co-ordinate the responses of less powerful states to superpower pressure through the establishment of a 'third way' – an independent posture aligned to neither the capitalist West nor the communist East. Together with the Group of Seventy-seven (G-77) economically less developed states (now numbering more than 120), the non-aligned lobby continues to promote the interests of its members at international forums, as was demonstrated at the June 1992 Earth Summit in Brazil.

Thus this period saw the division of the global system into

three 'worlds': the first world of developed capitalist states; the communist bloc, or second world; and the less developed third-world states of the southern hemisphere. The image of three distinct worlds dominated thinking about global politics for almost forty years (see chapter 7). Such a conflictual, yet relatively stable, world-view has been shattered by events since the late 1980s. The end of the Cold War has invalidated the three-world image, although 'third-worldism' retains relevance as an ideological position supportive of third-world interests. Of more immediate significance to the practice of global politics, however, was that the end of the three-world view also heralded the end of the duopoly of superpower domination of the global system.

Initial optimism that the end of the Cold War would lead to a more harmonious world order was rapidly dissipated. Global politics now appears less ordered, the future more uncertain (at least from a European perspective) than during the years of Cold War confrontation. Nevertheless, the processes identified at the start of this chapter – globalization, integration and fragmentation – are longer-term phenomena. These processes must be analysed if we are to gain understanding of global politics and to assess the relationship between global and domestic political systems.

## Globalization

The concept of globalization has been the subject of considerable debate (for example Luard, 1990; McGrew, Lewis et al., 1992). Globalization refers to the increasingly global scope of a range of phenomena and issues, some aspects of which have already been discussed above. The logic of the globalization thesis suggests a consequential reduction in the autonomy of individual states – nation-states will become increasingly ineffective in dealing with issues affecting the welfare of their citizens, and therefore their significance as separate political organizations will decline.

Decolonization was associated with the spread of ideologies of national self-determination and ultimately the near-universality of the sovereign nation-state. More recently, the ending of the Cold War and the introduction of measures of democratization in Russia, Eastern Europe and elsewhere has generated debate about the possible spread of liberal democratic forms of government (for example Held, 1992). The Cold War itself was a globalizing influence. The effects of superpower rivalry and associated ideological conflict were global in scope, while penetrating deeply into domestic societies and essentially linking domestic political issues with global processes. Today, external links with, and influences on, domestic societies are extensive, although unevenly distributed within and between states. While such links proliferate in affluent countries, the global scope of drugs-related crime, political violence and AIDS reminds us that poor countries are far from immune.

Technological developments have been essential to the growth of transnational links, especially in the areas of transport and communications. Individuals as well as groups, business corporations and government officials have access to high-speed travel, micro-technology and fax machines, and almost instant information about events world-wide via the news media. While problems of partiality and bias in news-reporting are, rightly, matters of concern, various issues that have attracted Western media attention have excited public opinion in the United States and Europe to the extent that governments have been obliged to respond. Recent examples include the plight of the Iraqi Kurds at the end of the Gulf War and the suffering of civilians in Bosnia-Hercegovina. The obverse of this phenomenon is, of course, the global influence of the technologically advanced Western news media – and hence of Western concerns, representations and ideas. The dissemination of ideas, particularly Western ideas, is a central aspect of globalization. Of great significance has been the influence of ideologies of modernization, both liberal and Marxist, which essentially equate progress with Western conceptions of social, political and economic development. Thus modernization implies commercialization of agricultural production, urbanization, industrialization and the development of political institutions based on secular, rational-legal authority.

Ideologies of modernization are divisive, ascribing values to 'development' and 'underdevelopment' of societies. They are also both gender- and culturally biased, representing an essentially male Western view of progress which has marginalized women and disregarded their interests. Development agencies, for example, have persistently involved men in agricultural-development projects in regions, particularly in Africa, where farming is the responsibility of women. The resulting harm, both to the status of women and to the production of food, is well documented (Sontheimer (ed.), 1991).

Liberal approaches to modernization are closely linked to economic globalization. The 'global' economy is essentially capitalist, but is not yet fully global in scope. The international economic institutions established after the Second World War (GATT, the International Monetary Fund (IMF) and the World Bank) were based on liberal premises unacceptable to the Soviet bloc, which remained, until recently, economically almost completely isolated. As this isolation ends the possibility arises of a fully global economy.

Economic globalization implies a great deal more than the development of extensive trade links. It implies the existence of a unified global economy that has a dynamic beyond simply the interaction of separate domestic economies. The principal agents of economic globalization are transnational business corporations (TNCs). Business corporations such as Unilever, ICI and Shell were operating transnationally in the nineteenth century, but their proliferation and freedom of operation has been greatly facilitated, since the Second World War, by technological development. Much discussion of the influence of TNCs has focused on their size, both in terms of the scale and scope of their operations and the fact that the turnover of the largest, notably the giant oil corporations, exceeds the gross national product of all but the richest states. The mobility of vast sums of transnational capital means that the investment strategies of TNCs are crucial to, but largely beyond the control of, domestic economic policy, and hence that state autonomy is reduced. While there are notorious cases of overt interference in domestic politics by TNCs – for example the role of ITT in the overthrow of President Allende of Chile in 1973 – fear of disinvestment is a more pervasive influence on government policy.

Perhaps even more significant for the globalization thesis have been changes in the operational strategy of many of the larger TNCs, involving both production and exchange. Production has been increasingly globalized, with processes located where it is most advantageous in terms of profit maximization. This has resulted in regional specialization and, effectively, the creation of a global division of labour. Examples of this include the separation of production and assembly in the motor industry and the location of low-technology, labour-intensive manufacturing processes in regions where labour is cheap and non-unionized (and frequently female). Goods and services produced according to global strategies now comprise more than half the total output, while by 1985 between a quarter and half of world trade (varying according to economic sector) was intrafirm, that is between buyer and seller within a single enterprise (Strange, 1991). Clearly, the operations of TNCs contribute significantly to globalization and also reduce the autonomy of states in terms of economic policy. Nevertheless, the relations between states and firms is complex and varied. While even the richest states are anxious to attract or retain TNC investment, they are more likely to be successful in imposing conditions on their operations than less developed states. The poorest states, particularly in sub-Saharan Africa, attract little TNC investment and are linked only tenuously to the global economy.

A further set of issues contributing significantly to globalization concerns the environment. Environmental degradation, whether resulting from pollution or from overuse of natural resources, does not respect the boundaries of states. The 1986 Chernobyl nuclear disaster in Ukraine provides a dramatic example of the transboundary impact of pollution, seriously affecting human and animal population over a wide area. The proliferation of disputes over scarce water resources, particularly between states bordering the Nile, Euphrates and Jordan rivers, attests to the impact of resource depletion, as does the relationship between deforestation and desertification. Despite their transboundary effects, however, these problems are not necessarily global in impact, although they may ultimately require global solutions. Nevertheless, two environmental issues are clearly global in scope – ozone depletion and climate change.

Depletion of the stratospheric ozone layer through the accumulation of chloro-fluorocarbons (CFCs), halons and a variety of other substances leaves the earth's surface increasingly exposed to harmful radiation from the sun. The discovery of a seasonal ozone 'hole' over the Antarctic in 1985 gave urgency to this issue, leading to a series of international agreements restricting the emission of ozone-depleting substances. The ozone-negotiations, conducted under the aegis of the United Nations Environment Programme (UNEP), marked an important stage in the globalization of issues and of policy-making. It involved not only states but also TNCs and environment pressure groups. Additionally, although production of ozone-depleting substances was largely confined to Northern, developed states, the essentially global nature of the issue was recognized by the inclusion of special provisions and (modest) funding to assist non-producers in the South to develop safer alternatives to CFCs.

The issues associated with climate change present a much greater, but apparently less immediate, challenge to global management, and the inconclusive outcome of the 1992 Earth Summit suggests that this challenge will not easily be met. There are, as yet, no adequate alternatives to the fossil fuels whose consumption is largely responsible for global warming, while the impact is likely to be delayed and unevenly experienced. Discussion of these issues is also complicated by the link between global warming and deforestation, which reduces the capacity for absorption of excess carbon dioxide. The essentially global scope of this issue is captured by a remark reputed to have been made by the Netherlands Foreign Minister to the Foreign Minister of Brazil: 'If you don't stop cutting down your forests my country will disappear.' The extent of linkage between issue-areas, and the global scope of contemporary problems such as environmental degradation, suggest the need for more effective global management. They demonstrate, too, the limitations of individual state action. Reduction of carbon dioxide emissions in the Netherlands would have little effect in preventing the submergence of that country.

## Integration

Increased co-operation between states has been a significant feature of the post-1945 world order, reflecting the reduced ability of states to act autonomously in the global arena. There has been a proliferation of regional organizations such as the Association of South-East Asian Nations (ASEAN) and the Organization of American States (OAS), economic groupings such as the G-7 (most economically developed countries) and G-77 (less economically developed countries), and military alliances such as NATO. Despite the end of the Cold War, military alliances seem likely to continue in some form – the Gulf War demonstrated the inability even of the United States to fund a medium-scale war unaided, and illustrated, again, the limitations to state autonomy.

While it is significant as a response to globalization, increased co-operation, is not necessarily indicative of integration. Integration implies a process whereby the economies and decision-making procedures of participating states become progressively linked, to the point of fusion, and to the development of institutions whose powers, in transcending those of the individual member states, become supranational. Despite plans for market integration in Latin America and between the United States, Mexico and Canada, it is only in relation to the European Community that integration can properly be discussed at present.

The creation of the European Community was a response to the changed economic and strategic situation of Western Europe after 1945 – the devastation of war, the loss of empire and the apparent threat of the Soviet bloc. European reconstruction, in the face of new global realities, was to involve an 'ever closer union' of its peoples. Great Britain, however, chose initially to pursue closer links with the United States rather than support the European initiative. Since it eventually joined the Community in 1973, Britain has remained an 'awkward partner', supporting completion of the single market but opposing closer political, monetary and social integration (George, 1990).

Despite differences between the member states, the development of the community clearly demonstrates a process of integration. The successful creation of the European Coal and Steel Community in 1951 was followed by formation of the European Economic Community and Euratom in 1957, and the introduction of a customs union and the Common Agricultural Policy in 1968. The early years were, nevertheless, characterized by excessive preoccupation with 'harmonization' – involving standardization of tractor-tyre dimensions and the noise emissions of domestic lawnmowers – and the progress of political integration was limited. Direct elections to the European Parliament added a measure of democratic legitimacy, while creating a significant source of pressure for further integration, but it was not until the passing of the 1987 Single European Act that real impetus was given to the integration process. The Single European Act provided for completion of much of the single-market process by the end of 1992 and introduced cautious moves towards political union. It also generated pressure from the European Parliament, and several member states, for the single market to be accompanied by closer political and monetary union and a more fully developed social policy. Such measures were included in the December 1991 Maastricht draft treaty. Also included were proposals for the development of a common foreign and security policy and, ultimately, common defence. The inclusion of these areas of 'high politics' challenges even the traditional security role of the member states.

The controversy that followed the publication of the Maastricht

Treaty highlighted significant differences between and within member states over the extent to which the process of integration should proceed, and over whether the proposed union rather than individual member states should be the principal location for decision-making in the future. The issues raised are fundamental, casting doubt on the continued existence of member states in their present form. Reactions to the Maastricht Treaty demonstrated that, despite the pressures from above emanating from the processes of globalization and integration, there is continued vitality in the nation-state.

## Fragmentation

Fragmentation is a process involving the disintegration of existing states and the formation of new states in an attempt to produce conformity between the boundaries of peoples and territories – to create 'genuinely' national states. Within the European Community the threats to the nation-state from above are accompanied by disintegrative pressures from below. The reduced autonomy and effectiveness of individual states resulting from globalization has undermined their authority in regions where the claims of minority 'stateless nations' provide an alternative focus for allegiance.

Demands for national self-determination, from Scotland to Catalonia, have been stimulated by the development of the European Community, which has both exacerbated perceptions of distance from the decision-making process and provided a familiar and supportive framework within which the newly independent states could operate. Thus, in Scotland, for example, implementation of the Scottish National Party's policy of 'independence in Europe' would mean that decisions on Scottish affairs, which are increasingly taken in Brussels, would no longer be made in collaboration with British government ministers without direct Scottish representation. Instead, Scotland, in common with other small member states, would be fully represented at all community institutions and have direct access to the Court of Justice.

Nationalist movements within the European Community have not yet succeeded in fragmenting the states within which they operate. Elsewhere, however, the process of fragmentation is advanced. In the Soviet Union and Eastern Europe the ending of the Cold War and the subsequent loss of central government authority have generated support for the claims of ethno-cultural nationalist movements. The disintegration of the Soviet Union, of Yugoslavia and of Czechoslovakia have been the most obvious results, but serious intercommunal tensions are also evident in Bulgaria, Romania and elsewhere.

Unlike the integration process, which threatens the concept of the sovereign state, fragmentation threatens the integrity of existing states but is strongly supportive of the idea of statehood. Fragmentation also opposes the process of globalization: its emphasis on ethnic and cultural particularism, and traditional, religious values reacts against the globalizing, secular ideologies of modernization.

## Conclusion

The ending of the Cold War initiated a period of rapid change, instability and uncertainty in the global political system. It did not, however, initiate the longer-term processes discussed above, although it affected them in different ways – contributing to the globalization of liberal political ideas and economic policies, posing new challenges to the European integration process as the East European states seek to participate therein, and stimulating the process of fragmentation.

How, then, are we to conceptualize the three distinct, yet interrelated, processes apparent in contemporary global politics? To what extent can the traditional models of global politics, outlined in chapter 20, help us to understand these processes? And what are the implications for the future viability of the nation-state as the principal unit of political organization?

Fragmentation is the process most supportive of the concept of sovereign, independent statehood which is central to realist analysis. Nevertheless, the processes of fragmentation are, for realists, internal to states and hence matters of domestic security. The power-politics model conceptualizes rather poorly the fragmentation of large states and the ensuing proliferation of small states.

Integration poses a fundamental challenge to the nation-state and to the traditional models of global politics. The liberal pluralist model of complex interdependence is useful, but fails to capture the dynamism of integration as a process. Failures in this process, however, are explicable in realist terms as the protection of national sovereignty. British policy towards the European Community could be said to involve careful application of realist principles – the pursuit of national self-interest, narrowly defined, through participation in the single market but opting out of the social chapter.

Globalization has been characterized as the overarching global political process. While integration in Europe can be seen as a response to this process, globalization does not necessarily promote co-operation. Its impact is partial and uneven, exacerbating global inequalities and potentially generating conflict. It is associated with the dissemination of Western ideas of progress, and involves a multiplicity of links between societies, across state boundaries, such that the impact of events reverberates globally and the distinction between domestic and foreign policy is blurred. Above all, globalization is a political process, involving issues that demand decision and action at a level higher than the individual nation-state. The development of a global economy dominated by the operation of transnational corporate capital, and the complex issues associated with global environmental change, suggest the need for management at the global level. This necessitates the strengthening of existing international institutions, such as the United Nations, or the creation of new institutions capable of meeting the challenge of globalization.

While liberal pluralist models best conceptualize the globalization process, no model is adequate. The cobweb model highlights the complexity of global interconnections, but globalization involves more than the proliferation of links. Models of interdependence deal with mutual vulnerability between states rather than shared vulnerability to global processes. As the feminist and structuralist critiques remind us, liberal pluralist models also fail adequately to conceptualize political and economic power, and the patterns of inequality that result from its operation. The realist state-centric model may seem least appropriate to analysis of contemporary political processes. Nevertheless, national security issues and the incidence of military conflict remain highly significant. Apart from the agreements on ozone depletion, which reflected the urgency of the issue, there has been little progress towards global management of global issues. The 'great powers', led by the United States (which retains pretensions to superpower status despite serious domestic problems), continue to dominate international institutions, from the Security Council of the United

Nations to the World Bank, and seem unlikely to countenance a change in this situation in the foreseeable future. Recent decisions in Japan and Germany permitting deployment of their armed forces outside their national territories appear to support the realist view that, in the conduct of global politics, economic status must be backed by military capacity.

Each of our models continues to provide some insights, although none is wholly adequate. In practice, a variety of perspectives is likely to be employed in analysis of global politics, although the need for refinement of existing models and development of alternatives is evident. Similarly, the practice of global politics requires reform. States remain important global actors but their struggle to retain independent status precludes solutions to global problems. In the words of the Brundtland Report, *Our Common Future*: 'The earth is one but the world is not. We all depend on one biosphere for sustaining our lives. Yet each community, each country, strives for survival and prosperity with little regard for its impact on others' (World Commission, 1987, p. 27).

## Questions for Discussion

1   Which factors are most likely to limit the spread of liberal democracy following the end of the Cold War?
2   Do the operations of TNCs bring benefits to the communities where they are located?
3   Why may environmental degradation be an issue of particular concern to women?
4   How could the United Nations be reformed to facilitate global management of global problems?

## Further Reading

George, S. (1989), *An Awkward Partner: Britain in the European Community*. Basingstoke, Macmillan.
Held, D. (1992), Democracy: from city-states to a cosmopolitan order. *Political Studies*, 40, pp. 10–39.
Hocking, B. and Smith, M. (1990), *World Politics: An Introduction to International Relations*. Hemel Hempstead, Harvester Wheatsheaf.
Luard, E. (1990), *The Globalization of Politics: The Changed Focus of Political Action in the Modern World*. Basingstoke, Macmillan.
McGrew, A.G., P.G. Lewis et al. (1992), *Global Politics*. Cambridge, Polity.

Sontheimer, S. (ed.) (1991), *Women and the Environment: Crisis and Development in the Third World.* London, Earthscan.

Strange, S. (1991), An eclectic approach. In C.N. Murphy and R. Tooze (eds), *The New International Political Economy.* Boulder, Colo., Lynne Reiner, pp. 33–49.

World Commission on Environment and Development (1987), *Our Common Future* (The Brundtland Report). New York, Oxford University Press.

# 22

# Nationalism, Federalism and Devolution

## Introduction

Most modern nation-states of any size have some form of political or administrative devolution of authority to smaller units of government within the whole. Politically, there is a variety of reasons why decentralization may be desirable or even inevitable. There is a widespread belief that people have a right, in principle, to control their own affairs and that authority and legitimacy are more effectively maintained when they do. This fits in well with the individualistic ideas of liberal democracy and with the communist principle of the withering away of the state. It was important, therefore, for both types of regime at least to pay lip-service to the idea, although implementation might often give rise to practical problems and be more formal than actual.

## Nationalism

Nationalism and the idea of national self-determination have been a strong component of political aspiration and activity throughout the world in the twentieth century. 'Nationalism' as a concept refers to the idea that people identify with a collective entity based on a belief in a (real or otherwise) common inheritance or experience of history, myth, tradition, language, culture, former or existing independence – or some combination of these. Although it manifests itself in various ways, it has proved a powerful motivation for action (Kellas, 1991, pp. 34–50). No country is immune from its influence. The consciousness of a separate history or a distinctive national culture (and especially a common religion or language) frequently induces a desire for a significant degree of independence. The great empires have broken up into smaller independent units under the impact of nationalism – the last of these to go being the Soviet Union. Alternatively, people may be conscious of a common identity because of geographical boundaries that highlight their separation from others, or for economic advantage or artificial political reasons which harden into real national consciousness. In contrast, others may find themselves absorbed by a more powerful neighbour, or agreeing to a union with another political entity. The United States is one example of this, and the union of England and Scotland in 1707 another.

But actual conditions do not make the political expression of national aspirations easy. The republics of the former Soviet Union have many ethnic minority groups within their territories as do the countries of Eastern Europe and the Middle East. For example, the republic of Moldova (formerly Moldavia) not only has a majority population of Romanians, but sizeable minorities of Gauguz (Christian Turks), Russians and Ukrainians, all of whom are very assertive and demand autonomy. Russia itself has many ethnic minorities living in its vast territory. Great Britain not only has the four nationalities of the English, Scots, Welsh and Irish, but also ethnic minorities with distinctive cultures who have emigrated to Britain from the former empire.

## Devolution and Federalism

Devolution may simply be convenient for administration. Beyond a point, administrative organization becomes impossibly clumsy and complex, with the result that delays and muddle occur; people become increasingly frustrated and may begin to seek unofficial and possibly illegal ways of circumventing the system. One way of mitigating such tendencies is to decentralize, that is to set up regional or local offices with enough authority to cope with a broad range of problems on the spot. This has taken place on an increasing scale in Great Britain since the Second World War. There are now regionalized areas of government administration for bodies like the National Health Service and British Rail, as well as utilities like electricity and water which were privatized by the Thatcher government in the 1980s. In addition, there are regional offices for the administration of Wales from Cardiff and of Scotland from Edinburgh. Nevertheless, Britain has been characterized by strong centralized political control in London, which is unusual for a country with its size of population. There are no regional political authorities and local government is weak.

In the context of the European Community, the debate on centralization and devolution has been intense. The community has strong policies for aid to regions, but many feel that its policy-making process is too centralized and excessively influenced by unelected officials. Hence the adoption of the principle of 'subsidiarity' – that decisions should be taken at the lowest practical and effective level – which is favoured by those who wish to democratize the community and those who wish to preserve the powers of national parliaments (Wallace, 1990, pp. 150–72).

In the former Soviet Union extensive administrative devolution was necessary, due to the vast area and considerable number of nationalities involved. The main units were the fifteen union republics and various autonomous regions and territories. Theoretically, the Soviet Union was a federal state – that is based on a decentralized system made up of a central government with substantial powers, and of units (the fifteen union republics) with constitutional powers of their own. But, in reality, the Soviet communist system was highly political and was characterized by bureaucratic central control from Moscow. It became clear in the period of *glasnost* and *perestroika* that this centralization was a source of considerable discontent and resentment among the republics and smaller nationalities. As soon as the centre showed signs of weakening, the centrifugal pressures for more autonomy, and even independence, became overwhelming.

The United States, too, has a federal system of government, although recent years have seen a growing central dominance, some would say almost to the extent of making the United States a unitary system. The American federal structure was originally conceived as a major means of defending liberty by preventing the emergence of a centralized tyranny. Although the states and, particularly, the localities now operate much as administrative agencies, the opportunities for them to influence politics at the federal level are undoubtedly greater than they are for local authorities in Britain, which is not a federal state.

Decentralization involves the inevitable problems of deciding the acceptable levels of decentralization (local, regional or federal), the extent of the power of each unit at each level and, perhaps most important of all, the political and administrative relationship between the various authorities at different levels. In particular, it has to deal with questions such as whether the central authority or the decentralized unit takes the ultimate decisions, the extent of overlapping power and how differences between different units are resolved. Such problems are exacerbated by demands that are considered excessive or impossible by one side or the other, which can give rise to militant home-rule or separatist movements, which may even resort to political violence. Each political system has to sort out these problems as best it can. We shall take the examples of our case-studies in order to show the sorts of problems that may arise and how they can be solved or at least tolerated.

## Devolution in the United Kingdom

The Scottish National Party (SNP) did not make much impact on national politics until 1974, when much of the significant falling away of support for the two main parties in Scotland (especially the Conservatives) went to them. At their peak in October 1974 they were able to win 30 per cent of the Scottish vote in the seats that they contested and eleven seats in the House of Commons. It is not easy to account precisely for the growth in support or to determine how deep national sentiment went or what it implied. Various explanations for the growth of Scottish nationalism in the 1970s have been put forward, none of which is wholly satisfactory. The Scots probably shared the general disaffection that accompanied Britain's economic decline, and may have regarded the discovery of oil off the Scottish mainland as something that should benefit Scotland more directly than Whitehall would wish. It is clear that the campaign for devolution – the establishment of a Scottish parliament with significant powers – did not capture the imagination of most Scottish voters still less were they enamoured of the official SNP policy of independence for Scotland. According to the opinion polls, they were primarily concerned with the usual economic issues of prices, housing and unemployment. However, there seemed to be wide support for a limited form of devolution, falling short of full independence. The SNP was in something of a quandary, for, although they had gained votes as a result of support for devolution, their official policy – independence – was one that fewer of the Scots supported.

This change in the electoral fortunes of the British parties revealed hitherto unsuspected depths of support for the union of England and Scotland among the establishment. The controversy cut across party lines and, as time went on, the question of the desirability of the union foused on the workability of the proposals contained in the bill brought forward by the Labour government after and as a result of the considerable SNP gains in the 1974 general election. The government was fearful, on the one hand, of losing more support in Scotland but, on the other, of a major party split at Westminster and in the mass party organization. It was clear that many MPs did not support devolution in the form proposed, or at all. In the end, a referendum defeated the modest proposals for Wales, while the slight majority in favour in Scotland was less than the 40 per cent of the electorate deemed necessary by the majority of antidevolutionists in Parliament. This required the government to ask the Commons to repeal the Act, which they duly did. After the referendum defeats in 1976 the issues died down for some years, but during the 1980s the SNP again made progress in Scotland as the Conservative vote continued to decline. The Labour Party was now proposing some form of devolution not only for Scotland and Wales, but also for regional assemblies in England beginning with the North-West and the North-East. The decline in support for the Conservative government in Scotland (at the 1992 election it held only nine seats out of seventy-one) and the commitment of the Labour Party to devolution made the issue central to the Scottish election campaign in 1992. The SNP demanded independence but the Conservatives fiercely supported the union. In the event, the Conservatives increased their support in Scotland a little, gaining two seats, but about three-quarters of the voters had supported devolution or independence parties. It appears that the new Conservative government will not be able simply to leave things as they are.

The case of Northern Ireland illustrates the severe political problems that arise when no acceptable consensus can be found within a community. The difficulties of the situation lie deeply embedded in Irish history and Irish relations with Britain. Protestants – most of whom are known politically as Unionists, the most militant being known as Loyalists – are in a majority in Northern Ireland but fearful of their position as a small minority in Ireland as a whole. Catholics – known politically as Nation-alists and represented by the Social Democratic and Labour Party (SDLP), or Republicans and represented by the political wing of the Provisional IRA, Sinn Fein – on the other hand, are a minor-ity in Northern Ireland but part of the large Catholic majority in Ireland as a whole. The problem is seriously exacerbated by the presence of paramilitary activity by the Provisional IRA (or Provos) and various Unionist paramilitary groups. The government of the Irish Republic wants Irish unity but does not wish to inherit a divided and war-torn province. The Westminster government is legally responsible for the province but cannot find a solution that is acceptable to all parties to the conflict. Meanwhile, direct rule has been imposed as a negative interim solution while the British government seeks to encourage talks between the con-tending parties, the development of an effective local government (as something on which to build) and a successful policy against political violence. Successive British governments have committed themselves to the policy that there can be no union of Northern Ireland with the Irish Republic unless such a move is supported by a majority of the inhabitants of Northern Ireland. The Irish government now also holds this view.

The situation in Northern Ireland seems not to lend itself easily to explanatory analysis based on economic and class conflict, although it has been argued that the Protestant bourgeoisie have used the Protestant working class to maintain Unionist domina-tion. The province seems to be divided vertically rather than horizontally, on socio-cultural rather than class lines. Some organ-izations (like churches and trade unions) exist on an all-Ireland basis and there are other manifestations of an Irish dimension to society. But in significant areas, such as education, or on certain political problems, such as the policing of the border, the division remains clear and irreconcilable. The British government there-fore not only has a major political conflict on its hands, but the problem of a breakdown of law and order perpetrated by the paramilitary on both sides. This has led to various measures to combat violence, which some have argued have tended to aggravate rather than mitigate the problem. The suspension of normal legal procedures with respect to detention, the exclusion of jury trial and the right to silence, together with allegations of a shoot-to-kill policy by security forces have all provoked considerable controversy and been used for propaganda purposes by both sides. Any incumbent British government inherits the consequences of the activities of the contending parties and the policies of its predecessors which, with hindsight, may be seen as mistaken or unwise.

Political parties, like the Alliance Party and Workers' Party, that espouse a policy of reconciliation have limited impact. The major British parties did not compete in elections in Northern Ireland until the Conservatives began to do so in the 1992 general election. Progress towards more co-operation between the Protestant and Catholic communities is very slow but some movement can be detected, at least at the local level. The latest government initiative is the Anglo-Irish Agreement between the Irish and British governments which gives the former a consultative role in some policy decisions concerning Northern Ireland and is intended to improve the co-ordination of security matters with respect to the border. It is strongly opposed by the Loyalists (Jones (ed.), 1991, pp. 501–20).

## Federalism in the United States

The United States of America consists of fifty separate states whose autonomous powers were entrenched in the 1787 Constitution. As we saw in chapter 11, nationalism has not been a divisive political issue in the United States in spite of mass immigration in the twentieth century. The financial and political relationships between the federal (central) government, based in Washington, DC, and the governments of the fifty states have fluctuated considerably throughout history and remain exceedingly complex. Generally, however, power has shifted to the centre and it is the federal government that has provided most of the initiatives as American governments have intervened more in the general attempt to regulate a highly urban and industrial society.

Since the 1970s, a conservative reaction to the liberal-inspired social policies of the 1960s has led to an attempt to increase the choice open to state and local governments by supplying them with federally raised money, more through block grants and General Revenue Sharing (GRS) which allow them to decide how the money will be spent, and less through categorical grants where the federal government directs the policy. Nixon achieved little change, but under Carter, a fiscal conservative, grants to state and local governments began to level off. Reagan sought to revive Nixon's original idea and in 1981 the Omnibus Budget

Reconciliation Act ended sixty federal programmes and merged another seventy-seven into just nine block grants. Even more radical proposals were made by the administration in 1982 for cuts and a return to state autonomy but these foundered on the opposition of the 'intergovernmental lobby'.

What is interesting about this development is that it can be seen as reversing the normal model of the political process – that pressure groups (called 'the lobby' in the United States) influence governments to get the programmes they want – to one in which the creation of expensive policies of social and economic inter- vention, developed mainly by professionals and technocrats, has promoted the growth of a large lobby consisting of state and local officials (Beer, 1978). Thus it was the massive increase in federal spending in the 1960s that gave rise to the intergovernmental lobby which, once established, played an important role in the initiation of GRS in the 1970s. The 'Big 7' which made up the lobby (the United States Conference of Mayors, the National Governors Conference, the National Association of Counties, the Council of State Governments, the National League of Cities, the International City Management Association and the National Legislative Conference) were by no means new arrivals on the Washington scene, but what was new was the sophistication of their lobbying and the size of their interest as federal expenditure increased throughout the 1970s.

There has always been immense variety among the patterns of politics found within the fifty states, and generalizations are therefore very difficult to make as well as being potentially mis- leading. Many changes have been made in state constitutions in the past twenty years with effects on legislative, executive and judicial branches. Legislatures meet more regularly and more frequently, members are more likely to be professionals and to possess greater staffs and authority to raise taxes. Executive au- thority has been strengthened by electing governors for longer terms and giving them greater control of state budgets. Addition- ally, with the greater involvement of state governments in social policy, governors have been able to imitate presidents to some extent and gain greater attention from the media. This can be used as a tool of influence with state legislators, federal officials and outside interests. Many state judges are elected, but greater strides have been made in many states to professionalize the judiciary.

Until the 1950s, there was no real competition between the

two main parties in most states. In the majority of states, which were effectively one-party, the only competition would occur in the organizations that were factionalized around particular personalities or interests. The nationalization of issues such as poverty, urban redevelopment and civil rights in the past thirty years has increased the extent of two-party competition. As can be seen from table 22.1, in 1989 the Democrats controlled most governorships (twenty-eight), but in only half of these did they also control both houses of the state assembly. In the other states the Republicans controlled one or both houses. The Republicans enjoyed control of all three in only four states.

**Table 22.1**  Party control of state politics in the United States, 1989

|  | Democrats | Republicans |
|---|---|---|
| Party has governor and controls both houses of assembly | 14 | 4 |
| Party has governor and controls one house of assembly | 10 | 3 |
| Party has governor, and controls neither house of assembly | 4 | 13 |

*Notes*: Nebraska had a Republican governor with a unicameral, non-partisan assembly; in New Mexico the governor was Republican, the Democrats controlled one house and the other was hung.

*Source*: adapted from Grant (1991), pp. 200–1.

## Federalism in the Soviet Union

In Russia there was chronological and geographical continuity in the building of the state and empire. The result was an insensitivity to ethnic problems, which tended to be seen by the central authorities as reactionary or enemy-inspired. During the period of communist rule many of the minorities were very small in number and the Soviet government attempted either to assimilate or to exaggerate their ethnic differences in a divide-and-rule policy. Only a dozen or so nationalities really counted politically (for example the Russians, Ukrainians and Georgians). Among them the sense of cohesion varied from one nationality to another. Tests of cohesion included awareness of previous independence, the proportion of people professing to speak the national language as a mother tongue, territorial concentration and the proportion of the ethnic population actually living in the national territory.

The Soviet Union consisted of fifteen union republics. Smaller national groups that did not form an all-union republic (which the Constitution once required to be on the border of the Soviet Union) were administratively organized into so-called autonomous units – autonomous republics, regions, provinces or districts – depending on size. The degree of administrative control varied according to the size and significance of the nationality. Many of these national groups were in the Russian Republic (sometimes called the Russian Federation), but many also existed in other republics or were to be found in more than one area. Still other groups, like the Jews, were sufficiently scattered to have frustrated the central authorities' desire for them to set up more than a nominal administrative unit of their own. Others were in dispute with the central government over which territory they should occupy. Although the union republics were referred to as sovereign, significant policy decisions were taken by the all-union Communist Party and government. But it must be said that major party leaders of the union republics were likely to be members of the Central Committee of the CPSU or, occasionally, of the Politburo. Party and government organization at national level were virtually duplicated at republic level and also lower down, with some simplifications. Much of the activity of republic and regional politicians was devoted to requests for more funds from the central government, and to pressing for a prominent place in education for the local language and culture. A good deal of energy was taken up with disputes over the degree of autonomy permitted in the spending of funds or in the making of appointments. By far the most significant problem (and thus the one least openly discussed) was the nationality question.

The authorities tended to be hidebound by the Marxist-Leninist formula 'national in form – socialist in content' which constituted part of the official ideology. But it appeared that feelings of nationalism in the Soviet Union grew more quickly than the rate of assimilation into the national value system. Why did such nationalist sentiment survive? Resistance to Russification is only part of the answer, since nationalist sentiment is only partly to do with ethnicity. Such resistance is more a result than a cause of nationalism. The policy of dividing the country administratively along national lines kept alive national consciousness or even created it where it had not existed before (as in Central Asia). Other nationalities tended to see themselves as being second best to the Russians and tried to assert themselves by preserving their cultural heritage, gaining economic advantage and (in the case of dissidents) promoting political nationalism (Smith (ed.), 1990, pp. 1–20; Dixon, 1990, pp. 21–37). There had long been a tendency for Russians to migrate to the other republics (especially those to the west), which led to growing tension between Russians and non-Russians. The proportion of Russians in the Russian Republic diminished but the proportion residing in the many other republics continued to rise. The rapid population growth in some republics (especially in Central Asia) put increased pressure on resources and services. Another related source of tension was the fact that Russian immigrants had, in some republics become a sizeable proportion of the urban population, leaving the countryside populated largely by the local nationality.

As in many other areas of Soviet life, the forces released by Gorbachev's policies of *glasnost* and *perestroika* created hope in the nationalities, who wanted more autonomy and in some cases (like the Baltic republics and Georgia) independence from a union that they claimed they had been forced into against their will. At first, Gorbachev believed that far-reaching economic and social reform could be achieved without endangering the union. But economic and social problems worsened dramatically and the central government showed itself unable to deal with them. The Baltic republics began a policy of attrition in an attempt to compel the centre to grant (or, in their eyes, restore) their independence. Central authority was increasingly undermined and Gorbachev's attempt to negotiate a new union treaty with the republics was seen as unrealistic (Gitelman, 1992, pp. 122–46). Even the republics and nationalities that wished to preserve the union wanted essentially a confederal structure – that is one where the final authority lay with the constituent republics rather than the centre. After the failed *coup d'état* in August 1991 the authority of the centre was irretrievably damaged. Attempts continued to negotiate new union and economic treaties, but the republics were less and less interested. The crunch came on 1 December 1991 when Ukraine voted for independence. A union without Ukraine was considered unfeasible. Thus the Baltic republics found their independence restored far earlier than they had expected, while other republics, which had not really wanted full independence, found it foisted on them anyway.

Thus a new era began for the whole region. Many of the new republics have artificial boundaries and ethnic-minority problems of their own. These are especially acute in Russia, Georgia and Moldova. Serious disputes resulting in armed conflict have arisen in the republics of Central Asia and the Caucasus. The old Soviet regime left them economically interdependent, yet they prefer to assert their new independence rather than to co-operate. The Commonwealth of Independent States – an organization designed to facilitate their co-operation over economic and defence issues – is weak and undermined by controversy between Russia and Ukraine. Its future is uncertain as is the future of all the new republics. Nationalism has triumphed but the full cost has yet to be discovered.

## Conclusion

Although there is more international and supranational political activity, movements that identify with smaller political units have a powerful attraction. Although this is sometimes based on administrative necessity, it also carries the appeal of various forms of nationalism. The federal system in the United States is not based on national identity, the policy of integrating immigrants having been largely successful in the past. Whether it will continue to be so in the future is not so certain. In Britain and the Soviet Union nationalist pressures have been evident in different circumstances and to different degrees. They have precipitated the breakup of the Soviet Union into fifteen independent states, all with nationality problems of their own. In the United Kingdom administrative necessity seems likely to lead to some regional devolution, while Scottish devolution remains an issue that divides the political parties.

Political struggles over the question of centralization and devolution are bound to continue, as conflicts over cultural and economic interests rage between different areas in almost all countries. Nationalism can generate strong emotional responses, but it can create many economic and social problems for the newly independent entity; for example, it is often based on quite artificial criteria. Federalism seems to be the main form within which conflicting interests can be institutionalized relatively successfully, and it is therefore worth enquiring whether the United Kingdom, for example, would gain anything from adopting a federal structure.

# Questions for Discussion

1 Is a federal government more democratic than a centralized one?
2 What are the positive and negative aspects of nationalism as the basis for exercising political power?
3 Is the principle of deciding issues at the lowest practicable level one that enhances legitimacy?

# Further Reading

Bogdanor, V. (1979), *Devolution*. Oxford, Oxford University Press, esp. ch. 1.

Denenberg, R.V. (1992), *Understanding American Politics*, 3rd edn. London, Fontana, ch. 3.

Gitelman, Z. (1992), Nations, republics and Commonwealth. In S. White, A. Pravda and Z. Gitelman (eds), *Developments in Soviet and Post-Soviet Politics*, 2nd edn. Basingstoke, Macmillan, pp. 122–46.

Hough, J.F. and M. Fainsod (1979), *How the Soviet Union is Governed*. Cambridge, Mass., Harvard University Press, ch. 13.

Kellas, J.G. (1991), *The Politics of Nationalism and Ethnicity*. Basingstoke, Macmillan, chs 6 and 7.

King, D.S. (1992), The changing federal balance. In G. Peele et al. (eds), *Developments in American Politics*. Basingstoke, Macmillan, pp. 190–209.

Lane, D. (1992), *Soviet Society under Perestroika*, rev. edn. Boston, Unwin Hyman, ch. 6.

McKay, D. (1989), *American Politics and Society*, 2nd edn. Oxford, Blackwell, ch. 4.

Stoker, G. (1990), Government beyond Whitehall. In P. Dunleavy, A. Gamble and G. Peele (eds), *Developments in British Politics 3*. Basingstoke, Macmillan, pp. 126–49.

Wallace, H. (1990), Britain and Europe. In P. Dunleavy, A. Gamble and G. Peele (eds), *Developments in British Politics 3*. Basingstoke, Macmillan, pp. 150–72.

# 23

# Local Politics

## Introduction

We understand local government to mean government below the level of the region or federal unit. The structures of local government vary widely between our three case-studies and therefore we require some yardstick by which to make useful comparisons between them. We have seen how questions of nationalism and regionalism pose problems for central state organizations and how structures of federalism and devolution have been developed to try to alleviate those problems. When questions of local politics arise on the basis of perceived local interests, our analysis again needs to concentrate on the extent to which power is fragmented or concentrated within the polity. Therefore our central questions in this chapter will be: how autonomous of the central state are or were local governments in Great Britain, the United States and the former Soviet Union, and what are the main factors that affect the balance of power between centre and locality?

The question of autonomy usually takes rather different forms with respect to local government than it does with nationalism or regionalism. Occasionally, there are movements for local self-government but the more usual question is the extent to which local areas can determine for themselves the nature and extent of local services which, in all three countries, tend to be dominated by matters of housing, education, welfare, roads and recreation. We shall examine, first, questions of organization and what local governments actually do; secondly, matters of finance; and then attempt to draw some conclusions.

## Organization

The dominant characteristic of local government in the United States is its extreme fragmentation – over 1,000 in some of the larger cities, and over 80,000 separate units in all. The units exist at various levels: municipalities and towns, which tend to be responsible for services such as the police, the fire brigade and roads; counties, which are responsible for such things as public health, airports, hospitals, welfare, the police and parks; and special districts, which are responsible for just one service, most often education but they also exist for housing and transport. Such extreme fragmentation reflects the strong localist sentiments that still characterize American politics and which have generally overridden attempts to rationalize the system based on notions of 'efficiency'. In the large urban areas the main suggestion has been to develop metropolitan government to replace the present patch-work of counties, towns, and special districts with a single structure responsible for all services. This has been introduced in only a few areas, however. More often, such plans have foundered on a combination of opposition from above and from below. Politicians at the state level fear the competition from a united metropolitan level, while local interests fear the loss of influence at the level of small towns and neighbourhoods.

The structure of local government in Great Britain is quite straightforward to comprehend, due to the relative smallness and cultural homogeneity of the country on the one hand, and, on the other, to the greater centralization of state power. This has meant that localism, while still present, has been nowhere near as strong a political force as the wish of the central state for what it sees as better means of administration. Much of the present structure dates from the early 1970s, although there have been significant changes since then. In much of the country the system is two-tier, with county councils (regional councils in Scotland) and district councils sharing service-delivery. In metropolitan areas there is a single-tier metropolitan district system, with some services (like the fire brigade and the police) run by boards jointly serviced by the metropolitan districts. In the metropolitan areas the districts are also responsible for major services such as education, which elsewhere are dealt with by the counties. There have been hints from the Conservative government that it may move towards single-tier authorities for all areas. Of greater long-term significance was the (Conservative) central government's creation of urban-development agencies which are specifically designed to bypass elected (Labour) local authorities in the major cities. They are seen by the government as more appropriate for its policies of urban regeneration, relying on a combination of central-government and private-sector capital. Being non-elected, and with their budgets ultimately set by central government, such agencies are generally seen as further evidence of centralization (Stoker, 1990, pp. 126–49).

The structure of local government in the Soviet Union was also diverse. Below the level of the union republics were the *krai* (area), *oblast* (region), *gorod* (city) and *selo* (village). The largest cities, like Moscow and Kiev, were independent of the oblast, and were divided into boroughs. At each of these levels, and in the villages in rural areas, there was a soviet which shared the main features of the Supreme Soviet at the national level: election of deputies in uncontested elections and Communist Party supervision of the nomination and legislation process. But whereas at national level the specialized administrative agencies were called ministries, at the local level they were called administrations or departments, and the soviet had an executive committee rather than a council of ministers (Hough and Fainsod, 1979, pp. 485–6). Not surprisingly in a polity in which the reach of state power in general was greater than in the United States or Great Britain, local governments had more extensive functions than in the West, and a large city in the Soviet Union would have had about a dozen agencies covering, for example, finance, planning, education, culture, housing and capital construction. Nevertheless, the extremely centralized nature of the Soviet system left little room for local initiative, with quite minor decisions having to be approved by the centre. A major task of the new republics will be to evolve an effectively decentralized regional or local government system. Power will also, in many places, have to be prised from the grasp of local communists who have continued to exercise control throughout the period of *glasnost*, *perestroika* and the coup attempt (albeit abandoning the 'communist' label) (Smith, 1992, pp. 173–80).

## Functions

However diverse their structures may be, it can still be argued that the major functions of local governments, at least as far as the central state is concerned, reveal a measure of common ground across our three case-studies. First, they are responsible for supporting the system of production by providing the necessary infrastructure in terms of roads, planning and technical education. Ownership and control of the system of production was, of course, different in the Soviet Union compared with Great Britain and the United States, but in all three countries there was a constant tension between the efforts of local governments to co-ordinate local service-delivery in the general public interest, and the efforts of productive industries, whether private or state-owned, to maximize the advantages and minimize the costs to them of siting in a particular area.

Second, they are responsible for the provision of services that relate to the quality of people's lives, and which thereby contribute further to supporting the production system, such as housing, education, libraries and museums. The provision of low-rent public housing on the one hand and control over the development of private housing for purchase (in the United States and Great Britain) on the other, remains one of the most basic and controversial of local-government activities. In the United States and Great Britain it was the inability of the market to provide decent accommodation at low cost that led to the development of public or council housing in the twentieth century and an improvement in living conditions for many people. However, the political consequences of this development were not all foreseen by their originators. In Great Britain the process of slum clearance, especially after 1945, led to the creation of large estates of council housing and flats which vary widely in quality. Local authorities have faced increasing problems in maintaining these estates as their financial freedom has been reduced. Since these estates have remained the source of large numbers of Labour votes in elections the Conservative government has sought to reduce the public role in the provision of housing. The Conservatives also believed that maintenance of the properties would be improved if tenants had a choice between different types of ownership. The first policy change was to oblige local authorities to offer their council houses for sale at a discount to their tenants and to prevent them from reinvesting the proceeds in new building. Thus local authorities have seen their stock diminish, and it was also their best stock. Then in November 1987 the government published a bill which aimed to eliminate altogether the notion of local authorities as providers of housing. Housing Action Trusts (HATs) were to be set up to take over the management of public housing and to dispose of it to private developers and housing associations. Like urban-development corporations, HATs would be non-elected; this amounted to a further effort to reinstate the market as provider of housing while centralizing such political control as remained.

Services have often been cut back significantly because of the restrictions on local-authority spending also imposed by the Conservative governments of the 1980s. Local control was restricted by measures such as privatization – the contracting out of services like refuse collection to private firms, and council-house sales. The 1987 Education Bill included further measures that impinged on local control of education, for example enabling schools to opt out of local-authority control, and the running of polytechnics and higher-education colleges independently of local government by governing bodies of whom at least half would be from commerce and business.

In the United States political fragmentation has permitted and then supported the segregation of housing along lines of class and race so that the development of suburbs has been a device for maintaining white, privately owned enclaves outside the old cities which were increasingly and disproportionately occupied by ethnic minorities in public housing or poor-quality privately owned tenements.

In the Soviet Union housing controversies centred on rather different issues. City soviets had no major source of independent funding and a large proportion of housing (and other facilities such as roads) was financed by the national ministries specifically to serve their employees. Demands were then placed on the soviet to provide other support services to areas of housing constructed entirely outside of their control (Hough and Fainsod, 1979, p. 345).

The third area of local-government responsibility is the maintenance of order and social-cohesion. Routine policing is the responsibility of local authorities in Britain and the United States, and was so in the Soviet Union. However, there are significant differences in the degree to which the police are subject to local political control, while political policing is more subject to central direction (see chapter 19). But in addition to the more overt forms of social control, other legitimating functions performed by local authorities include the provision of emergency welfare, temporary accommodation and so on.

The role of local government in encouraging more widespread involvement of people in the political process is also important.

Relatively low turnouts in local elections in both the United States and Great Britain suggest that this should not be over-emphasized, but the multiplicity of local agencies provide both greater opportunities for participation and, in all three countries, training-grounds for politicians intent on reaching the national political stage.

## Finance

The question of finance is crucial in assessing the autonomy of local governments. It can be argued that local governments wield independent power to the extent that they can raise their own revenue and dispose of it as they wish. Given this, it is clear that local governments in none of these countries has full independence. In the Soviet Union local soviets were subject to CPSU control and central financing; in the United States state law restricts the financial independence of cities and counties; and in Great Britain central government determines the limits of how much local authorities can raise and spend.

In the Soviet Union one of the few independent sources of funds enjoyed by city governments was the 'above plan' profits made by municipal enterprises, and there was some discretion available to city officials to shift funds around within the limited city budget. But each department, for example construction or roads, sought its funding from within its own ministerial hierarchy and therefore was in competition with similar departments in other cities rather than with other departments in its own city. The general dependence of city officials on the funds controlled by ministries led one expert to characterize towns and cities that were based primarily on one industry as 'company towns', although the postwar growth in the number of large cities and the greater diversification of industry reduced the numbers of these (Hough and Fainsod, 1979, pp. 345–8).

In Great Britain and the United States the financial problems of local governments, especially in cities, have been no less acute than they were in the Soviet Union, although they derive from different causes. At its simplest, as the twentieth century has progressed and the state in both countries has taken increasing responsibility for the provision of housing, education, welfare, roads and so on, the local levels of government have found their limited financial resources unable to meet the demands being placed on them. Their financial autonomy has declined for two main reasons: first, the central state has granted them extra responsibilities and the money to deliver the service but with strings attached; and secondly, their ability to raise finance locally has diminished because, in the cities, changing economic structure and housing patterns have produced a decline in the local tax base. These factors produced a crisis for many cities as their populations came increasingly to consist of those who were most dependent on local services, like welfare and transport, but were least able to pay for them.

This pattern has gone further in the United States where the fragmentation of structure and the relative unwillingness of state governments to subsidize the cities led to the bankruptcy of New York City in the 1970s and a consequent large reduction in city employment and services. The election of the Reagan administration in 1980 brought proposals for massive cuts in federal aid to the cities (partly, of course, because they were not exactly Republican strongholds). During 1981–2, when the Republicans had wrested control of the Senate from the Democrats (in 1980) and a coalition of Republicans and conservative Democrats controlled the House of Representatives, some cuts were made. Thereafter, the Democrats' restored position in Congress meant that they were able to resist further large-scale cuts in spending on the cities, but during the 1980s local authorities were obliged to become much more entrepreneurial and have had to look to joint programmes in the private sector for economic regeneration.

Current restrictions on levels of local-authority spending in Great Britain began in 1976 when the then Labour government found itself obliged to cut public spending in order to meet the requirements of the International Monetary Fund from whom the government was seeking help. In 1979 the newly elected Conservative government saw the reduction of public expenditure as positively desirable rather than as an unfortunate necessity, and proceeded with a series of Acts which first attempted to curtail local-government spending and then set about removing local control of some of the services they had traditionally administered. Spending was restricted both by the reduction in the proportion of local expenditure met by central grants and by restrictions on the ability of local authorities to make up the loss of grant by increasing their own revenue-raising (rate- or charge-capping).

One reason why central governments in both the United States and Great Britain have been quite successful in curtailing the financial independence of local governments, in spite of survey evidence suggesting that there is considerable support for the services that they provide, is that the means by which local governments raise their own revenue are extremely unpopular. Most unpopular of all are property taxes, which provide one of the main sources of independent local revenues in the United States and were almost the only source in Great Britain, in the form of rates. Dissatisfaction in the United States became so widespread that, in the space of a few years (by 1979) twenty-three states had enacted some form of limit on the extent to which local governments could increase their taxation.

In Great Britain most politicians were against the inequities of the rating-system but were unable or unwilling to propose an alternative. For the government, matters came to a head from 1984 onwards when a revaluation of property in Scotland (on which new levels of rates would be fixed) threatened to cause very large rises in rate bills. Ministers concentrated on the search for an alternative which was enacted in Scotland in 1989 and in England and Wales in 1990. This was what the government called the 'community charge' and what everyone else referred to as the 'poll tax'. It was to be levied at a flat rate per individual adult in each area, thus apparently replacing one form of inequitable taxation with another. One effect was that far more individuals were being required to pay the tax than under the rates. In any case, it proved even more unpopular than the rates and was soon replaced by a modified property tax – the council tax. Whatever its longer-term repercussions, an increase in local financial autonomy is unlikely. It is, clearly, not one of the British government's intentions.

## Conclusion

The evidence we have examined so far, of growing local reliance on central funding and the problems facing local governments as they are squeezed between central authorities on the one hand and the pressures of the production system on the other seems to suggest that the autonomy of local governments in our three case-studies is minimal. Yet commentators continue to question this conclusion; for example Sharpe discusses the 'central, and ineradicable ambiguity of the status of local government in a democratic state' (Sharpe (ed.), 1981, p. 5). On the one hand, it is constitutionally subordinate to the central state, but because it is regularly elected, raises money and employs staff, it retains the potential for independent power. More recently, Dunleavy and Rhodes observed that, despite the financial restrictions on local governments in Britain, 'they continue to retain a substantial autonomy about how they allocate both their tax and grant funds between services and in the development of new policies' (Dunleavy and Rhodes, 1986, p. 116). This underestimates the constraints on the budgetary process in British local authorities in the 1990s. The budget is not prepared from scratch each year. Because of a variety of legal, contractual and political commitments, they are able to make only marginal adjustments to the previous year's figures, and when the total available is the same or less than the previous year the freedom of manoeuvre is small indeed. Between 1990 and 1993 this was compounded by non-payment of the poll tax by significant numbers of people, simultaneously increasing the authorities' costs and decreasing their revenue.

It does seem, therefore, that in Great Britain, which has always had a relatively highly centralized, and constitutionally unitary system of government, the period since 1976 has seen a variety of financial and political developments combine to shrink even further what was always a heavily circumscribed autonomy. The involvement of private enterprise in local urban regeneration after the 1987 general election seemed to indicate clearly that local-authority autonomy in Great Britain was further diminished.

The different results of the battles over spending between local and federal governments in the United States since the 1970s provide an interesting comparison with those in Britain. Recent presidents have all tried to reduce the size of the federal bureaucracy and increase the influence of the states, rather than localities, on domestic spending. We noted in the last chapter that they had not been very successful with respect to the states. Similarly, they had problems with respect to the localities.

First, it is suggested, the Presidents underestimated the strength of the political alliances that develop around particular government spending programmes. Key actors in the political process – federal and local bureaucrats, members of Congress and local elected politicians – together can form a weighty alliance, particu-larly in view of the extreme fragmentation of the policy-making process which presents numerous opportunities to block some proposed change. Compared, for example, to members of parliament in Great Britain, members of Congress in the United States are much more susceptible to local pressures and thus more likely to vote against presidential initiatives, especially if the President represents the other party. McKay concludes his survey of contemporary intergovernmental relations in the United States: 'The ways in which federal aid is distributed were, and remain too political and complex to provide any one institution and political leader with complete control' (1989, p. 72). Therefore, the extent of local autonomy is much greater in the United States than in Great Britain, mainly because of the greater fragmentation of policy-making, but local governments in both countries face similar constraints that arise directly from their respective economies and it is perhaps these that constitute the greater threat to local autonomy in the United States.

In the Soviet Union, on the face of it, local soviets had little formal autonomy, subject as they were to the dual subordination of ministries and local industrial concerns on the one hand, and the local Communist Party on the other. On a more informal level, however, the local soviets may have been able to exercise greater autonomy, due to a number of factors. First, the local party organizations in some areas played an important role as brokers when production and construction bottlenecks occurred at the local level, and this may have given the soviet leverage in other areas of policy (Hough and Fainsod, 1979, pp. 509–10). Secondly, the local party, soviet and industrial interests may well have shared perceptions as to what was in the local interest. Local industrial expansion which gave rise to the desire for more socio-cultural facilities could have united the efforts of local managers and party officials in lobbying for increased central funds (Schulz, 1979, pp. 107–9). This feature of local political activity was very similar to the lobbying in the United States which has been partially successful in recent years in maintaining levels of local funding. Slider points out that in the early 1980s the rights and responsibilities of city governments in the Soviet Union to co-ordinate their economies were expanded but without an increase in the power of local soviets to carry out these responsibilities (Slider, 1986, pp. 495–511).

Some Soviet experiments may also be seen as remarkably similar to the British government's intention to extend the urban-development corporations. Both seem to have in common a belief that professional planning and co-ordination at the local level should be insulated as far as possible from the local party-political process. The crucial difference of course, is that while the Soviet government was proposing this kind of measure along with a greater democratization of local and workplace decision-making (in the spirit of *glasnost* and *perestroika*), the British government's policies leave decision-making at the centre and in the hands of local, nominated representatives of business.

A reorganization of local and regional government in many of the new post-Soviet republics is inevitable. The immediate problem for local government is wresting control from the communists who have held power for so long and built up significant patronage networks, and trying to create orderly policies out of a confused political, legal and economic situation. In some cities, like Moscow and St Petersburg, there have been accusations of illegal appropriation of property and funds. In some republics old and divisive local and tribal differences have re-emerged which give rise to tension and even violence.

## Questions for Discussion

1 Who benefits from a high degree of local autonomy from central government?
2 Does local government need to be elected?
3 Is the question of financing local government central to its efficiency and legitimacy?

## Further Reading

Budge, I. and D. McKay (1988), *The Changing British Political System: Into the 1990s*, 2nd edn. London, Longman, ch. 6.
Ross, C. (1987), *Local Government in the Soviet Union*. London, Croom Helm.
Sakwa, R. (1989), *Soviet Politics: An Introduction*. London, Routledge, ch. 8.
Smith, G.B. (1992), *Soviet Politics: Struggling with Change*, 2nd edn. Basingstoke, Macmillan, pp. 173–81.
Stoker, G. (1988), *The Politics of Local Government*. Basingstoke, Macmillan, chs 1, 10 and 11.
Stone, C.N. (1991), Urban issues in American politics. In P.J. Davies and T.A. Waldstein (eds), *Political Issues in America*. Manchester. Manchester University Press, pp. 62–72.

# Part V

## Links between Government and People

# 24

# Legitimacy

## Introduction

Legitimacy relates to the degree of recognition and acceptance that the political regime enjoys among the community (see chapter 3). In our earlier discussions of history, myth, tradition and ideology, we considered the important link between these factors which provides the context for the political process, and ensures the durability of that process. Myths, for example, provide selective interpretations of aspects of the political process, and ideology is intended to provide principles to guide and inspire both rulers and ruled. As long as such interpretations and principles are accepted and believed they will be a strong cement binding the ruled to the rulers. If they come to be widely perceived as distortions, then the legitimacy of the political process comes under threat.

## Maintaining Legitimacy

Using an over-simplified model, we may envisage the controlling group as seeking to maximize its legitimacy, for example by emphasizing manifestations of assent, expressions of loyalty, patriotism, nationalism and other emotional signs of support. But the existence of strong subcultures may inhibit the effective penetration of all sections of society by the dominant myths, ideology and so on; therefore, a regime must take other measures to safeguard its legitimacy. It will affirm, through public pronouncements and propaganda, that its particular political system is the envy of the world, that all its citizens believe that and have no other wish than to defend and strengthen it. At the same time, it has to take active steps to discourage, divert or suppress overt signs of discontent. No regime can be wholly legitimate in the eyes of its citizens, but some regimes can achieve a very high level of legitimacy.

The United States is a good example of a regime that, in spite of challenges, has not suffered a sustained or widespread campaign to undermine its position for at least 100 years. Its great success in recent years as a world political, economic and military power has sustained its hold on the citizens, although it may be wondered whether its self-conscious sense of superiority masks an underlying insecurity. Although a challenge to the regime seems as far away as ever, the legitimacy of the country's political system does not look as well founded as it once did. Defeat in the Vietnam War, growing economic difficulties, an intractable law-and-order problem at home, a huge rise in the number of poverty-stricken (often illegal) immigrants from South America, increasing scepticism and even cynicism about the political system (only half the electorate bother to vote in a presidential election) all indicate that legitimacy may have been significantly undermined.

In Great Britain the stability, and therefore the legitimacy, of the regime has long been a byword among commentators. It has become part of the official propaganda, a kind of self-fulfilling assertion. However, while avoiding actual revolution, the British political system has experienced significant movements of unrest in the twentieth century, as a result of industrial and political discontent and economic crisis. Above all, it has seen a large-scale rebellion in one part of the kingdom which led to not only the secession of the greater part of Ireland, but also considerable political disruption, civil war and extensive political violence. That this has been largely confined to one geographical area – Ireland, and in recent years Northern Ireland – cannot detract from the fact that Great Britain is one of the regimes in the world whose legitimacy is challenged by a significant minority of the population in one area, who are prepared to express that challenge by acts of violence. Other factors that may have weakened the legitimacy of the British political system in recent times include the inegalitarian policies of the Conservative government, under Margaret Thatcher, of the 1980s, which some claimed damaged the social fabric (others felt that it gave new dynamism and confidence to the country). The geographical polarization of support for the two main political parties (the Conservatives in the south, south-east and rural areas of England, Labour in the industrial cities, Scotland and Wales), together with growing criticisms of the power of the executive, the electoral system, the legal system, the police and so on, all reflect a decline in legitimacy. In addition, the question of some devolution of power to a Scottish parliament is seen by some as potentially undermining the very foundation of the regime – the Act of Union between England and Scotland of 1707 (Moran, 1991, pp. 93–108).

The developing political and economic policies of the European Community, of which Britain is one of the more important members, will have a significant impact on the British political system. Its effects are already evident in the limitations now placed on the initiatives of member governments in financial and economic policy, and on the influence over other members of the strongest economy in the community, Germany. The integration of the financial and economic policies of the members was epitomized by the establishment of the Single European Market on 1 January 1993. Meanwhile, negotiations continue with the aim of creating much greater political union within the community. Debate is taking place in Britain and other member states as to the implications of this for national sovereignty, which may be a little late as well as rather unreal, for the concept of sovereignty may change its meaning according to the context of actual relationships both between governments and between them and supranational organizations in the years to come. It certainly opens up the possibility that in the future legitimacy will be understood by the British people in a European rather than in a national context.

After the Russian Revolution the Bolsheviks had a long struggle to establish control over most of the Soviet empire. The degree of coercion used throughout the 1920s and 1930s did not suggest a regime that had been accepted by the mass of the people, although some saw it as affording great new opportunities. The Second World War (which the Soviet authorities, significantly, called 'the Great Patriotic War') reflected the situation. While Russians and some of the other peoples fought bitterly against the invader, many of the nationalities on the Soviet Union's western border welcomed the Nazis as liberators. Nevertheless, victory (as it often does) consolidated the Soviet regime. The dissident nationalities, now part of a great power, acquiesced in a situation they could do little about. Firm central control and a hard line towards any form of dissidence gave the impression of well-founded legitimacy. As the general standard of living rose throughout the 1950s and 1960s, the Soviet regime was probably enjoying as high a level of legitimacy as it had ever had. The failure to maintain this economic progress in the 1970s, together with an inability to keep up with technological advances, the debilitating effect of the arms race and the disaster of the war in Afghanistan, combined to generate frustration and cynical disillusion. However, such decline can drag on for a long time unless a catalyst is introduced to precipitate change. Gorbachev's policies of *glasnost* and *perestroika* did just this, unleashing many pent-up nationalist frustrations, and dissatisfaction with social and economic conditions, which revealed a serious weakness in the legitimacy of the regime. By the middle of 1991 it was clear the Soviet Union could continue in existence only as a loose confederation. Even that became impossible after the failed coup attempt in August and the vote for independence by Ukraine in December (Crawshaw, 1992).

The successor republics of the Soviet Union have to deal with many questions regarding their legitimacy. While some nationalities have a clear historically and culturally based sense of national identity, others have not. All face questions regarding their borders, the ethnic minorities within their republics and the attitude of other powers towards them. Some also have intra-ethnic tribal, regional or city-based divisions. The serious economic problems facing them can only exacerbate their difficulties.

The problem of legitimacy is made more severe by polarization within the state. Where a challenge is particular, diffuse or temporary, or where an individual's loyalties are likely to be divided, it does not pose a strong threat to the regime's legitimacy. To be strong, a challenge has to be single-minded and sustained. The Republican section of the community in Northern Ireland, for example, approaches a total opposition which denies all legitimacy to the regime. In such circumstances, as indeed the British government has found, it is all but impossible for the regime to maintain stability except by coercion. There are similar situations in some of the post-Soviet republics. In Moldova, to cite one example, both the Gagauz (Christian Turks) and the Russian-Ukrainian community have challenged the legitimacy of the Moldovan government (which is controlled by the majority Romanian community) to the extent of trying to set up their own republics.

Fortunately, for most governments the problem of legitimacy is not usually as severe as the above examples suggest. The attitude of many, if not most, citizens to the regime is, as we shall see, probably one of pragmatic, conditional acquiescence. It is what they are used to, its characteristics are accepted, if not always with enthusiasm, and there is generally a feeling that, due to familiarity if nothing else, it is preferable to any alternatives. That is not to say that the government cannot arouse more positive and overt expressions of support by appeals to the emotions in certain circumstances, such as a royal wedding or the external threat of war. But even in the case of war, people's attitudes are probably rather more subtle, complex and equivocal than is often supposed. The impact of the dominant ideology on the recipient population, conveyed through the education system and the media, appeals to the emotions and even the solid achievements of successive governments, is something of which we still know little. We can say that people often have conflicting and alternative values, priorities and achievements with which to compare the claims of the controlling groups, and this is likely to give rise to equivocal and even sceptical attitudes in the minds of many.

However, sceptical attitudes are unlikely to lead to action to undermine the legitimacy of the regime except after long periods of dissatisfaction and when a peculiar combination of circumstances gives rise to an opportunity for action. Non-acceptance of the regime, particularly in authoritarian regimes where opportunities for overt political action are limited, may be expressed negatively or indirectly by, for example, low productivity or pointed enthusiasm for ostensibly non-political organizations like the church (as in communist Poland) which can be seen as embodying an overt expression of national identity and ideals. A crucial factor in any challenge to a regime is how far people perceive that overt opposition will have a chance of achieving results.

## Challenges and Subcultures

A society may have an official myth and tradition, an accepted interpretation of its history and an ideology associated with the dominant culture of the ruling group, but there are also a number of subcultures and systems of ideas, associated with the working class in particular geographical areas, or work or age groups.

These subcultural values which are more firmly rooted in the mind than the dominant ideology and culture inculcated by education and the media, may well have a major effect on the political attitude and behaviour of the individual. This may lead to various results. A tension may be created in the individual's mind between the values of the subculture and those of the dominant ideology. This may not be so much of a problem in relation to the mass media, because the individual can select and adopt frivolous, sceptical or hostile attitudes as may be deemed appropriate. However, in the compulsory education system the individual may find it impossible to reconcile the values inculcated by teachers and books with those of the local society in which he or she lives. This may be the cause of some of the revolts evident in schools, particularly in working-class areas. Middle-class youth may also manifest such signs of revolt, particularly in the educational context of college and university, as they did in the late 1960s.

The reason why there is not more widespread political disruption is not because of the inculcation of deferential values; rather, it is because of social pressures towards a preoccupation with affairs regarded as of individual rather than of social concern, such as the maintenance of the family's living standards and the acquisition of a home. In addition, the individual's response to situations felt to be unsatisfactory is greatly affected by his or her perception of the possibility of change and the existence of other viable options. In the likely event of no feasible alternative offering itself, his or her attitude will be less a manifestation of discontent than a pragmatic acquiescence – an acceptance of a situation that he or she can see no practicable possibility of changing. A person's political role may be more than apathy and less than activism, but from the point of view of the authorities it serves the purpose of keeping protest and discontent down to a manageable level.

A clear manifestation of the existence of a subculture, usually accompanied by pragmatic acquiescence, is found in the situation of African-Americans. It is impossible to discuss the impact of political socialization on this group in the same terms as for the white majority. Historically, the dominant process reinforced the inferior status of African-Americans and the racism endemic in American institutions, and consequently, their political participation, where it has not actually been illegal, has tended to be slight. This pattern began to change first in the northern cities,

where African-Americans made their first real contact with the
political system other than as its victims. But the first time they
had more than a marginal impact on events was in the urban
riots of the 1960s. Explanations vary as to why these occurred
when they did, but it seems likely that the rising expectations
generated by the mass civil-rights movement and the readier
appreciation of the vast material gulfs between black and white
society provided the conditions in which riots could be sparked
off by almost any incident. Having been systematically excluded
from traditional 'legitimate' forms of political participation,
African-Americans, not surprisingly, employed other forms, notably the riot. Black and white perceptions of why the riots
occurred diverge widely, needless to say, but the evidence suggests that most African-Americans saw them as expressions of
genuine community protest which were seen as helpful in achieving their goals. But the questions remain: did the situation of
those who rioted improve and, if not, why did the riots not recur
in subsequent years? In the short run, much federal money was
pumped into the urban ghettos, welfare eligibility was eased and,
mainly because of the Vietnam War, employment prospects improved. But in the longer term little happened.

By the mid-1970s the situation for African-American inhabitants of the ghettos was as bad, if not worse, than it had been in
the 1960s. Inflation and recession had hit the poor hardest, as it
always does, and unemployment again rose. Meanwhile, the government was more conscious of conservative financial orthodoxy,
and so welfare eligibility and other programmes were reduced.
Furthermore, between 1981 and 1986 the Reagan administration
took the initiative in attempting to dismantle parts of the legal
structure by which the federal government had attempted to protect ethnic minorities since the 1960s. Appointments of key personnel, arguments in court and funding policies all played a part
in this. After the Democrats recaptured the Senate in 1986, and
rejected Reagan's nomination of Robert Bork to the Supreme
Court in 1987, the steam ran out of the New Right campaign.
Bush was less committed to an anti-civil-rights position: though
his 1988 campaign was marked by advertisements pandering
to white racism, while Congress has reasserted the liberal position. In 1989 the Supreme Court made a number of decisions
which increased the burden of proof on those – both minorities
and women – seeking to demonstrate that employers were engag-
ing in discriminatory practices regarding employment. Congress

responded to these decisions by passing a Civil Rights Act to reinstate employee protection but Bush vetoed the measure just before the 1990 mid-term elections. Congress reintroduced the bill in 1991 and, although Bush signalled continued opposition, he eventually signed into law a modified version in October 1991. However, there were early indications that enforcement of the new law may be less than energetic (*Guardian*, 22 November 1991, p. 12).

There were fewer riots during this period than there had been in the 1960s, but this can hardly be explained by an increase in positive support for the political system from minorities. While a growing ethnic minority middle class participated more in the political system, the relative quiescence of the growing numbers of extremely poor African- and Hispanic-American citizens was relatively pragmatic. Intracommunal violence and drug abuse took a rising toll and yet state violence against these people was still capable of provoking outbursts of serious rioting, as in Los Angeles in April and among Hispanics in New York in July 1992.

The episodic nature of riots in Britain during the 1980s suggests that certain groups do not accord much, if any, legitimacy to the system, but only occasionally is this manifested in physical attack. Most of the time a combination of factors such as economic survival, the creation of a life-style separate and distinct from the mainstream economy and society, and increasingly sophisticated policing ensure a lack of overt and sustained challenge.

## Conclusion

Controlling groups ignore at their peril the potential instability caused by the rejection of the legitimacy of their regimes. This is made doubly difficult for them by uncertainty as to what may trigger successful challenges to their legitimacy and when. In assessing the significance of challenges to the powers that be from outside the 'normal' political process, a regime has to discern whether they are actually challenges to its authority to govern, or manifestations of discontent at a particular shortcoming which can be assuaged by a relatively small change in policy.

It is important to try to assess the presence or absence of these factors, but it is frequently very difficult and, in any case, what starts off as a protest at a particular policy may, given particular conditions, escalate into a more generalized revolt. If we knew with more certainty what it is that sustains legitimacy in the first place, it would be easier to see how legitimacy may be eroded. For example, do regimes gain legitimacy by meeting the expectations of the people for a certain standard of living, or by pursuing procedures widely perceived as fair even if the results are not so bountiful? For Marxists, there can be no such thing as legitimacy for capitalist liberal democratic regimes.

If we accept that the primary objective of all regimes – whether they are liberal democracies, Marxist-inspired, third-world 'people's democracies' or military juntas – is to stay in power, then to maximize the citizen's acceptance of the regime will be paramount. The point would probably be accepted by all analysts. Where they would differ would be over whether this acceptance is given freely and genuinely by the citizenry, or is manipulated by the ruling group's use of such symbols as the queen, the flag and the country.

## Questions for Discussion

1  How far can governments foster their own legitimacy as opposed to merely neutralizing dissent?
2  Under what sorts of circumstances will the legitimacy of a regime (a) diminish and (b) collapse?
3  Discuss the view that acquiescence rather than legitimacy is a more realistic concept to describe the relationship between government and citizens.

## Further Reading

Bailer, S. (1991), The death of Soviet communism. *Foreign Affairs*, 70 (5), pp. 166–81.

Held, D. (1984), Power and legitimacy in contemporary Britain. In G. McLennan, D. Held and S. Hall (eds), *State and Society in Contemporary Britain: A Critical Introduction*. Cambridge, Polity, pp. 299–369.

Joll, J. (1977), *Gramsci*. London, Fontana, esp. ch. 9.

Jowitt, K. (1990), Gorbachev: Bolshevik or Menshevik?. In S. White, A. Pravda and Z. Gitelman (eds), *Developments in Soviet Politics*. Basingstoke, Macmillan, pp. 88–104.

McKay, D. (1989), *American Politics and Society*, 2nd edn. Oxford, Blackwell, pp. 23–32.

Mandelbaum, M. (1992), The end of the Soviet Union. *Foreign Affairs*, 71 (1), pp. 164–83.

Miliband, R. (1982), *Capitalist Democracy in Britain*. Oxford, Oxford University Press, pp. 76–93.

Moran, M. (1985), *Politics and Society in Britain*. Basingstoke, Macmillan, ch. 2.

Peele, G. (1992), Values, institutions and policy agendas. In G. Peele et al. (eds), *Developments in American Politics*. Basingstoke, Macmillan, pp. 14–36.

# 25

# Political Socialization

## Introduction

A major way in which those with political power attempt to create and maintain their legitimacy or acceptance in the eyes of the citizens is by the process of political socialization. 'Socialization' can be broadly defined as a learning process undergone by an individual to establish his or her position and role in society. From birth, an individual undergoes a very extensive process of learning which will affect all his or her relationships and thus the direction of his or her life. The process is continuous but early socialization, perhaps, has, a particular significance. Students of politics are concerned with the individual's relations with those in power, the degree and kind of political activity in which he or she is engaged and why different behaviour can be observed even though socialization processes are ostensibly similar. It is probably true to say that, so far, studies in political socialization have raised more questions than they have answered. The problem still is to clear the ground and to establish the most appropriate and useful questions to ask.

In our discussion of ideology in chapter 4, we saw that effective socialization for some analysts means the inculcation of the dominant ideology throughout all classes of society. The result of such socialization is that this 'dominant' set of ideas is taken to be self-evidently correct. Thus people see their place in society as being right and proper, in spite of their low expectations and rewards and lack of control over their own lives.

## Politics and the Child

Much study of political socialization has been based on the assumption that it is experiences and learning during early childhood which have the most profound effect on political attitudes and behaviour. This makes the family or family-substitute the most important unit of socialization. It should be noted, however, that the family can take on a variety of forms and significance within different social contexts. The patterns of attitudes and behaviour that the family and its immediate social context establish are seen to be the deepest and most lasting of the individual's life. Thus, whether a child is likely to take a positive and active, or a negative and passive, attitude to politics is thought to be influenced by the attitudes and activities of its parents, relatives and peers. They are seen as passing on the tradition which, in the great majority of cases, is one of acceptance of the received values and ideas of the ruling group and of the assumption of a passive, acquiescent and inactive role in the political system. Only a minority, born into the ruling group and brought up in special privileged circumstances, are likely to adopt an active, involved, leadership role. Activists not from the ruling group are likely to have been brought up in a politically aware family – for example those actively engaged in trade-unionism. Therefore, the habits acquired early in life are seen as the dominant influences on an individual's behaviour for the remainder of his or her life, and factors such as class background, education and work experience will simply reinforce the influence of the family. In the political process as a whole this serves to maintain established patterns of behaviour and thus contributes to the stability of the political process. If people are conditioned early into essentially passive or apathetic attitudes towards politics they are more likely to behave in predictable ways which constitute no threat to legitimacy and stability.

However, whatever the strength of childhood experiences and conditioning, the assumption of the great influence of childhood does not answer some difficulties which the evidence throws up. For example, how can perceived changes in the political behaviour patterns of adults be explained? Recent examples of this in Britain are the changes in party support and related voting behaviour, which have been shown to affect all age groups and which cannot be explained away by the replacement of generations.

Something more is needed to account for the weakening of the transference of the received tradition which has occurred perceptibly between one generation and the next. The child-socialization theory suggests a reinforcement of tradition rather than a weakening of it. The intensive socialization programme of the Soviet Union did not prevent a perceptible weakening of legitimacy in post-Second World War generations. Another difficulty that is not accounted for by the theory is the different development of individuals apparently brought up in very similar circumstances. Many British middle-class individuals educated in public schools show just as much apathy or cynicism towards politics as many members of the working class, while some of the latter develop a highly political consciousness. In American and former Soviet society, too, we can perceive acceptance or rejection of received values among people whose socialization has been ostensibly similar. Clearly, other factors, like personality and personal experience, must have an effect. Another shortcoming of the socialization-in-childhood view is its assumption that identical behaviour reflects both identical attitudes underlying that behaviour, and a similar understanding of the meaning of that behaviour in another context. The significance for a British voter of voting Labour in 1945 may be very different indeed from the similar act of voting Labour by the same individual in 1992. His or her depth of conviction, expectations, understanding of the meaning of the Labour Party in his or her life and in the political life of the country may all be profoundly different, yet according to this theory they are masked by apparently identical behaviour in the two instances.

Recently, it has been more commonly argued that, far from being primarily experienced in childhood, political socialization is a continuing process throughout life. It is profoundly affected by the more dramatic life experiences of the individual and his or her social group, like unemployment or war. For example, it would appear that a critical point in the establishment of partisan loyalties, which frequently last for a long time, is when a person is first able to vote. In the United States the catastrophic depression of the 1930s induced many more new voters to vote Democrat than would otherwise have done so. By and large, that generation's loyalties have endured up to the present time. In contrast, the generation that first voted in the 1960s and 1970s have shown a greater tendency to view themselves as independents and to switch their votes more readily from one party to another. An important factor in their political socialization was that the major political events as they reached maturity were the Vietnam War and domestic social unrest, neither of which was as susceptible to a simple 'party cures' as was the depression of the 1930s. The assumption that the older a person gets the more conservative he or she becomes is true only to a limited extent. The individual's adherence to habitual behaviour will be much affected by the pressures that he or she feels in life, by his or her sense of security, by the extent of his or her responsibilities, among other factors. A person may even be more cautious of change in middle life (because there is more to lose) than in old age. The point is that individuals are not fixed in their political attitudes in childhood – important as that period is – but are open to significant changes in attitudes and behaviour throughout their lives. Political socialization is a continuous process.

## Education

All political systems have some means, not necessarily public, of providing the education necessary for the attainment of the goals of the controlling groups. These arrangements may appear bizarre or eccentric to outsiders and there is a danger that the system and its methods can become outdated through inertia, inhibiting the ability of institutions to keep up with social change. The significant new feature of education systems in modern industrialized societies is the need to teach the entire population basic information and skills and how to convey equally basic but essential messages through the system. This is to equip the population to operate and understand the complex interlocking functions of industrialized society. Education, therefore, is seen as desirable by the controlling groups in so far as it contributes to the social and political cohesion they desire.

In Great Britain there is officially no overt political indoctrination. In practice this means that while the principles of liberal democracy are broadly upheld, no support is openly given to any particular (usually party) interpretation of them. It does not mean that there is not a good deal of implicit bias on occasions. Until recently, most arguments about education in Britain have centred on the question of access, but in the past few years the Conservative government and a number of local authorities have questioned the content of what is being taught. Some of the questions are related to the problem of racism, such as has been tackled in the United States; and the introduction of 'peace studies' has led to accusations of schools being used for propaganda. Attempts to examine syllabuses and books in order to eliminate sexism have also met with opposition. The Conservative government of the 1980s also set out to establish for the first time in Great Britain a national curriculum of courses for all schools. Controversy surrounded the teaching of history in particular, where the syllabus had been broadened to encompass the experiences of a variety of groups and classes. The new national curriculum aims to return history teaching to more traditional lines, centred around the 'great' events and prominent individuals of British history.

How is the 'dominant ideology' said to be inculcated into the population? Here the practice of Great Britain and of the old Soviet Union present an apparent contrast. In Britain a child's political attitude and behaviour are decided by the implicit information that the child receives indirectly from family, teachers, mass media and peer group. He or she may receive a consistent message from these sources which are steadily modified by the growth of knowledge and awareness. However, for most children the message is to some degree confused. Officially, the child is told that political awareness and activity are desirable attributes of the 'good' citizen, but other messages convey the impression that politics is 'boring', 'stupid' and generally irrelevant to most of his or her life's activity.

In the Soviet Union an elaborate system of political teaching in the principles of Marxism-Leninism was organized in schools, youth organizations, colleges and workplaces. In addition, there were many opportunities for people to pursue their political education on a voluntary basis. This approach arose out of the need to 'resocialize' a whole population after the revolution, but it owes far more to the Marxist-Leninist belief in the centrality of ideas as a means to action, and that all social action is political. Thus, from the 'Lenin corner' in a Soviet school to the compulsory Marxist-Leninist classes at university, the point was driven home.

It is debatable whether the British approach is any less effective than the overt, organized education programme in Marxism-Leninism which characterized not only the educational system but also the workplace in the Soviet Union. The emphasis on theory and the formality of the programme raised doubts in the minds of some Soviet commentators as to whether its results justified the large expenditure of money, time and energy. Its continuance was based mostly on the wishes of vested interests and their belief in such a programme as an essential 'revolutionary' activity. In spite of the political education programme, certain other values, such as religious belief and nationalism, continued to be successfully transmitted from one generation to the next, presumably via the family and the general cultural milieu of the various nationalities. Thus the Soviet political-socialization programme was a costly and ultimately self-defeating policy. People found it difficult to relate Marxist-Leninist theory to the reality of their daily lives which must have helped ultimately to undermine the credibility of the system. The role of education in the new republics will probably not be controlled in this way in most cases. It will not be easy for them to develop education systems that reflect their new-found self-conscious independence while retaining sufficient detachment to command credibility. The content of their educational programmes, especially the teaching of history and the social sciences, will, of course, undergo fundamental revision (Lane, 1992, pp. 289–314).

Political socialization in the United States provides another model which lies somewhere between those of Great Britain and the Soviet Union. Like the post-revolutionary Soviet elites, American elites have always been well aware of the importance of socialization. A major vehicle for the Americanization of the large numbers of immigrants was the comprehensive and publicly funded school system, which has been used more overtly than that in Great Britain for the inculcation of political attitudes deemed to be desirable. Civics classes are compulsory and concentrate primarily on early American history – the revolution, the founding fathers and early presidents. It is again questionable as to whether this more overt system of socialization is necessarily any more effective than the rather more subtle British system. Tension over the content of education has been greater in the United States than in Britain, particularly since the attempt to desegregate schooling in the post-1954 period. Growing black consciousness produced many criticisms of syllabuses which reflected white dominance. Therefore, in many areas today much more emphasis is given to studies reflecting the experiences and culture of minority groups. This in turn has given rise to reaction and the criticism that only 'politically correct' interpretations can be taught.

We are not yet in a position to come to definite conclusions about the actual political influence of education. What is certain is that education is usually a comparatively minor influence compared to that of the family and general social background. The factors in political socialization are many and complex, and cross-national comparisons and analyses may serve only to confuse the issue.

## The Media

Accompanying the other socialization processes of the individual in an industrialized society is the constant presence of the media. Of the various media the most significant, politically speaking, is television, followed by sound-broadcasting, newspapers, magazines and films. The characteristics of the media as opposed to other forms of socialization are that, by means of modern technology, they enable messages to be conveyed more quickly and more graphically to far larger numbers of people than before. The obverse of it is that the control of technological resources is restricted to only a few people, and the opportunity for dialogue is therefore much reduced. For example, a public meeting creates an opportunity for face-to-face dialogue, while a viewer normally has no immediate means of communicating with the people on television, 'phone-in' programmes and the like notwithstanding.

First, how do politicians themselves use the media? Clearly, the ability of the media to reach a very large audience provides politicians with a vehicle of tremendous potential propaganda value – hence their attempts to control them and the jealous negotiations that go on between the major parties in a country like Britain over the allocation of time for party political broadcasts. So far, the use of the media to persuade the population to support one political party or group rather than another is less highly developed in the former Soviet republics. Their full potential has yet to be recognized. But is the widely held belief in the political impact of the media (especially television) justified? Certainly, politicians can reach large audiences through the media, but how easy is it for them to convey the intended political message, or to be sure that the recipient understands the message in the way intended? The predominance of television in electoral politics now means that the main energies of the political parties are directed towards sending highly simplified messages which are intended to create the desired *image* of the party and its candidates rather than indulging in detailed policy debate. However, all messages have to be filtered through a conceptual framework which preconditions the recipient to understand the message in a particular way. Hence political messages are likely to be rejected altogether by the uninterested recipient. This is more easily done in newspapers where the reader chooses what to read; than on television where an uninteresting item cannot so easily be excluded from conscious reception, but has to be accepted in the flow along with the other messages. In the United States election candidates make great use of television advertising (which they have to pay for) of no longer than fifteen or thirty seconds, while in Britain great efforts go towards the creation of a daily media 'event' tailored to the requirements of the main news programmes. Thus politicians aim to present brief, simple, reassuring images of themselves.

Second, how are politicians reported by the media? Politicians make increasingly strenuous efforts to achieve favourable coverage. For example, so-called 'spin-doctors', who first appeared in the United States but now also operate in Great Britain, speak privately to journalists after, say, the President or Prime Minister has made a speech, to ensure that they 'understand' the politician's preferred interpretation. With Reagan this was needed on some occasions to make the President's meaning comprehensible and to correct his frequent errors; but, in general, it represents an attempt to manipulate the information process. There were also many complaints of manipulation of the media (including the depriving of opponents of access to it) by politicians in the Soviet Union.

The fundamental issue here is that of control. It is misleading to think in terms of an absolute ideal of objectivity, but rather, we should ask who can and should control the media in order that society's best interests are served? It depends on the sense in which society as a whole can be said to have interests and how far we have to reconcile ourselves to an accommodation with particular vested interests (see discussion of interests in chapter 4). Many would argue that at the present time journalism reflects the preconceived opinions of proprietors and journalists, while broadcasting is basically controlled by the professionals – the station managers, producers and so on, a self-perpetuating elite of untypical educational and social background. Attempts to suggest policy changes that would open up broadcasting media and provide greater access to a wider range of individuals and social groups have so far received only token recognition. Any more fundamental change in the structure of control of the broadcasting media and of its relationship with the rest of society is extremely difficult to achieve in a planned, far-sighted way owing to vested interest and the control of the application of new technology (the latter itself governed by political and social pressures). New technology (such as the availability of more television channels) has the potential to enhance the democratic contribution of the media, but there are difficulties as to how a consensus may be reached on the way in which such opportunities are to be used. On the other hand, the development of satellite television appears to reduce the ability of states to control broadcasting in pursuit of general 'public' interest. Increasingly, the market rules the media (Jones, 1991, pp. 200–23).

The old Soviet Union had a system of communication that was closely supervised by the state. Once again, this was in line with an understanding of the media as primarily a means of propaganda rather than a purveyor of news and comment. The organization of broadcasting, newspapers and magazines was a vast undertaking, which covered the huge geographical area of the country. By Western standards, the political attitudes found in this vast output were tightly controlled by a system of syndicated material which was vetted and censored by the appropriate authorities to ensure that it was in line with official policy. No adverse criticism of a general nature was allowed except, in an indirect way, in learned journals with small circulations, although a good deal of criticism of specific aspects of the working of the administrative system was permitted, especially in the newspapers. The restrictions on communications in the Soviet Union contributed significantly to the atomization of society and was thus an important means of social and political control. Anyone who wished to circumvent such extensive state control had to find ways and means of publishing or broadcasting so-called *samizdat* material, which meant resorting to illegal private means of publication rather than using the official printing- and publishing-houses. The circulation of such material was inevitably limited, but it could sometimes have an impact out of proportion to the size of its circulation.

However, we cannot apply Western criteria to the Soviet media. The reluctance of the Soviet media, until the advent of *glasnost*, to report disasters such as air crashes was not self-evidently 'wrong'; rather, a different set of priorities existed as to what constituted 'news'. Soviet media aimed to present a positive and optimistic image of Soviet society. News and information that did not fit in with this aim had to be dealt with by the appropriate bodies, but it did not have to be blazoned abroad for all the world to read and see. Soviet dirty linen was not washed in public; instead, the media aimed to convey an image of order and unity. What is significant, perhaps, is that this almost undiluted diet of positive, pro-regime news and information did not prevent the legitimacy of the regime being undermined. The difference between the media image and perceived everyday reality became too great.

The censorship that existed did not need to be obtrusive in newspaper and television offices. The people employed in editorial positions knew what was expected of them – as, indeed, they usually do in Western countries too. If editors, or programme producers were doubtful about something, they occasionally took a chance. An interesting example of this was the stories that appeared in the literary magazine *Novy Mir* in the decade following the death of Stalin. More usually, however, they would await guidance which would come in official party speeches or statements printed in *Pravda*, then the party newspaper. What *Pravda* said was taken as official party policy throughout the country. Its editorials gave media personnel everywhere the guidance they needed as to the interpretation of official policy. Where a major dispute remained unresolved in top circles, politicians might utilize different journals or newspapers to support their line, and the assiduous reader was able to note the subtle changes of emphasis from different sources which indicated top-level disagreement. Such matters were likely to pass the general reader by.

The media face considerable challenges in the new situation following the collapse of the Soviet Union. Although they look to the Western media for models, it is by no means certain that they can achieve effective levels of freedom of expression. The new governments of the republics are sometimes authoritarian, often insecure and hence do not yet take criticism in their stride. Another immediate difficulty is the need to establish means of financing the media, which was hitherto supported by state subsidy. This, together with the serious shortage of newsprint and equipment makes for an uncertain future for the media in the former Soviet republics (Lane, 1992, pp. 315–33).

# Conclusion

The majority of citizens are persuaded by their place in the structure of the social system, and the priorities this engenders, that political activity is not relevant to changing their lot significantly. However, because socialization is a continuing process throughout life and is much affected by experiences of the individual or of social groups, no particular attitude to the social system can be seen as permanent and inevitable. The concepts related to socialization, for example legitimacy, stability, apathy, participation and acquiescence need to be constantly revised by the student of politics as circumstances change. They should never be taken for granted by politicians who wish to maintain a secure basis of support for the existing political system. Indeed, a great deal of political activity must be concerned with securing that base and ensuring that discontent is not activated into real political threats.

On the face of it, the education process must be an important socializing influence on individuals, although it is difficult to assess just how important it is relative to other influences such as the family and the workplace. We also need to ask why apparently very similar processes of education can produce a wide variety of political responses in different people. It is doubtful whether the much greater emphasis on overt political education in the Soviet Union was successful in persuading people that politics and public life are more important areas of endeavour than the acquisition of private material benefits. In the context of industrialized societies education has a double-edged role. On the one hand, such societies need an educated work-force, 'factory fodder' for the industrial machine. But, on the other hand, literacy and education can be great liberators of people's minds and may stir them to political activism. Thus, while debates surrounding education in Britain have concentrated on the question of access to the system, the question of the content of that education is equally, if not more, important in terms of its socializing effect.

There is no 'right' policy as to control of the media, just as there is no 'right' way to present news and comment. These questions can be resolved only in the context of the prevailing political and social values. For Marxists, these must be based on the existence of economic classes in conflict, and the need for a society which has abolished the conflict between them. For liberal democrats, various kinds and degrees of qualified elitism may be more accurate and desirable. The medium will mostly reflect the dominant values of or the clash of values in society. It cannot be realistically considered apart from these questions.

## Questions for Discussion

1   Do you consider that the structure of education necessarily reflects a particular ideological stance? If so, what are the implications for political activity?
2   How may the media contribute to wider political participation?
3   To what extent are socialization processes under the control of regimes?

## Further Reading

Curran, J. and J. Seaton (1981), *Power without Responsibility*. London, Fontana, ch. 14.
Denenberg, R.V. (1992), *Understanding American Politics*, 3rd edn. London, Fontana, ch. 8.
Dowse, R.E. (1978), Some doubts concerning the study of political socialisation. *Political Studies*, 26 (3), September, pp. 403–10.
Lane, D. (1992), *Soviet Society under Perestroika*, rev. edn. Boston, Unwin Hyman, chs 6 and 7.
Newton, K. (1988), Mass media, In H. Drucker, P. Dunleavy, A. Gamble and G. Peele (eds), *Developments in British Politics 2*, rev. edn. Basingstoke Macmillan, pp. 313–26.
Smith, G.B. (1992), *Soviet Politics: Struggling with Change*, 2nd edn. Basingstoke, Macmillan, ch. 4.

# 26

# Representation and Elections

## Introduction

Legitimacy is concerned with the relationship between those with political control and the people subject to them. As we have already noted, this is a matter not simply of attitudes but of behaviour. Political behaviour resolves itself into the question of the type and degree of participation or, conversely, the degree of non-participation or apathy tolerated or encouraged by the political system. In principle, both liberal democracy and communism place a high value on widespread political participation. There are, however, practical and political difficulties to hinder the implementation of this principle.

The practical difficulties revolve around the size of the population and the geographical area of many nation-states in the world. Although any ideas of an optimum or at least a minimum size for independent state existence have been abandoned in recent years, there are few states that do not number their population in hundreds of thousands, and most count them in millions. It seems impossible for the total population of states like Great Britain (56 million), Russia (148 million) and the United States (249 million) to play a significant political role in contemporary circumstances, even given the capabilities of modern technology. Attempts to take decisions and govern by means of large public meetings (where possible) is very cumbersome and is liable to produce inconsistent or bizarre results. It has frequently been shown that large meetings can be manipulated by demagogues and by those who are prepared to master the rules of procedure.

The political difficulties of greater participation revolve around the stability of the power structure. Participation on a large scale can involve delay, inconsistent and even arbitrary decisions, the upsetting of carefully negotiated agreements and the intrusion of short-lived emotional responses with long-term consequences.

## Representation

One of the most significant and widespread means of dealing with these problems is by some system of representation. In principle, the 'power of the people' is temporarily transferred to (usually) elected individuals to speak and act on their behalf. Representation is essentially a means of overcoming the difficulties of participation in decision-making where large numbers effectively preclude everyone from being involved. But, even though opportunities for manipulation and difficulties of coherent and consistent decision-making in mass meetings are evident, to transfer decision-making to a limited number of people – while keeping them in significant contact with the larger group – also gives rise to problems. For example, what are the terms of reference within which the representatives operate? Who should be represented and to what degree? What structures and procedures are appropriate? Once again, we have to refer to the values and presuppositions of the society in which the system of representation exists. In some societies the monarch represented the people by virtue of his or her appointment being ratified by God. No means of election or accountability were necessary. (This did not stop kings, even god-kings, from being deposed, however.) In eighteenth-century Britain only those who were considered to have a stake in society through the ownership of property were entitled to be directly represented, and the right to elect was even more restricted. Throughout the eighteenth and nineteenth centuries, however, an individualistic and egalitarian philosophy gained ground, and it was argued that almost all men were entitled to an equal say in the choice of decision-makers. (Not until the twentieth century was the same argument applied to women.) In practice, this meant one vote of equal value per person (universal suffrage and equal electoral districts). One vote per person in Britain was not achieved until the 1940s, but practical difficulties have prevented the attainment of votes of equal value expressed by electoral districts of equal numbers of voters from being anything like fully implemented even today. There is, however, nothing self-evidently right or proper about the principles behind this system of voting. It simply reflects and expresses a certain understanding of society.

There are also various ways of looking at the terms of reference within which representatives operate. For example, whom do deputies to the soviets, American members of congress and British members of parliament represent? That they are elected from a particular constituency or electoral district suggests that they represent the people living there and, indeed, they do take up problems on behalf of constituents regardless of their party allegiance. Alternatively, Edmund Burke, the eighteenth-century political philosopher, argued that representatives should support only those policies they believed to be in the 'national interest'. This means that they should have complete freedom to decide what is in the interests of their country, even if it conflicts with their constituents' particular interests. A quite different notion of what representation involves, which is accepted by few MPs, members of congress and deputies in the soviets, is the idea of representatives as delegate, that is they have no authority to decide anything themselves. Rather, they have to promote and support what has been specifically agreed at meetings of those whom they represent. In other words, they are mandated to speak and vote on behalf of particular policies. Clearly, this attitude reflects a greater concern with the possibility of representatives losing touch with their electors. But it could make the representative forum itself very inflexible and slow in operation as delegates find themselves having to report back for fresh instructions.

## Electoral Systems

Elections are a manifestation of political participation, and they provide analysts with vast amounts of quantitative information which can now be manipulated, with ever-increasing statistical complexity, with the aid of computers. As a result, elections and voting behaviour have provided a massive field of study within the analysis of politics generally. As we examine some of the findings of this research, we shall consider what it is that we want to know and why, and just how effective elections are in influencing what governments actually do. If we regard politics essentially as a process of power and the making of decisions, it may be that elections have been given a disproportionate importance in recent studies. But their legitimating role, the opportunities they give to those who win and form governments, and the re-evaluations that take place among the defeated cannot be dismissed as trivial or meaningless in the political process.

Just as different ideas and practices of representation reflect different relationships of power, so do different ways of counting votes. As was suggested in chapter 4, voting systems are by no means neutral methods of totalling preferences. Electoral systems can basically be divided into variations on the simple majority (first-past-the-post) system, the proportional representation system, and some combination of the two. In the simple majority system the person who gets a majority of votes in each constituency or electoral district wins the seat. With proportional representation there is, as the name suggests, a close proportional relationship between votes cast in favour of a particular party and seats won. The particular system that is adopted will depend not so much on theoretical principles or on what is considered 'right' or 'fair', as on the way in which the system is likely to reflect the interests of those in power in staying there.

Four broad types of political contests between parties in an election have been identified by analysts, based on a notion of a 'normal' vote, that is if everyone were to vote for the party with which they are identified. The first and most frequent type is the 'maintaining', election in which the party with the largest 'normal' vote wins. Second, there is the 'deviating' election, in which for some reason the minority party wins but without affecting the basic support for the parties. Third, we have the 'reinstating' election, in which the majority party returns to power. Fourth, there is the 'realigning' election, in which some major events disrupt the majority coalition and replace it with a new coalition through the vehicle of the other main party.

## Voting

Universal suffrage was originally seen as a direct link between the mass of the citizens and those chosen to be decision-makers. The voter was seen as making a rational choice between candidates on the basis of their personal qualities and the policy proposals of the parties to which they belonged. The ability to understand the options and to make a rational choice was assumed, and those who did not accept such an assumption tended to be unenthusiastic about universal suffrage, preferring some limitation of it, for example an educational qualification. This comparatively simplistic rational theory of voting behaviour eventually took several knocks. It was noticed between the two world wars that people were sometimes prepared to vote into office advocates of apparently irrational behaviour like Adolf Hitler. Other evidence emerged, for example that a large proportion of the electorate remained consistent in their voting behaviour, irrespective of candidates and policies, while another large proportion was unaware of what the policy proposals of the parties were or, even if they were aware, were unable to attribute policies to the parties that advocated them. Thus modifications of the theory took place. At first, it was agreed that, while the majority of voters acted out of habit, a relatively well-informed minority did consider the issues and acted rationally. The results of elections were thought to turn on the decisions of this minority.

A much more sophisticated analysis of the non-rational theory of voting behaviour eventually developed, emanating from the so-called Michigan School. It forms the basis of the major study of British voting behaviour in the period 1964–70 by David Butler and Donald Stokes (1974). In this analysis, voting behaviour is seen largely as a habitual activity which can be explained by the early socialization experiences of the electorate. Thus voters who underwent their early childhood socialization before the First World War are more likely to be Conservative Party supporters than Labour supporters, because in that period there were comparatively few established Labour-supporting households. This means that the apparent, disproportionate tendency of older people to vote Conservative is due to people remaining fixed in their attitudes and habits rather than to a transference of loyalties as they grew older.

David Robertson (1976), of the Essex School, has argued the need for a new rational theory of voting behaviour to explain the voting behaviour of the 1970s. The electorate in Great Britain and the United States seemed more volatile and less inclined to stick to habitual voting behaviour. The problem with previous rational theories, Robertson argues, is that the concept of rationality was defined too narrowly to be helpful in the field of voting behaviour. If we redefine the concept more flexibly we may understand the voter as acting rationally in accordance with his or her perceived best interests, based on a general idea of party image and policy, his or her personal experiences and circumstances, and the emotional relationships and responses he or she has in relation to politics.

## Elections and Voting in Great Britain

In Great Britain the simple majority (or first-past-the-post) system has a built-in bias in favour of the larger parties so long as votes for minority parties are not too geographically concentrated (see table 26.1). It is usually the two biggest parties – Conservative and Labour – which benefit from a first-past-the-post system at the expense of the smaller parties. Nationally, the Liberal Party (now the Liberal Democrats) has suffered primarily, with even the Scottish National Party receiving a better ratio of seats to votes because their vote is relatively concentrated compared to that for the Liberals. Proportional representation has been used in Northern Ireland, but it is not necessarily considered a precedent for the rest of Britain because of the unusual political circumstances prevailing there. To concede proportional representation in elections to the European Parliament or to devolved assemblies, may be seen as an admission of the acceptability of such a form of voting for the Westminster Parliament. Thus it has so far been resisted by those in power, who perceive that they may well lose from such a change.

The prospects for change in the British system seem unlikely in spite of the Conservative government having been returned in the 1979, 1983, 1987 and 1992 elections, with parliamentary majorities on the basis of the votes of just over two in five voters (one in three of the total electorate). Previous Labour governments had also been elected on a minority of votes cast. Because the Conservative governments so elected adopted radical and controversial policies on the basis of their simple majority, the desirability or otherwise of proportional representation has come increasingly to be discussed. The Labour Party is prepared, reluctantly, to discuss the issue. But any change is not likely to be implemented while a Conservative government is in power.

In British elections since the 1970s an average of one person in four who was entitled to vote did not do so. Since this is the absolute minimum of representation available to the individual, why is it that a sizeable percentage of the electorate do not vote? It seems that non-voting is accounted for as much by factors like being away or sick, or having moved, as it is by apathy or a

Table 26.1 Votes cast and MPs elected, by party, in Great Britain, 1974–1992 (%)

| | 1974 (Feb.) | | 1974 (Oct.) | | 1979 | | 1983 | | 1987 | | 1992 | |
|---|---|---|---|---|---|---|---|---|---|---|---|---|
| | Vote | MPs | Vote | MPs | Vote | MPs | Vote | MPs | Vote | MPs | Vote | MPs |
| Conservative | 38.2 | 46.6 | 35.8 | 43.5 | 43.9 | 53.4 | 42.4 | 60.8 | 42.3 | 57.5 | 41.9 | 51.6 |
| Labour | 37.2 | 47.4 | 39.3 | 50.2 | 36.9 | 42.4 | 27.6 | 31.8 | 30.8 | 34.9 | 34.4 | 41.6 |
| Lib/SDP/LD | 19.3 | 2.2 | 18.3 | 2.0 | 13.8 | 1.7 | 25.4 | 3.6 | 22.6 | 3.4 | 17.8 | 3.1 |
| Plaid Cynru | 0.6 | 0.3 | 0.6 | 0.5 | 0.4 | 0.3 | 0.4 | 0.3 | 0.4 | 0.5 | 0.5 | 0.6 |
| SNP | 2.0 | 0.1 | 2.9 | 1.7 | 1.6 | 0.3 | 1.1 | 0.3 | 1.3 | 0.5 | 1.9 | 0.5 |
| Other | 2.7 | 2.3 | 3.0 | 2.1 | 3.4 | 2.0 | 3.1 | 3.2 | 2.6 | 3.2 | 3.4 | 2.6 |

*Note*: Columns may not add up to 100% because of rounding.

*Sources*: 1974: *Social Trends*, 1977. London, HMSO.
1979: *Guardian*, 6 May 1979.
1983, 1987: *Keesing's Contemporary Archives*
1992: *Keesing's Record of World Events*

conscious decision to withhold a vote as a protest. There are no significant differences in socio-economic characteristics between non-voters and voters.

Up to the 1960s, the best predictor of a person's voting behaviour in twentieth-century Britain was social class. Labour was supported predominantly by the working class, and the Conservatives by the middle class (with, however, up to a third of the working class voting Conservative). Butler and Stokes (1974) note that this class-based voting behaviour was then tending to become less significant. Why, and in what circumstances, do people change their voting habits? It was found that a much higher proportion of the voters than analysts had realized changed their voting behaviour at some time during their lives and that this volatility was on the increase. However, habitual behaviour was still the dominant factor, as there was a strong tendency for voters to revert to their habitual voting pattern after a comparatively short period of volatility.

The growing volatility in voting behaviour during the 1970s, the period following that studied by Butler and Stokes, raised questions about their thesis (see figure 26.1). In the last four elections (1979, 1983, 1987, 1992) support for the two largest parties has settled at around 55 per cent of the electorate. Where were the lost votes going? Up to 1970 a significant part of the loss was the result of declining turnout after 1950, but since 1970 the votes have been going primarily to other parties, in particular to what is now the Liberal Democrats in England and to the nationalist parties of Scotland and Wales. The steady change in voting habits reflected in this series of election results cannot be explained by the Butler and Stokes analysis. We can approach the problem in part by recognizing that political socialization is not confined to childhood but is a lifelong process, and that this can sometimes result in major shifts of attitude and behaviour. For example, Crewe, Fox and Alt (1977) suggest that the apparent failure of successive governments of both parties in the 1960s and early 1970s led to a decline in the number of people identifying strongly with the two major parties, resulting in a drop in support and declining turnout.

Thus even the built-in bias of the simple-majority electoral system cannot sustain indefinitely the predominance of the two main parties in the face of continued decline. At some stage a 'realignment' election may occur, in which the electoral relationship between the parties will be permanently altered. This may

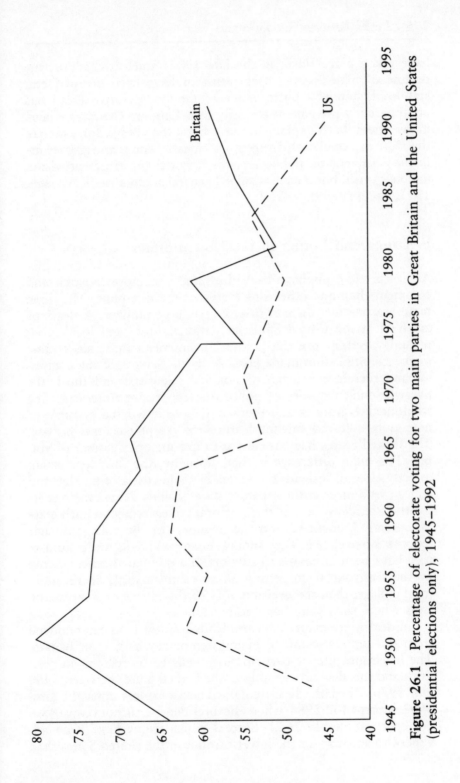

**Figure 26.1** Percentage of electorate voting for two main parties in Great Britain and the United States (presidential elections only), 1945–1992

have taken place since, in the late 1980s and early 1990s, the decline of major-party votes seems to have been arrested and stabilized, but in a position where the Conservative Party has an apparently permanent majority over Labour. There have been many attempts to explain the new basis for voting, for example the shift in population from inner cities to suburbia, greater affluence, reliance on public services rather than private provision and vice versa, but none has gained general acceptance (Kavanagh, 1991, pp. 179–99).

## Elections and Voting in the United States

American elections have been the subject of more research and comment than any other single area of the discipline. The three main reasons for this are: first, a very large number of elections are held in the United States at national, state and local level; second, elections are the political phenomena most susceptible to the quantification made possible by the advent of the computer and therefore beloved of political scientists; and third, the overwhelming majority of political scientists are American. The resulting literature is enormous and here it will be possible to note only a few dominant features of recent electoral history. The United States has basically a simple-majority system of voting. The main difference is that, formally, the President is not directly elected. Instead, the voters elect members of an electoral college who meet in the separate state capitals to cast their votes for the President. In fact the electoral college votes in each state are already committed and the members of the college do not exercise a free choice. They simply register a vote for the candidate they have been delegated to support. If a popular third candidate prevents anyone from getting an absolute majority in the electoral college, then the decision goes to the House of Representatives where each state has one vote.

Political representation in the United States is as far removed from the supposed aim of liberal democracy as it is in Britain. The basic measure of participation tends to be turnout in elections and this declined steadily in the United States between 1960 and 1976. Then the level remained more or less constant until 1992, except for 1988 when the presidential turnout was 48.6 per cent. (see table 26.2). Several explanations have been advanced to account for the lower turnout in the United States than

**Table 26.2  Turnout in British and American elections, 1966–1992 (% of electorate)**

| Great Britain | 1966 | 1970 | 1974 (Feb.) | 1974 (Oct.) | 1979 | 1983 | 1987 | 1992 |
|---|---|---|---|---|---|---|---|---|
|  | 75.8 | 72.0 | 78.8 | 72.8 | 76.0 | 72.7 | 75.4 | 77.7 |

| United States | 1966 | 1968 | 1970 | 1972 | 1974 | 1976 | 1978 | 1980 | 1982 | 1984 | 1986 | 1988 | 1990 | 1992 |
|---|---|---|---|---|---|---|---|---|---|---|---|---|---|---|
| Presidential[a] |  | 60.9 |  | 55.7 |  | 53.3 |  | 52.4 |  | 53.0 |  | 48.6 |  | 54.0 |
| Mid-term[b] | 45.4 |  | 43.4 |  | 38.0 |  | 37.0 |  | 40.0 |  | 37.0 |  | 36.4 |  |

[a] In addition to the President, the whole House of Representatives and one-third of senators are elected at the federal level.
[b] No president is elected, but the whole House of Representatives and a further one-third of the Senate are selected.

in comparable European systems. First, registering to vote is more difficult and restrictive, so that only about three-quarters of those eligible to vote are actually registered. Second, the groups among whom turnout is relatively low – the young, the poor and those who do not identify strongly with a party – are a growing proportion of the population as a whole. But there remains the question of why turnout has been declining while general education and voter awareness of candidates and issues has been increasing. It may be that people simply recognize that the political parties present such indistinct policy alternatives that other forms of participation are more likely to be fruitful. As we shall argue in chapter 27, other forms of participation seem to be increasing.

The national nominating conventions of each party which take place in July or August of each presidential-election year used to be real decision-making bodies as far as the nomination was concerned, but since the Second World War they have rarely done more than ratify the choice that has emerged from the long series of state primary elections, in which the candidates attempt to demonstrate their ability to win and accumulate convention delegates pledged to their support. By 1980 thirty-seven states held primaries; in 1992 there were thirty-six and, because they include most of the large states, the significance of the primaries remains great.

The first major modification in voting behaviour in recent times has been the gradual encroachment of the Republican Party in the South, particularly in presidential elections. A main factor in this has been the association of the Democratic Party with liberal civil-rights measures, while the South has remained essentially conservative. Another factor has been the drift away from the Democrats of some of its working-class base; in particular, white working-class support for the Democrats has declined as ethnic-minority working-class support solidified. These were both significant factors in the defeat of Carter by the Republican candidate, Ronald Reagan, in the 1980 presidential election. In 1976 Carter, a Southerner, swept the board in the South, but in 1980 he was able to win only in his home state, Georgia. Even Bill Clinton won only two Southern states in 1992. Carter's support from traditionally Democratic groups, such as Catholics, Jews and union members, also declined from around 60 per cent in 1976 to less than 50 per cent in 1980. Only in 1992 did enough of these so-called 'Reagan Democrats' return to support Clinton to enable the Democrats to win the presidency for the first time since 1976 (See table 26.3).

Both parties have been seriously affected by another important

**Table 26.3** Presidential-election results in the United States, 1964–1992 (% of votes cast)

|  | 1964 | 1968 | 1972 | 1976 | 1980 | 1984 | 1988 | 1992 |
|---|---|---|---|---|---|---|---|---|
| Democrat | 61.1 | 42.7 | 37.5 | 50.0 | 41.6 | 41.0 | 45.7 | 43.2 |
| Republican | 38.5 | 43.4 | 60.7 | 47.9 | 51.7 | 59.0 | 53.4 | 37.7 |
| Other | 0.5 | 13.8[a] | 1.7 | 2.1 | 6.7[a] | —[b] | 0.9 | 19.0[a] |

*Note*: Columns may not add up to 100% because of rounding.

[a] In 1968 the 'other' vote was for George Wallace's American Independence Party, in 1980 for John Anderson and in 1992 for Ross Perot.
[b] There was no significant third-party vote in 1984.

change which has been noticeable since 1964 – the declining strength of party identification. One in three people of all ages now identify themselves as independents, and the trend has been greatest among the younger and white, well-educated voters. This greater independence has been manifested in an increase in 'split ticket' voting, that is a voter does not vote, say, Democratic, for all the offices to be filled, but votes for, say, a Republican president, a Democratic senator, a Republican governor and so on. It is this phenomenon, of course, that largely explains why Bush (Republican) won the presidency in 1988 while the Democrats held large majorities in Congress. Half of all Democrats elected to the House of Representatives won in districts that were also won by George Bush (Grant, 1991, p. 32). Whereas during most of the post-war period switches in support to the Republicans have been limited mainly to presidential elections, in 1980 the Republicans succeeded also in gaining a majority in the Senate for the first time since 1972. Ticket-splitting remained an important phenomenon, however, with control of the House of Representatives staying with the Democrats, though with a reduced majority, so that for the first time since 1917–18 the two houses were not controlled by the same party. In 1986 the Democrats regained control of the Senate.

## Representation and Elections in the Soviet Union and the New Republics

Elections in the Soviet Union were, theoretically, democratic but, because, in effect, only one candidate was permitted, they became mostly a formality. However, it was possible to cross out the name of the candidate and to write in the name of someone whom the voter preferred. Only a tiny proportion of voters ever did this. In addition, a candidate had to get 51 per cent of the vote in order to be elected. When more than one candidate was permitted to stand for election in the Gorbachev period, these rules still applied. Hence some candidates found themselves defeated even though no other candidate was standing, and run-offs were often required.

Western commentators have often dismissed old-style Soviet elections as a meaningless formality in which there was no choice of candidate and voting levels were supposed to be around an improbable 99 per cent. Such elections also gave rise to cynicism among Soviet citizens and attempts to exercise electoral rights – as when Roy Medvedev and another dissident tried to have their names entered on the ballot paper as alternative candidates in the 1979 elections to the Supreme Soviet – were effectively scotched by the authorities. However, as elections in the Soviet Union were taken very seriously by party and governmental authorities, it is important to understand their operation and significance. Rejection of the chosen candidate at an adoption meeting or even at the election itself (by crossing out the name on the ballot paper) did occur but it was very rare, and was seen to reflect on the competence of the local party which did not realize that a particular candidate would arouse such opposition. Traditionally, candidates were chosen on criteria like good production records and notable sporting achievements. In recent times, however, the need for some administrative competence had been recognized.

The election campaign was conducted energetically and assiduously. Activists came together in voters' clubs to organize the election, register voters and whip up support generally. What evidence there is suggests that, far from explaining current policy issues to the voters as required, many activists confined themselves simply to reminding voters of the date and place of voting. They were usually regarded with passive tolerance by the citizenry. Election meetings were held, at which complaints could be made and registered. Formal mandates could also be registered at the election meeting, although discussion on them was reserved for the soviet so as to preserve the non-conflictual atmosphere of the election. Defeat of the one official candidate was rare, and occurred mostly in the local soviets, where comparatively few votes were involved. The recall of elected members by their disgruntled constituents was also practised occasionally and the deputy could be dismissed if he or she could not defend his or her conduct. Apart from elections, an element of direct democracy was found in the holding of public meetings where, at least sometimes, genuine public discussion took place. In spite of the formal quality of Soviet elections, they were regarded as an important socializing activity by the authorities as well as an effective loyalty check. They had legitimating and communicative functions, and provided a means of comparatively easy public service which was demanded of every citizen. Finally, it should be realized that the role of elected deputies was not merely formal, but involved considerable administrative activity and in the public service of representing their constituents to the authorities and explaining government policies to the citizens.

In the atmosphere of *glasnost* and *perestroika* Soviet politicians had to get used to campaigning for votes and facing rival candidates. No firmly established party system emerged, so personality and reputation still counted for much. The new republics have broadly taken over the system inherited from the Soviet Union. Parties exist but are relatively weak, campaigning is low-key compared with the West, and the exact role of the deputy has still to be decided. Many of these questions will be resolved with experience, if democracy survives the economic and social crisis engendered by the collapse of the Soviet Union. None of the republics has a strong democratic tradition and some (like the Central Asian republics) have none at all. Initial enthusiasm for free voting has given way to disappointment and disillusion. Hence the proportion actually casting their vote in most elections has fallen considerably since those first held under the new system (Lane, 1992, pp. 66–73).

## Conclusion

The initial assumptions as to how people exercised their vote was that they acted as 'rational maximizers', that is, having thought about what policies they wanted, they then voted for the person they believed most likely to deliver them. The first sophisticated studies of voting behaviour carried out in the mid twentieth century presented a very different picture. If people voted, they did so in response to very basic cues such as how their parents voted or what major social pressures they perceived from work colleagues. What they did not do, it seemed, was think in a coherent way about the policies of parties. Later, this somewhat extreme view of the 'irrational' voter was modified to one in which the citizen votes in accordance with some general views on policy issues and with a prior identification with a particular party. People are likely to vote according to these dispositions, if at all, depending on generalized feelings of satisfaction or dissatisfaction with parties' performances in or out of government.

What light have these studies of voting and elections shed on the relationship between decision-makers and the mass of citizens? Elections are only a crude method of keeping decision-makers in touch with the people, but it would be wrong to dismiss them as being *only* of symbolic value. Voting consists of millions of individual acts which often bring about changes in political control on the basis of quite small simple majorities. For example, in Britain the votes of about one in three of the total electorate in 1987 and 1992 were enough to return a Conservative government with a majority over all other parties in the House of Commons. This was not an unusual occurrence. And in the presidential election in the United States in 1992 the votes of fewer than one in four of the total electorate were enough for the Democrats to win. Thus phrases such as 'the people's will' must be treated with great caution. But although elections do not give governments the mandate to do any particular thing, they do provide them with general authority to act over a given period of time.

Reforms, such as compulsory voting and proportional representation, may remove some of the worst inconsistencies from the process but, since nothing better has been proposed, it is likely that elections will continue to be the major means by which decision-makers seek to legitimate their position as they try to exercise influence, power and authority. Marxists and elitists will emphasize the symbolic aspects of elections, while pluralists will be more concerned to demonstrate a positive link between government performance and election results.

## Questions for Discussion

1 What social and economic conditions are required for the holding of 'free and fair' elections?
2 What useful political information can political analysts gain from election results?

3 What is the significance of elections from the point of view of prac-
tising politicians?

# Further Reading

Davies, P.J. and F.A. Waldstein (eds) (1991), *Political Issues in America*. Manchester, Manchester University Press, chs 7–9.

Husbands, C.T. (1986), Race and gender. In H. Drucker, P. Dunleavy, A. Gamble and G. Peele (eds), *Developments in British Politics 2*. Basingstoke, Macmillan, pp. 295–312.

Lane, D. (1992), *Soviet Society under Perestroika*, rev. edn. Boston, Unwin Hyman, ch. 3.

McKay, D. (1989), *American Politics and Society*, 2nd ed. Oxford, Blackwell, pp. 101–22.

Miller, W.L. (1990), Voting and the electorate. In P. Dunleavy, A. Gamble and G. Peele (eds), *Developments in British Politics 3*. Basingstoke, Macmillan, pp. 42–68.

Moran, M. (1989), *Politics and Society in Britain*, 2nd edn. London, Macmillan, ch. 3.

Sakwa, R. (1990), *Gorbachev and his Reforms, 1985–1990*. Hemel Hempstead, Philip Allan, pp. 133–51.

# Other Forms of Participation

## Introduction

In chapter 4 we suggested that there are three basic ways in which choices can be made – by means of numbers, violence and words. Elections are just one way by which governments come and go. An examination of a wider variety of systems than we have undertaken here will reveal a plethora of combinations of the use of numbers, words and violence. The question of how regimes on the one hand, and particular governments within a stable regime on the other, succeed one another represents a kind of choice by a society, and all three of these methods have been and are employed. The elections, or 'numbers', method of choosing governments has been dealt with at some length. Just as all governments like to call themselves 'democratic', so they would all prefer to come to power via elections, since it then becomes relatively easy for them to demonstrate their legitimacy. However, sometimes elections are not available for aspiring ruling groups, or they may be deemed unsatisfactory for some reason – such as the likelihood of its producing an undesired result!

## Succession other than by Election

In discussing violent methods of succession political analysts tend to distinguish between 'revolution' and 'coup d'état'. The former is seen as refering to the violent overthrow of regimes, the latter to the violent overthrow of governments, leaving the regime essentially unchanged. Examples of the former are the American War of Independence in which colonial rule from Britain was replaced by independent American democracy, the Russian Revolution of 1917 in which tsarist autocracy was replaced by the 'dictatorship of the proletariat' and the Iranian Revolution of 1979 in which the modernizing monarchy of the Shah was overthrown by the radical theocracy of Ayatollah Khomeini. Examples of coups have been more numerous throughout history – dynastic clashes in the Middle Ages were coups rather than revolutions because the prize was the Crown, that is the regime stayed the same. Today coups are most frequently the replacement of a civilian by a military government or vice versa, or the replacement of one military regime by another.

In practice, incidences of succession may not easily be classified, because elements of more than one method may be present. This is particularly true where there is no formalized process of succession and where the death or demise of a leader leaves a vacuum to be filled. How the resulting instability and uncertainty is finally resolved will depend very much on the conditions of time and place, but certain patterns are observable. In monarchical regimes succession is hereditary and frequently stable, but struggles can develop where the right to succession is disputed. The succession may be settled peacefully or violently, but even in a peaceful settlement there is a strong tendency for the victors to ensure the defeat of the losers by their death or exile. A modern variation of this could be seen in communist regimes where elections might take place but they were not significant in terms of governmental succession. The deaths of Lenin and Stalin in the Soviet Union and of Mao Zedung in China were followed by considerable struggles involving both words and violence. However, the succession in Yugoslavia after the death of Tito was entirely orderly and the succession of general secretaries following the death of Brezhnev in the Soviet Union were peacefully resolved.

There are also regimes in which succession is determined mainly by a combination of numbers and words. Here we are thinking primarily of liberal democracies where elections take place that do not produce a clear-cut majority for one or another party, and hence are followed by a period of negotiation in order to form a coalition of groups which can maintain a government. In Italy, for example, between 1945 and 1992 there were over fifty governments but only twelve elections. Thus many governments have been the outcome of discussions and deals over policy rather than

of an election. Finally, of course, there are states in which numbers
and violence are the form of choice, where elections are held in
a climate of considerable violence, intimidation and fraud.

## Methods of Participation in Democracies

The adequacy of both participation and representation in liberal
democracies has been called into question in recent commentary
and analysis. It is clear that a comparatively high level of participation can be achieved, provided that the type of participation
called for is purely formal and symbolic, as in elections to the
soviets in the former Soviet Union, or is limited to a narrow
choice, as is provided in many liberal democratic elections. But to
many people participation means some significant involvement in
the decision-making process itself. At the least it has meant an
opportunity not simply to choose but also to influence decision-
makers at a point in the process where such influence will have
a measurable effect on the decisions ultimately taken and their
implementation. The difficulties inherent in mass participation
has led to its being impracticable beyond a certain level, but very
little consideration has been given to what may be an appropriate
level or how it may be measured. Thus political societies have a
tolerance level of participation which is set either arbitrarily or
by criteria that suit the convenience of ruling groups. Much discussion as to whether Britain and the United States are really
democracies or whether they need 'more participation' is vitiated
by its ignoring of the criteria for measuring an acceptable level of
participation. (For turnout in post-war elections see table 26.2.)

The advocates of greater participation believe that realistic involvement in the decision-making process will make such decisions
more relevant, and therefore more acceptable, to the participants.
Thus the greater the degree of participation the higher the level
of legitimacy is likely to be. It can further be argued that new
information and communications technology, such as interactive
television systems, will enable some of the long-standing practical
difficulties of obtaining immediate and unmanipulated opinions
from large numbers of people to be overcome. Whether those in
power are anxious that participation be increased by these means
is, of course, debatable. A central question is whether greater political participation is conducive to an enhancement of the legitimacy

of the regime. That the opposite is likely can be strongly argued. According to this view, participation is seen as introducing practical complications into the decision-making process, the frustrations of which are likely to reduce the efficacy and therefore the legitimacy of the decisions and of those who make them. Furthermore, it is suggested that 'excessive' participation can create the structure and conditions for the manifestation of discontent and dissension that would not have surfaced in the first place, or even have existed at all. This argument has been applied even to elections in liberal democracies where it has been suggested that larger than usual turnouts in elections (implying that the normally apathetic have become sufficiently aroused to vote) indicate a crisis in the political process. It would probably be more fruitful, however, to look at other forms of participation for better indications of crisis.

Participation has so far been interpreted primarily as involvement in the selection of representatives, and for the majority of people in liberal democracies this is the extent of their participation in the political process. However, it may be argued that, for participation to have much significance in terms of what governments actually do, more than the act of voting is required. In both Britain and the United States those who do more than just vote are generally better-educated and more affluent. Conventionally, this minority of relatively active citizens will communicate their ideas more regularly to representatives through organized pressure groups and within the political party organizations (see chapters 12 and 13), but there are also other ways. Here we discuss the referendum and forms of direct action.

## Referendums

A fairly recent innovation in British national politics has been the use of the referendum to decide on continuing membership of the European Community and on the devolution question in Scotland and Wales. Nothing could seem more straightforward than the practice of putting a direct question to the electorate as a way of ascertaining the wishes of the people, but in reality it is not that simple. The fundamental difficulty is the framing of a simple question concerning issues that do not lend themselves to simplification, and on which a simple direct answer is either equally inappropriate or fails to reflect the variations in opinion among the electorate.

In Britain the referendum sits awkwardly in the political system because, constitutionally, the existing Parliament is sovereign and cannot be bound by any other institution. The referendums of 1975 and 1979 were, strictly speaking, consultative only, but everyone recognized that in practice it would be impossible to overthrow a clear referendum result such as those achieved on the question of remaining in the European Community and on devolution for Wales. An understanding of why referendums have come to be used in Great Britain, however, must consider the context of prevailing party politics. On issues such as joining the European Community and devolution, the division of opinion did not coincide with party lines and this was exacerbated by the presence in the Commons of the Liberals and several nationalist parties. In other words, the referendum – like elections, parliamentary procedures, party politics and so on – is a device to be used to maintain the government in good working condition in accordance with the preferences of powerful vested interests. These two intentions – good working condition and the preferences of powerful vested interests – are not always easily compatible, nor do the political devices always work in the way intended. Thus politics is a serious game of calculated risks within an ideological context, and the referendum is simply a device that can be used for its legitimating authority but it may backfire. The possibility of using the referendum has arisen again in the 1990s. Broadly, the same contentious issues are involved – devolution of power to Scotland and the development of the European Community.

In the United States frequent use is made of referendums. The ballot paper at election time in half the states will contain a number of questions in addition to the names of candidates for office. In recent years these have included attempts to limit the number of times politicians can be re-elected and to limit levels of taxation. There was also constitutional provision for referendums in the Soviet Union but it was not used until the spring of 1991 when Gorbachev held a union-wide referendum on the continuing existence of the union. It was part of his attempt to preserve the union but, in spite of a large pro-union vote (the question put to the people was rather loaded) he could not ultimately halt the breakup of the country into its constituent republics.

# Direct Action in Great Britain and the United States

Since the Second World War there has been some significant decline in committed support for the established political parties in both Great Britain and the United States, particularly in terms of voting. But this has been accompanied by an apparent increase in people's readiness to participate in other ways, which have frequently been disruptive, and are condemned by most conventional politicians as unnecessary or illegitimate. There is a spectrum of such unconventional activity, from orderly demonstration, strike, blockade, march and sit-in to riot and organized violence, such as bombing and arson. The action taken in a particular situation depends very much on local circumstances and traditions. At the same time, the decline in the support for the main parties was also accompanied by a much greater proliferation of single-issue groups whose memberships were often very small but whose potential for influence over politicians increased as general turnout in elections fell or stabilized.

It is difficult to generalize about the extent of the resort to such direct forms of political action. In the United States protest seemed to be almost the norm in the late 1960s but declined rapidly in the early 1970s. Since then it has erupted occasionally, usually sparked by police racism, as in Miami and Chattanooga in 1980 and Los Angeles and New York in 1992. As we saw in chapter 18, violent direct action has also become associated with the abortion issue. In Britain since the 1970s conflicts between governments and trade unions have given rise to many marches and demonstrations, and sometimes resulted in violence, most recently during the miners' strike of 1984–5 and the printers' picketing of Rupert Murdoch's new newspaper plant at Wapping in London. Other issues that have given rise to direct political action in the 1980s in Britain include the nuclear one: demonstrations and peace camps at cruise-missile bases, and in 1986 the blockade of sites being explored for the dumping of nuclear waste. Towards the end of the 1980s public protest in the streets manifested itself over such issues as the 'poll tax' and the question of devolution of some political power to Scotland.

A major question in the discussion of such unconventional behaviour revolves around whether or not it achieves its ends. Denials of the effectiveness of direct action are frequently loudest from those most inconvenienced by it. Those in political control have, of course, a direct interest in minimizing such unconventional forms of participation. However, it is equally difficult for the proponents of such action to show clearly that it does work. Sometimes it does work at little cost to the protestors, at other times it does not, and people may lose a great deal by it. But there seems to be a more general predisposition today to employ unorthodox methods of political action either as complements or alternatives to more traditional forms of group and party activity.

## Participation in the Soviet Union and the Successor Republics

The party and political authorities in the Soviet Union claimed to have solved many of the problems of conventional participation. A high degree of participation was achieved by a comparatively large proportion of the population, many of whom were elected for short terms to the various levels of soviets in a representative capacity. Until the arrival of Gorbachev, some 18 or 19 million of the population were members of the Communist Party. Others gave up time and energy for various forms of political and social service. The system of soviets and, more importantly, the Communist Party itself, formed the vehicles of communication and contact between governors and governed. The elaborate hierarchical structure, the systematic elections, meetings and conferences were designed to provide ample opportunities for widespread participation and discussion so that the party leaders could not help but be in touch with the desires and aspirations of the people. Thus the CPSU was officially seen as truly the party of the people, and the people were represented in the organs of government through the soviets.

Little criticism of this sort of analysis was allowed in the Soviet Union itself or in other communist countries, until Poland led the way. But Western commentators have generally taken the view that, while neither the soviets nor the CPSU were entirely ineffective as channels of communication and participation in decision-making, the degree of effective communication from the bottom up was extremely limited, due to the over-bureaucratized nature of the system which caused delays and acquired vested interests of its own. In addition, any real discussion and participation that did take place had to do so in private. It was considered imperative to preserve a show of outward unity. To Western eyes, the lack of a political arena for public discussion was a serious disability in any regime that aimed at influential and widespread participation. In reality, participation was confined to administrative chores with little input into policy-making. Any serious attempt to discuss or criticize official party policy would have incurred social or even legal sanctions.

In spite of these criticisms, it is clear that from the time of Khrushchev onwards some effort was made to involve a significant proportion of the population in some participation, albeit subordinate, in the administration. Two principles were involved – that of control of the bureaucracy by the people, and that of the replacement of the bureaucracy by a people's administration. Khrushchev encouraged these activities with enthusiasm, which led to confusion and resentment. His successors, however, continued the process in a more limited way, while providing a more effective organizational framework. Central to this was the revival of the local soviets as the main supervisory bodies for administrative effectiveness. The soviets were ideal for this role because they were representative, nation-wide in extent and embodied a high degree of legitimacy. They were assisted by a multitude of organizations at the national and community levels. These included the comrades' courts and *druzhinii* (voluntary patrols) which aimed to control deviant behaviour; house, street and neighbourhood committees which mobilized citizens for public-spirited action; and a growing number of voluntary supplementary services. The professional bureaucracy itself was supplemented by public unpaid participation in subordinate roles where great expertise or professionalism was not required. All this was supervised by standing committees of the local soviets. One of the most interesting organizations was the people's control committee which checked the work of factory and office administration. It relied heavily on volunteers but its usefulness was often severely curtailed by its close co-operation with management. Needless to say, the organization of such a vast amount of public participation involved problems. Vested bureaucratic interests often resisted the incursion of the citizens on to their terrain. Local soviets were sometimes reluctant to do more than rubberstamp executive decisions, in spite of encouragements to greater participation. It could be difficult to find the right balance between professional administrators and volunteers – too many of the latter could cause administrative chaos. Finally, the overall supervision and control, which was at all times exercised by the CPSU, could also develop into a usurping of the responsibilities of the local soviet by the local party. This tendency had to be resisted. Nevertheless, whatever the difficulties, such policies and developments did represent an adherence at least in principle to the revolutionary ideal of the commune as the basic and significant unit of government.

From the death of Stalin to the advent of Gorbachev there were dissenting groups who at some risk to themselves expressed views at variance with the official communist line. There were liberal democrats (like Andrei Sakharov), conservatives looking for a restoration of what they believed to be prerevolutionary values (like Alexander Solzhenitsyn), nationalist and religious groups, and those who wanted a return to 'true' communism which they believed had been perverted by the regime. Overall, these dissidents had little practical impact (except when they could invoke international pressure on the Soviet government), but their courage and persistence helped to keep their causes alive.

The opportunities afforded by the policy of *glasnost* after 1985 showed that the Soviet people were prepared to express themselves, given the opportunity to do so without fear of reprisal. There was a vast amount of comment in the media, in the popular fronts for the support of *glasnost* and *perestroika* and in a multitude of new 'informal' organizations which the Communist Party soon gave up trying to control. These ranged through the political spectrum, from anarchists to Stalinists, monarchists and neo-Fascists. The political impact of these groups was limited by the vast number of them, their inexperience of political activity and the tendency for many of them to be dominated by intellectuals. However, there were some more popularly based organizations, like the miners' trade union, which did have political significance. Huge political demonstrations were held, often consisting of over 200,000 people. The economic and social crisis of the old Soviet Union continues in the new republics, and public demonstrations of protest and discontent will remain a feature of their politics (Lane, 1992, pp. 107–44; Remington, 1992, pp. 147–73).

## Conclusion

Why do people not always make full use of the opportunities for participation that exist? We do not know for sure, but various explanations have been offered. It used to be frequently argued by proponents of liberal democracy that many people did not participate simply because they were content to leave politics to others and also content with their lot. An increased tendency for political action to take more direct forms in recent years has raised serious questions about this theory, as has the fact that many people who are non-active receive relatively few benefits from the political process by any definition of 'interest'.

So we return to debates over whether 'non-actives' have been 'bamboozled' by the ruling ideology or people have simply realized that their chances of achieving anything are slight. This argument has been put in more formal terms by analysts employing models of rational choice, which are based on the assumption that people act rationally and, therefore, do not participate in politics because they calculate that the costs of doing so in terms of time, money and energy will outweigh the benefits they receive as a result of their activity. Whether or not we concur with the individualistic assumptions of this approach, the question remains as to whether greater participation is likely to alter the distribution of benefits by any political process and, if so, why?

## Questions for Discussion

1  What is the rationale for greater political participation?
2  Discuss the relative significance of 'conventional' and 'unconventional' modes of political participation in the United Kingdom, the United States and the Soviet Union.
3  Can genuine mass participation be achieved within the framework of a pluralist political process with respect to either domestic or foreign-policy issues?

## Further Reading

Birch, A.H. (1971), *Representation*. London, Pall Mall, ch. 1.
Kavanagh, D. (1983), *Political Science and Political Behaviour*. London, Allen & Unwin, ch. 9.
Lane, D. (1992), *Soviet Society under Perestroika*, rev. edn. Boston, Unwin Hyman, ch. 9.
McKay, D. (1989), *American Politics and Society*, 2nd edn. Oxford, Blackwell, pp. 122–5.

Marable, M. (1984), *Race, Reform and Rebellion*. London, Macmillan, esp. chs 4, 5 and 6.
Smith, G.B. (1992), *Soviet Politics: Struggling with Change*. Basingstoke, Macmillan, ch. 8.

# References

Ackroyd, C., K. Margolis, J. Rosenhead and T. Shallice (1977), *The Technology of Political Control*. Harmondsworth, Penguin.

Allison, G. (1971), *Essence of Decision*. Boston, Little, Brown.

Aristotle (1962 edn), *The Politics*. Harmondsworth, Penguin.

Bailey, C.J. (1992), Congress and legislative activism. In G. Peele et al. (eds), *Developments in American Politics*. Basingstoke, Macmillan, pp. 115–37.

Barghoorn, F.C. and T.F. Remington (1986), *Politics in the USSR*, 3rd edn. Boston, Little, Brown.

Barry, N. (1990), Ideology. In P. Dunleavy, A. Gamble and G. Peele (eds), *Developments in British Politics 3*. Basingstoke, Macmillan, pp. 17–41.

Beer, S. (1978), Federalism, nationalism and democracy in America. *American Political Science Review*, 72 (1), pp. 9–21.

Beer, S. (1982), *Britain against Itself*. London, Faber.

Beetham, D. (1974), *Max Weber and the Theory of Modern Politics*. London, Allen & Unwin.

Benn, A. (1980), The mandarins in modern Britain. *Guardian*, 4 February, p. 9.

Benvenuti, F. (1991), Reforming the party: organisation and structure, 1917–1990. In C. Merridale and C. Ward (eds), *Perestroika: The Historical Perspective*. London, Edward Arnold, pp. 117–37.

Blondel, J. (1973), *Comparing Political Systems*. London, Weidenfeld & Nicolson.

Blondel, J. (1990), *Comparative Government: An Introduction*. Hemel Hempstead, Philip Allan.

Borcke, A. von (1990), The KGB and *perestroika*. In Federal Institute for Soviet and International Studies, Cologne (ed.), *The Soviet Union, 1987–1989: Perestroika in Crisis?*. London, Longman, pp. 61–6.

Burton, J.W. (1972), *World Society*. Cambridge, Cambridge University Press.

Butler, D. and D. Stokes (1974), *Political Change in Britain*, 2nd edn. London, Macmillan.

Buzan, B. (1991), *Peoples, States and Fear: An Agenda for International Security Studies in the Post-Cold War Era*, 2nd edn. Hemel Hempstead, Harvester Wheatsheaf.

Campbell, C. (1992), Presidential leadership. In G. Peele et al. (eds), *Developments in American Politics*. Basingstoke, Macmillan, pp. 88–114.

Castles, F.G., D.J. Murray, C.J. Pollitt and D.G. Potter (eds) (1976), *Decisions, Organisations and Society*, 2nd edn. Harmondsworth, Penguin.

Cater, D. (1964), *Power in Washington*. New York, Vintage.

Cawson, A. (1978), Pluralism, corporatism and the role of the state. *Government and Opposition*, Vol. 13, spring, pp. 178–98.

Collender, S.E. (1992), The budget deficit. In G. Peele et al. (eds), *Developments in American Politics*. Basingstoke, Macmillan, pp. 280–93.

Crawshaw, S. (1992), *Goodbye to the USSR: The Collapse of Soviet Power*. London, Bloomsbury.

Crewe, I. (1987), A new class of politics. *Guardian*, 15 June.

Crewe, I., T. Fox and J. Alt (1977), Non-voting in British general elections 1966 – October, 1974. In C. Crouch (ed.), *Participation in Politics*. London, Croom Helm.

Crick, B. (1982), *In Defence of Politics*, 3rd edn. Harmondsworth, Penguin.

Crosland, A. (1956), *The Future of Socialism*. London, Cape.

Crossman, R. (1975–7), *Diaries of a Cabinet Minister*, 3 vols. London, Hamilton.

Crouch, M. (1989), *Revolution and Evolution: Gorbachev and Soviet Politics*. Hemel Hempstead, Philip Allan.

Davies, R.W. (1991), Soviet reform in historical perspective. In C. Merridale and C. Ward, *Perestroika: The Historical Perspective*. London, Edward Arnold, pp. 117–37.

Deutsch, K. (1966), *Nerves of Government*. London, Free Press.

Dixon, S. (1990), The Russians; the dominant nationality. In G. Smith (ed.), *The Nationalities Question in the Soviet Union*. London, Longman, pp. 21–37.

Dolbeare, K.M. and M.J. Edelman (1977), *American Politics*, 3rd edn. Lexington, D.C. Heath.

Dunleavy, P. and B. O'Leary (1987), *Theories of the State: The Politics of Liberal Democracy*. Basingstoke, Macmillan.

Dunleavy, P. and R.A.W. Rhodes (1986), Government beyond Whitehall. In H. Drucker, P. Dunleavy, A. Gamble and G. Peele (eds), *Developments in British Politics 2*. Basingstoke, Macmillan, pp. 107–43.

Easton, D. (1969), The new revolution in political science. *American Political Science Review*, 63 (4), pp. 1051–61.

Edelman, M.J. (1964), *The Symbolic Uses of Politics*. Urbana, University of Illinois Press.

Enloe, C. (1988), *Does Khaki Become You? The Militarization of Women's Lives*. London, Pandora.

Friedgut, T.H. (1979), *Political Participation in the USSR*. Princeton, Princeton University Press.

George, S. (1990), *An Awkward Partner: Britain in the European Community*. Basingstoke, Macmillan.

Gitelman, Z. (1992), Nations, republics and Commonwealth. In S. White, A. Pravda and Z. Gitelman (eds), *Developments in Soviet and Post-Soviet Politics*, 2nd edn. Basingstoke, Macmillan, pp. 122–46.

Grant, A. (1991), *The American Political Process*, 4th edn. Aldershot, Dartmouth.

Griffith, J.A.G. (1991), *The Politics of the Judiciary*, 4th edn. London, Fontana.

Hayek, F. von (1944), *The Road to Serfdom*. London, Routledge & Kegan Paul.

Heclo, H. (1978), Issue networks and the executive establishment. In A. King (ed.), *The New American Political System*. Washington, DC, American Enterprise Institute for Public Policy Research.

Held, D. (1987), *Models of Democracy*. Cambridge, Polity.

Held, D. (1992), Democracy: from city-states to a cosmopolitan order. *Political Studies*, 40, pp. 10–39.

Hindess, B. (1987), *Freedom, Equality and the Market*. London, Tavistock.

Hogan, J. (1992), Economic policy. In G. Peele et al. (eds), *Developments in American Politics*. Basingstoke, Macmillan, pp. 210–28.

Home Office (1984), *Guidelines on the Work of a Special Branch*. London, HMSO.

Hosking, G. (1992), *A History of the Soviet Union*, rev. edn. London, Fontana.

Hough, J.F. and M. Fainsod (1979), *How the Soviet Union is Governed*. Cambridge, Mass., Harvard University Press.

House of Commons Select Committee on Home Affairs (1985), *Fourth Report: Special Branch*. House of Commons Paper No. 71. London, HMSO.

Jones, B. (1991) The Mass Media and Politics. In Jones, B. (ed.) *Politics UK*, Hemel Hempstead, Philip Allan, pp. 200–23.

Jones, B. (1991) The Policy Making Process. In Jones, B. (ed.) *Politics UK*, Hemel Hempstead, Philip Allan, pp. 501–20.

Jósza, G. (1990), The heart of Gorbachev's reform package: rebuilding the party apparatus. In Federal Institute for Soviet and International Studies, Cologne (ed.), *The Soviet Union, 1987–1989: Perestroika in Crisis?*. London, Longman, pp. 23–9.

Kaplan, A. (1964), The *Conduct of Inquiry*. San Francisco, Chandler.

Kavanagh, D. (1991), Elections and voting behaviour. In Jones, B. (ed.), *Politics UK*. Hemel Hempstead, Philip Allan, pp. 179–99.

Kellas, J.G. (1991), *The Politics of Nationalism and Ethnicity*. Basingstoke, Macmillan.

Keohane, R.O. and J.S. Nye (1977), *Power and Interdependence: World Politics in Transition*. Boston, Little, Brown.

Kober, S. (1990), Idealpolitik. *Foreign Policy*, 79, pp. 3–24.

Kuhn, T.S. (1962), *The Structure of Scientific Revolutions*. Chicago, University of Chicago Press.

Kuhn, T.S. (1977), *The Essential Tension*. Chicago, University of Chicago Press.

Lane, D. (1985), *State and Politics in the USSR*. Oxford, Blackwell.

Lane, D. (1992), *Soviet Society under Perestroika*, rev. edn. Boston, Unwin Hyman.

Lea, J. and J. Young (1984), *What is to be Done about Law and Order?*. Harmondsworth, Penguin.

Lees, J.D. (1975), *The Political System of the United States*, 2nd edn. London, Faber.

Locke, J. (1929 edn), *Second Treatise on Civil Government*. London, Dent.

Luard, E. (1990), *The Globalization of Politics: The Changed Focus of Political Action in the Modern World*. Basingstoke, Macmillan.

Lukes, S. (1974), *Power: A Radical View*. London, Macmillan.

McGrew, A.G., P.G. Lewis et al. (1992), *Global Politics*. Cambridge, Polity Press.

McKay, D. (1989), *American Politics and Society*, 2nd edn. Oxford, Blackwell.

McKeever, R.J.M. (1993), *Raw Judicial Power? The Supreme Court and American Society*. Manchester, Manchester University Press.

Mackenzie, W.J.M. (1975), *Power, Violence, Decision*. Harmondsworth, Penguin.

Merkl, P. (1977), *Modern Comparative Politics*, 2nd edn. Hinsdale Ill., Dryden.

Merridale, C. (1991), Perestroika and Political Phuralism: Past and Prospects. In Merridale, C. and C. Ward (eds) (1991), *Perestroika: The Historical Perspective*. London, Edward Arnold.

Miller, W.L. (1990), Voting and the electorate. In P. Dunleavy, A. Gamble and G. Peele (eds), *Developments in British Politics 3*. Basingstoke, Macmillan, pp. 42–68.

Mills, C.W. (1956), *The Power Elite*. New York, Oxford University Press.

Moran, M. (1991), Political culture and participation. In B. Jones (ed.), *Politics UK*. Hemel Hempstead, Philip Allan, pp. 93–104.

Morgenthau, H.J. (1978), *Politics among Nations: The Struggle for Power and Peace*, 5th edn. New York, Knopf.

Mullen, W.F. (1976), *Presidential Power and Politics*. New York, St Martin's.

Neustadt, R.E. (1976), *Presidential Power*, rev. edn. New York, Wiley.

Norton, P. (1985), *Parliament in the 1980s*. Oxford, Blackwell.

Norton, P. (1991), The judiciary. In B. Jones (ed.), *Politics UK*. Hemel Hempstead, Philip Allan, pp. 475–98.

Nove, A. (1989), *Glasnost' in Action: Cultural Renaissance in Russia*. Boston, Unwin Hyman.

Oberländer, E. (1990), 'The history of our country is not the biography of Stalin!': restructuring and history. In Federal Institute for Soviet and International Studies, Cologne (ed.), *The Soviet Union, 1987–1989: Perestroika in Crisis?*. London, Longman, pp. 47–53.

Olson, M.E. (1965), *The Logic of Collective Action*. Cambridge, Mass., Harvard University Press.

Peele, G. et al. (eds) (1992), *Developments in American Politics*. Basingstoke, Macmillan.

Rahr, A. (1991), Yeltsin sets up a new system for governing Russia. *Report on the USSR (RFE/RL Research Institute)*, 3 (34), 23 August, pp. 9–12.

Rapoport, A. (1960), *Fights, Games and Debates*. Ann Arbor, University of Michigan Press.

Remington, Thomas F. (1992), Towards a Participatory Politics?. In S. White, A. Pravda and Z. Gitelman (eds), *Developments in Soviet and Post-Soviet Politics*, 2nd edn. Basingstoke, Macmillan, pp. 147–73.

Reshetar, J.S. Jr (1989), *The Soviet Polity: Government and Politics in the USSR*, 3rd edn. New York, Harper & Row.

Robertson, D. (1976), *A Theory of Party Competition*. London, Wiley.

Ross, D. (1980), Coalition maintenance in the Soviet Union. *World Politics*, 32 (2), January, pp. 258–80.

Sakwa, R. (1989), *Soviet Politics: An Introduction*. London, Routledge.

Sakwa, R. (1990), *Gorbachev and his Reforms, 1985–1990*. Hemel Hempstead, Philip Allan.

Saunders, P. (1980), *Urban Politics: A Sociological Interpretation*. Harmondsworth, Penguin.

Schmid, K. (1990), Legal reform as a means of perestroika. In Federal Institute for Soviet and International Studies, Cologne (ed.), *The Soviet Union, 1987–1989: Perestroika in Crisis?*. London, Longman, pp. 54–60.

Schneider, E. (1990), The Nineteenth Party Conference: reform of the political system. In Federal Institute for Soviet and International Studies, Cologne, (ed.), *The Soviet Union, 1987–1989: Perestroika in Crisis?*. London, Longman, pp. 30–9.

Schulz, A. (1979), *Local Politics and Nation States*. Oxford, Clio.

Schwarzmantel, J. (1987), *Structures of Power: An Introduction to Politics*, Brighton, Wheatsheaf.

Seldon, A. (1991), Northern Ireland. In B. Jones (ed.), *Politics UK*. Hemel Hempstead, Philip Allan.

Sharpe, L.J. (1981), Is there a crisis in Western European Local Government: A First Appraisal. In Sharpe, L.J. (ed.) (1981), *The Local Fiscal Crisis in Western Europe*. London, Sage.

Slider, D. (1986), More power to the Soviets? Reform and local government in the Soviet Union. *British Journal of Political Science*, October, pp. 495–511.

Smith, G. (1990), Nationalities Policy from Lenin to Gorbachev. In

Smith, G. (ed.) (1990), *The Nationalities Question in the Soviet Union*. London, Longman, pp. 1–20.

Smith, G.B. (1992), *Soviet Politics: Struggling with Change*, 2nd edn. Basingstoke, Macmillan.

Sontheimer, S. (ed.) (1991), *Women and the Enviroment: Crisis and Development in the Third World*. London, Earthscan.

Stoker, G. (1990), Government beyond Whitehall. In P. Dunleavy, A. Gamble and G. Peele (eds), *Developments in British Politics 3*. Basingstoke, Macmillan, pp. 126–49.

Strange, S. (1991), An eclectic approach. In C.N. Murphy and R. Tooze (eds), *The New International Political Economy*. Boulder, Colo., Lynne Reiner, pp. 33–49.

Swingewood, A. (1975), *Marx and Modern Social Theory*. London, Macmillan.

Tickner, J.A. (1991), Hans Morgenthau's principles of political realism: a feminist reformulation. In R. Grant and K. Newland (eds), *Gender and International Relations*. Buckingham, Open University Press, pp. 27–40.

Truman, D. (1951), *The Governmental Process*. New York, Knopf.

Wallace, H. (1990), Britain and Europe. In P. Dunleavy, A. Gamble and G. Peele (eds), *Developments in British Politics 3*. Basingstoke, Macmillan, pp. 150–72.

Westwood, J.N. (1987), *Endurance and Endeavour: Russian History, 1812–1986*, 3rd edn. Oxford, Oxford University Press.

White, S. (1978), Communist systems and the iron law of pluralism. *British Journal of Political Science*, January, pp. 101–17.

World Commission on Environment and Development (1987), *Our Common Future* (The Brundtland Report). New York, Oxford University Press.

# Index